KT-221-445

THE DEN OF GEEK!

GUIDE TO THE MOVIEVERSE

MOVIE GEEK

SIMON BREW

WITH RYAN LAMBIE & LOUISA MELLOR

An Hachette UK Company
www.hachette.co.uk

First published in Great Britain in 2017 by Cassell,
a division of Octopus Publishing Group Ltd
Carmelite House
50 Victoria Embankment
London EC4Y 0DZ
www.octopusbooks.co.uk

Design and Layout Copyright © Octopus Publishing Limited 2017
Text Copyright © Dennis Holdings Limited 2017

Distributed in the US by
Hachette Book Group
1290 Avenue of the Americas
4th and 5th Floors
New York, NY 10104

Distributed in Canada by
Canadian Manda Group
664 Annette St.
Toronto, Ontario, Canada M6S 2C8

All rights reserved. No part of this work may be reproduced or utilized
in any form or by any means, electronic or mechanical, including
photocopying, recording or by any information storage and retrieval
system, without the prior written permission of the publisher.

ISBN 978-1-84403-935-7

A CIP catalogue record for this book is available from the British Library.

Some of the material in this book has previously been featured on
www.denofgeek.com

Printed and bound in China

10 9 8 7 6 5 4 3 2

Publishing Director: Trevor Davies
Editor: Pollyanna Poulter
Copy Editor: Alison Wormleighton
Senior Designer: Jaz Bahra
Designer: Siaron Hughes
Picture Research Manager: Giulia Hetherington
Senior Production Manager: Peter Hunt

THE DEN OF GEEK!
GUIDE TO THE MOVIEVERSE
MOVIE GEEK

SIMON BREW
WITH RYAN LAMBIE
& LOUISA MELLOR

CASSELL ILLUSTRATED

CONTENTS

FOREWORD
A FEW WORDS
ON WHY I LOVE
DEN OF GEEK

BY MARK KERMODE

Some years ago, I wrote a book called *Hatchet Job* which was described (quite correctly) by one reviewer as the sound of someone "worrying out loud" about his profession.

Having started out in film journalism back in the 1980s, at a time when magazines were designed and edited with scalpels and spray-glue (rather than on laptops and desktops), I'd become somewhat anxious about the future of film criticism in an age when online content was rapidly superseding print journalism. Everywhere you looked, people were blithely declaring that old-school film criticism was dead, and the internet had killed it. In the age of Twitter and Facebook, did anyone really need (or want) the kind of specialist knowledge that once thrived in movie magazines?

As part of my research, I started subscribing to diverse movie websites, trying to find out what movie fans were getting from the internet that they weren't getting from the printed word. I asked around about which sites people found to be the most reliable, the most useful, the most entertaining. Among the numerous responses, one name popped up over and over again: Den of Geek. As one respondent to my questions noted, "They're pretty much the gold standard here in the UK. They take it seriously. But they're funny with it…"

In the years since I first visited DoG, I have found this assessment to be absolutely on the money. Not only has the site supported and encouraged some of the best upcoming film writers on the net, it has also become a proud flag-waver for the kind of old-fashioned journalistic integrity that we are blithely assured no longer exists. With their winning blend of well-researched news and unashamedly nerdy humour (smart without ever being snide), DoG have built up an impressive readership; at the time of my writing and researching *Hatchet Job* in 2013–14, they were attracting nearly three million unique users per month, a figure that has doubtless grown since then.

Eschewing anonymous snark in favour of accountable wit, the DoG editors – under the leadership of the estimable Simon Brew – also adhere to a code of conduct that puts many of their printed contemporaries to shame. Championing "a sense of equality and community", they have a healthy disdain for anything that smacks of clickbait, and an eagerness to seek out the alternative view. Their features (many examples of which you'll find collected in this book) balance a delightful interest in obscure movie trivia with a prevailing desire to seek out the best, rather than the worst, in movies.

That sense of enthusiasm and positivity was evident when I invited Simon to join me as a guest at one of my regular onstage movie talks. I'd asked him to speak about online movie journalism in general – a broad remit, admittedly, but one about which I knew he could hold forth with passion. In fact, he turned up with a string of carefully chosen clips from *Superman III*, a film which is generally regarded (with some justification) as being quite terrible, but which Simon had decided to re-watch in the hope that he might find something of value lurking therein.

And somehow he did. Even when delighting the crowd by pointing out how utterly shoddy the entire production had been, and how little sense the movie made (not just scene-by-scene, but line-by-line), Simon still managed to inspire in the audience a desire to rush out and re-watch *Superman III* forthwith. His enthusiasm was infectious, his responses honest, his attention to detail frankly alarming. It was an irresistible combination, and the crowd responded with glee. In short, Simon was the star of the evening, and I became little more than a warm-up act.

That blend of surprising fact and quirky opinion runs throughout the DoG site, as does their enduring love of Jason Statham – another thing we have in common. As an unabashed devotee of The Stath, I was delighted to discover that DoG was similarly infatuated with the silver screen's most entertainingly muscular presence. Debates about whether *Hummingbird* or *Wild Card* represents the zenith of Statham's underrated oeuvre flourish at DoG, along with discussions of the iconic clifftop striptease sequence from the otherwise uneven *Transporter 3*. When Paul Feig's satirical romp *Spy* proved to mainstream critics that The Stath had always had a wry awareness of his on-screen persona, DoG was one of the few outlets that could rightly claim to have got on board this particular train years ago, leaving other, more cumbersome publications playing catch-up.

When it comes to their reviews, DoG writers tend to strike an admirably uncynical balance between hoping for the best while being ready to call

out the worst, always remembering that an enthusiasm for the medium should lie at the heart of criticism. From its news reports to its long-running "Geeks vs Loneliness" strand, DoG has fostered an air of collegiate co-operation which fans clearly appreciate.

As journalism moves increasingly from the printed word to online content, it's encouraging that sites like DoG are thriving, reminding us that while the medium may have changed, the message ("good work will rise") remains essentially the same. Back in 2000, the American site Film Threat (which began life as a printed fanzine) published its own "Acceptable Code of Behaviour", which included such basic ground rules as a pledge not to review films until they are finished, and a rejection of anonymous content – rules that clearly distinguished it from less reputable sites. Writing about DoG's editor in *Hatchet Job* 14 years later, I stated that "the fact that Brew has a name worth protecting is of course the key to his integrity, and indeed to good criticism".

That's a claim by which I stand, not just for Simon, but for DoG as a whole. The irony of this book being a rare foray into "dead tree" journalism is not lost on me, and I'd be lying if I said I wasn't quietly reassured by the site's desire to produce something substantial in print after all these years in cyberspace. But whether I read them on the page or on the internet, I'll proudly wear the T-shirt as a die-hard DoG fan.

DEN OF GEEK!
AN INTRODUCTION

FROM SMALL INDIE FILMS TO BIG BLOCKBUSTERS, LITTLE DRAMAS TO MASSIVE SCI-FI EPICS, WE'RE ABOUT TO VENTURE ON A MOVIE GEEKDOM CRASH COURSE IN THE COMING PAGES. BUT WHERE DID IT ALL BEGIN?

There was a point, just a few months after the Den of Geek website came to life in 2007, that I got access to an analytics tool for the first time. My background is in print magazines, where you used to have to wait weeks to find out how many copies of your latest issue had sold, but this newfangled tool would tell me how many people had read our work the previous day! Within a day of publishing something, I'd have an idea as to whether we were on the right track, and whether people were reading it! It felt new. It felt exciting.

It was soul-destroying. The number on that screen is burned into my brain: 14 people, in one day – 12, if you discount myself and my mum. Several new articles had gone up on the site, but only 14 people had popped by to read them. It was a crossroads: do you battle on, and believe in what you're doing? Or take advantage of the hostelry on the corner, and re-evaluate a few life goals? But then what would, say, Jason Statham do? The Stath would surely stay on and fight. And so did we.

As I'm writing this, the analytics tool lets me see how many people are on the site at the exact second I'm looking. I checked. Right now, as I write these words, there are 1,742 people browsing Den of Geek. On the eve of our tenth birthday, nearly nine million people a month are willing to give the site a try. There have been bumps along the road, there have been days where there's been nowhere to hide. But, mostly, it's been the adventure of my life.

Kevin Costner was instructed, in the outstanding *Field of Dreams*, that "if you build it, he will come". Well, we did build it, to the point where we now have teams in both the UK and the US. We're not sure if Costner himself came but many others did. In doing so, every one of those visitors proved that you don't have to play negative to get people through the front door.

It's all a bit humbling, not least because the ethos of what we did on the day those beloved 14 people turned up hasn't markedly changed between then and now. The site was born out of a passion for films, television, books, games and generally nerdish stuff. But also it was our response to the fact that entertainment reporting and reviewing had an undercurrent of snark, of attacking people and of not giving sufficient love to the oeuvre of Jason Statham. Something, clearly, had to be done.

GEEKS VS LONELINESS

This book is just a flavour of what happened next. Over the past ten years, Den of Geek has run tens of thousands of articles, including a good dozen or so long reads every week. In this book you'll find some of our favourites, rewritten and updated to take out old typos and to put new ones in. A lot of what you're reading here is brand-new, and exclusive to this book, too.

If you like it, pop by and say hello to us at www.denofgeek.com. If you don't? Pop in the Christopher Lambert sci-fi treat Fortress, and imagine giving us all random intestinations. Heck, even the cardboard sequel to that film is a hoot.

On behalf of myself, Ryan Lambie, Louisa Mellor, Mike Cecchini and Andrew Blair, whose words you are about to read, thank you. Join us in our printed festival of movie geekdom, while we help ourselves to a biscuit.

SIMON BREW
@simonbrew

JUST WHILE WE'VE GOT YOU, ONE OTHER LITTLE THING WE'D LIKE TO CHAT ABOUT...

On 11 August 2014, as you probably know, the much-loved actor, comedian and human being Robin Williams took his own life. In the years that followed, more details have come to the fore, and it's a sad, sad story. One of the factors in there is the depression that Williams had been battling throughout his life.

To try and find a positive in the midst of such a tragedy, Den of Geek launched Geeks Vs Loneliness, a weekly series that used the audience we're lucky to have to talk about things that may be affecting some of us, or people we know. You can find the full archive here: www.denofgeek.com/geeks-vs-loneliness.

But for the purposes of right here, right now: if you're in a tough place in your life, if you're struggling, if you're feeling lonely, even if something just doesn't feel quite right, please talk to someone. A common theme throughout all of our articles is that things tend to only get better when you let things out, and tell another person. A family, a friend, a stranger on an internet comment board, a Samaritan: please, find a way to stop internalizing your pains, and let other human beings help you.

Life is inevitably a lot, lot more complicated than the above paragraph makes it sound. But please know there are people rooting for you, however lonely you feel, and however dark the world looks. Stay awesome, and thank you for reading.

DEVELOPMENT
&
PRE-PRODUCTION

BRILLIANT OPENING CREDITS SEQUENCES IN MOVIES

Let's start right at the beginning. Once the ads have played, the trailers are over and you've tutted at the person using a smartphone in front of you, a movie's first chance to make an impact has traditionally been with its opening credits. But in recent times, there's been a paucity of these, as films opt instead for an opening scene, slamming the name of the film on the screen, and getting on with the action.

"I think these things go in fashionable waves," muses Richard Morrison, who has designed titles for the likes of *Quadrophenia* and *Sweeney Todd: The Demon Barber of Fleet Street*. "It's just down to the director, it's down to the script." However, Morrison remains a staunch fan of the title sequence, noting that "when people are rustling around with popcorn, it's quite good as an interlude to get them to have two minutes to realize the film is about to begin!"

It's been left primarily to the likes of the James Bond films to keep the flag flying for exquisite title sequences in recent times (see *The Spy Who Loved Me* and *Skyfall* for excellent 007 examples), but there have been some other notable instances. You more than likely know classics such as *Reservoir Dogs*, *Raging Bull*, the "spaghetti westerns", *GoodFellas* and suchlike. But do dig out a few of the following if you get the chance.

THE ADVENTURES OF TINTIN (2011)

This isn't a film that gets talked about much in the pantheon of Steven Spielberg movies, yet in the midst of it is a brilliant chase sequence, and the opening titles are a delight, with a silhouette of Tintin dancing through the list of names, giving you a bit of a bonus action sequence.

GET OVER IT (2001)

The Kirsten Dunst-headlined teen movie *Get Over It* (loosely based on Shakespeare's *A Midsummer Night's Dream*) puts the song "Love Will Keep Us Together" to good use, as a young Ben Foster (who would go on to play Lance Armstrong in *The Program*) walks away from his newly ex-girlfriend's home with his possessions in a cardboard box, while a dance number gradually comes together in the background.

ALIEN (1979)

That old mantra that less is more has rarely been better proved than with the chilling opening to Ridley Scott's original *Alien* film. As Jerry Goldsmith's score gradually sinks its claws deep into your skin, the name of the film slowly appears. The 1986 sequel *Aliens* would repeat the trick, and *Alien 3* (1992) has an opening that is brutally effective.

LORD OF WAR (2005)

One of the more chilling modern openings to movies, for its sheer matter-of-factness. Nicolas Cage gives a quick to-camera introduction, before we follow the cold, clinical manufacturing of a bullet as it goes through a factory production line.

LOCK, STOCK AND TWO SMOKING BARRELS (1998)

As the credits kick in, director Guy Ritchie wisely focuses the opening of *Lock, Stock and Two Smoking Barrels* on Jason Statham – more to the point, Jason Statham selling tat on a market stall. One glare from the mighty Statham and all stock will surely be sold in double-quick time.

SUPERMAN RETURNS (2006)

It was the surprise element of the opening titles for Bryan Singer's belated *Superman* sequel *Superman Returns* that gave so many such joy when moviegoers filed in to see the film. Singer's movie replicated the original title style from *Superman* and *Superman II*, and when you watch them you get a fresh appreciation of just how joyous the originals were. To see such titles done badly, meanwhile, dig out *Superman IV: The Quest for Peace*, in which they are sped up to the point of WTF.

BARBARELLA (1968)

Well, you can't say this one doesn't attract attention. When the opening sequence of *Barbarella* kicks off, it looks like we've got

Jane Fonda in *Barbarella*. Saluting the fact that someone appears to have stolen her goldfish.

the standard convention of a space dweller floating in zero gravity. But what we actually get is Jane Fonda deciding that clothes are somewhat of a luxury. Best not go searching for the clip on YouTube, though – someone's bound to have a policy against that sort of thing.

DOCTOR STRANGELOVE OR: HOW I LEARNED TO STOP WORRYING AND LOVE THE BOMB (1964)

Stanley Kubrick's funny, surgically precise black comedy about the Cold War is best known – rightly – as an acting tour de force for the late, great Peter Sellers. But give the credits another look if you get a chance. The film opens by aiming its sights at the newsreel reporting of the era, with soft, soothing music playing over imagery of planes flying off to drop bombs.

Watchmen: comfortably one of the most divisive comic book adaptations, but few quibble with its stunning opening.

THE NAKED GUN TRILOGY (1988, 1991, 1994)

Each of the three *The Naked Gun* films opens with a variant on the same title-sequence gag: that we're following a police car with its light flashing, before said car takes, er, a few turns. By the end of the trilogy, the cop car in question has driven through a shower, gone through someone's house and attacked the Death Star. This is all accompanied by Ira Newborn's score, for which his aim was "get it as close to the 1950s' *M Squad* theme tune as I could without plagiarizing it and getting sued".

THREE MEN AND A BABY (1987) AND THREE MEN AND A LITTLE LADY (1990)

The opening credits to *Three Men and a Baby* play against the backdrop of Miami Sound Machine's "Bad Boy". But the skill here is that the drawings and artwork of Steve Guttenberg's character are setting the foundations of the three leads. You get Tom Selleck, Tom Selleck's facial hair, Ted Danson and a host of, well, short-term female visitors to their apartment, too. The sequel, *Three Men and a Little Lady*, would repeat the trick.

WATCHMEN (2009)

The *Watchmen* comic-book series was always deemed impossible to film, but that didn't stop director Zack Snyder from choosing it as his follow-up to his smash hit 300. The resultant film varies according to which of the three available cuts you opt for, but there's little question that he nails the feel of it in the excellent opening sequence.

FLASHDANCE (1983)

Jennifer Beals goes for a bike ride. Irene Cara sings a song. And then the opening to the iconic 1980s box office hit *Flashdance* gets down to business. By the time the names of producers Jon Peters and Peter Guber are up on the screen, we're into some serious welding action. It's never looked better.

CATCH ME IF YOU CAN (2002)

Steven Spielberg's breezy caper – albeit one that runs to nearly 2½ hours – follows con artist Frank Abagnale Jr (played by Leonardo DiCaprio). It's a whole lot of fun and the tone is very much set by a terrific, quirky animated sequence that quickly establishes the tone of the film. John Williams's score is hugely underrated, too.

HOW *THE GIRL WITH THE DRAGON TATTOO* HELPED *DEADPOOL*

Director David Fincher's movies tend to include hugely arresting opening sequences. Take, for example, *Panic Room*'s wrapping of titles around architecture, and *Seven*'s demonstrating of things that come to prominence later on. But the urgent, visually stunning animation – the work of Tim Miller – that greets the opening of the English language take on *The Girl with the Dragon Tattoo* (2011) is hugely unsettling from the off. David Fincher recalled that he told Miller, "You're an animator, you've got eight weeks" and that he was looking for a "melange of nightmarish imagery". Miller obliged. He also turned around the opening for Marvel's 2013 film *Thor: The Dark World* on a tight deadline.

Unsurprisingly, 20th Century Fox was impressed. From 2011 onward, it had Miller in place as the director of the *Deadpool* feature, which it ummed and aahed about greenlighting. It took the leaking online of test footage that Miller had overseen to persuade Fox to give the go-ahead. Even then, Miller needed the skill and nimbleness he'd deployed in his earlier title sequences to bring *Deadpool* to the screen in 2016, on time and on budget.

COMEDIES WITH ANIMATED OPENING CREDITS SEQUENCES

In a trend kick-started in earnest by Blake Edwards's *The Pink Panther* (1963) and its sequels, a small subset of comedies opted to open up with an animated sequence as the titles played. If you're looking for a fun one, check out 1991's hit comedy *City Slickers* (the film that finally won *Shane* star Jack Palance an Oscar), although the less seen *Honeymoon in Vegas* – a film that was repackaged when its plot similarities to *Indecent Proposal* became notable – is worth seeking out, too.

Mind you, for animated openings, the classic 1978 musical *Grease* really is hard to beat (right through to the gloopy appearance of the film's title), as is the work of Terry Gilliam – *Monty Python's Life of Brian* (1979) being a prime example.

THE CLASSICS

It'd be remiss not to namecheck some of the outright classics of the opening title sequence, so might we also recommend you try the following?

- *BATMAN* (1989)
- *DO THE RIGHT THING* (1989)
- *THE SHINING* (1980)
- *STAR WARS* (1977)
- *TO KILL A MOCKINGBIRD* (1962)
- *TOUCH OF EVIL* (1958)
  VERTIGO (1958)

The subversive, hilarious opening of 2016's *Deadpool* movie.

THE THINGS THAT INSPIRE MOVIES

•••

The genesis of a blockbuster movie may be in a posh Hollywood boardroom, but the ideas that flesh out a movie can come from all sorts of places. Here are but a few examples.

One of the better-known instances of this centres on the 1997 comedy *In and Out*, starring Kevin Kline: a story of a teacher, played by Kline, whose former student wins a top acting prize and accidentally reveals that Kline's character is gay. It was a moment inspired by Tom Hanks's acceptance speech at the 1994 Academy Awards, when he took home the Best Actor Oscar for *Philadelphia* and unwittingly outed his former drama teacher.

Another example is the 1996 film *Jerry Maguire*, written and directed by Cameron Crowe. Arguably Tom Cruise's most popular role, certainly this side of *Top Gun*, the movie earned him a Best Actor Oscar nomination and proved to be a massive box office hit. But it actually came about as a strange side effect of another film. When, in 1990, Disney's *Dick Tracy* movie failed to have the box office impact that the studio was hoping for, the then-Disney movie boss Jeffrey Katzenberg penned a now legendary extensive memo outlining his views on the movie industry as it stood, and where the future lay. Something resonated with Cameron Crowe, because the "mission statement" that Katzenberg had written would spark the mission statement that Jerry Maguire pens in the film, and the story took hold from there. To paraphrase (badly and not particularly appropriately)

Jeff Goldblum in *Jurassic Park*, that's a sort of chaos theory at work.

Noel Clarke, meanwhile, was at one time a one-man British film industry, having a large part to play in no less than three features that landed in 2012. The last of the three – following *Fast Girls* and *Storage 24* – was *The Knot*, a wedding comedy that Clarke co-wrote and starred in. He'd been toying with writing a romantic comedy around the time he

Jerry Maguire probably wouldn't exist if *Dick Tracy* had been a massive hit movie.

Jingle All the Way: Arnie hunts for a toy. And funny jokes.

sprung to the attention of moviegoers with the 2006 film *Kidulthood*. But the catalyst for Clarke knocking the script into workable shape and pressing ahead with the movie was actually a dispute with the Australian actors' union. Clarke had been hired to star in Stephan Elliot's 2011 Aussie wedding feature *A Few Best Men*, but, Clarke recalls, "The Australian immigration committee only wanted three British actors. So when they had to lose one, I was the one that got lost. When that happened, I thought f--k 'em, we're going to make our own one." He did. The script for what became *The Knot* was reworked and updated, and the movie got its release.

Something far more mundane was the unlikely catalyst for Mark Herman's 1997 hit *Brassed Off!*. While making his way across England, the writer–director got stuck in a traffic jam. As a result, he took an unplanned turn and found himself back in the South Yorkshire town of Grimethorpe where he had sold bacon – yep, really – in his younger years. The place was now very different, though. "Seeing the shops I used to visit all boarded up, seeing these places like ghost towns, seeing that it was now easier to buy drugs than bacon, made me want to write something about it." He did. He penned the script for *Brassed Off!*, which duly told the story of the closure of the local mining colliery and the impact it had on the community, through the prism of its brass band.

These examples give a small indication of how unlikely events can come together to form a film idea, whatever the genre. Even something insignificant can prove inspirational. Composer Robert Kraft, for instance, was already mulling a story he'd read in a local paper that told of the strong wind, nicknamed the Hawk, that blows into Chicago from Lake Michigan. When a bracing gust hit him as he walked past New York's Hudson river (where the wind has much the same nickname), the movie that came out of it was called – yes – *Hudson Hawk*.

AND QUICKLY...

The 1993 film *In the Line of Fire* was inspired by producer Jeff Apple's memory of meeting, as a child, the US Vice President Lyndon B Johnson, surrounded by Secret Service agents in sunglasses and dark suits.

●●●

Writer Randy Kornfield came up with 1996's film *Jingle All the Way* when his in-laws spent the build-up to one Christmas hunting for a Power Rangers toy.

●●●

Sylvester Stallone started working on the 1976 movie *Rocky* after watching underdog Chuck Wepner fight Muhammad Ali in March 1975. Ali won, but Wepner went almost 15 rounds with him. Wepner's fighting qualities were said to have inspired the character of Rocky.

●●●

Co-director Pete Docter was inspired to begin work on what became the 2015 film *Inside Out* by observing the shyness of his preteen daughter. He related this back to his own childhood and began questioning how the human mind processes emotions.

UNDER-APPRECIATED MOVIES OF MAJOR MOVIE STARS

Let's take a quick breather and chat about some films that may have slipped off your radar. A lot of movie stars tend to be known for their big hits. But dig down into their list of credits and some interesting, occasionally more off-piste films are waiting to be found. Here are a few to get you going...

ARNOLD SCHWARZENEGGER

Key film: *Terminator 2: Judgment Day*
Underappreciated gem: *The Last Stand*

CLINT EASTWOOD

Key film: *The Good, the Bad and the Ugly*
Underappreciated gem: *The Beguiled*

BETTE DAVIS

Key film: *Whatever Happened to Baby Jane?*
Underappreciated gem: *The Nanny*

ELIZABETH TAYLOR

Key film: *Cleopatra*
Underappreciated gem: *Under Milk Wood*

CARY GRANT

Key film: *North by Northwest*
Underappreciated gem: *Mr. Blandings Builds his Dream House*

GEORGE CLOONEY

Key film: *Ocean's Eleven*
Underappreciated gem: *Good Night, and Good Luck*

JAMES STEWART

Key film: *It's a Wonderful Life*
Underappreciated gem: *The Shootist*

JENNIFER LAWRENCE

Key film: *The Hunger Games*
Underappreciated gem: *The Beave*

JOHN WAYNE

Key film: *The Searchers*
Underappreciated gem: *The Cowboys*

JOHNNY DEPP

Key film: *Pirates of the Caribbean*
Underappreciated gem: *Ed Wood*

KATHARINE HEPBURN

Key film: *Guess Who's Coming to Dinner*
Underappreciated gem: *Adam's Rib*

Far left: James Stewart; Left: Marilyn Monroe;
Above: John Wayne; Right: Johnny Depp

MARILYN MONROE

Key film: *Some Like it Hot*
Underappreciated gem: *Clash by Night*

PAUL NEWMAN

Key film: *Butch Cassidy and the Sundance Kid*
Underappreciated gem: *Slap Shot*

RUSSELL CROWE

Key film: *Gladiator*
Underappreciated gem: *The Insider*

TOM CRUISE

Key film: *Jerry Maguire*
Underappreciated gem: *Magnolia*

WILL SMITH

Key film: *Independence Day*
Underappreciated gem: *Six Degrees of Separation*

WHERE DOES A MOVIE BUDGET GET SPENT?

•••

We often hear about the mind-boggling costs of making a movie, with tens of millions of dollars seemingly thrown around as if it were small change. Even low-budget movies rarely seem to cost less than a million or two, and that kind of cash is huge by most people's standards. So where does the money get spent?

The 2005 film *Sahara*, starring Matthew McConaughey, became embroiled in a legal dispute, and as a consequence its budget was revealed in detail by the *Los Angeles Times*. This is just one example of one film, but it gives a fascinating insight into where the money goes. Here are just some of the highlights of the $160m expenditure – and that's before promotion and marketing costs.

(*Above*) *Sahara* cost a reported $160m to make, including $1.6m that was spent on accountants to keep track of it all.

(*Right*) Just a flavour of some of the budgeted costs for 2005's *Sahara*. Actual expenditure may have varied slightly.

THE FURTHER COST OF A STAR

On top of Matthew McConaughey's $8m payday, a total of nearly $1m was spent to pay for his entourage's travel, stunt double, assistant, personal trainer, chef, stand-in, security and gym room, among other costs.

EXTRA COSTS ASSOCIATED WITH A 7-MINUTE ACTION SCENE:

- **$915,415 for two powerful boats**
- **$548,162 for two gunboats**
- **$131,950 to build the shell of another**
- **$28,314 for helicopter rental, for aerial shots**
- **$288,285 for boat guns, weapons and 44,000 rounds of ammunition**
- **$211,120 for stunt performers**
- **$173,700 for boat fuel**
- **$60,231 for boat site rental fees**
- **$38,785 for set construction**

(The boats would all be resold for $803,049)

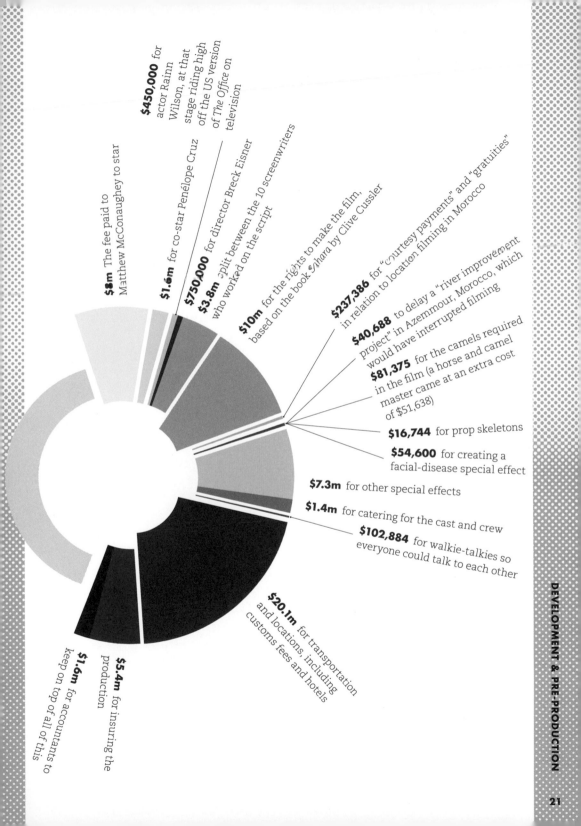

$8m The fee paid to star Matthew McConaughey

$1.6m for co-star Penélope Cruz

$750,000 for director Breck Eisner

$3.8m split between the 10 screenwriters who worked on the script

$450,000 for actor Rainn Wilson, at that stage riding high off the US version of *The Office* on television

$10m for the rights to make the film, based on the book *Sahara* by Clive Cussler

$237,386 for "courtesy payments" and "gratuities" in relation to location filming in Morocco

$40,688 to delay a "river improvement project" in Azemmour, Morocco, which would have interrupted filming

$81,375 for the camels required in the film (a horse and camel master came at an extra cost of $51,638)

$16,744 for prop skeletons

$54,600 for creating a facial-disease special effect

$7.3m for other special effects

$1.4m for catering for the cast and crew

$102,884 for walkie-talkies so everyone could talk to each other

$20.1m for transportation and locations, including customs fees and hotels

$5.4m for insuring the production

$1.6m for accountants to keep on top of all of this

HOW *X-MEN* KICK-STARTED THE SUPERHERO BOOM

•••

Bryan Singer's 2000 film *X-Men* was a major turning point in the era of the comic-book movie. The ramifications of it, and the confidence it gave Hollywood, mean that this movie was indirectly responsible for the fact that modern multiplexes are filled with superheroes.

Before the first of the *X-Men* series landed in cinemas, superhero movies had already had their moment. In the 1970s, uber-producers Alexander and Ilya Salkind had gambled hard on bringing Superman to the movies. They embarked on an ambitious plan to film *Superman* and *Superman II* back to back, and they very nearly managed it, save for running out of cash and falling out heavily with director Richard Donner. For those reasons, the focus went into finishing the first film, and the director Richard Lester would ultimately be hired to finish work on *Superman II*.

The two films hit big but fell short of kick-starting a trend. The decision to take the focus in *Superman III* off the title character and put it onto Richard Pryor's Gus Gorman stalled the series, which led to *Superman IV: The Quest for Peace* being budget-starved.

Throughout the 1980s plans were in place for an X-Men movie that would bring together the collection of mutants found in the comics by Marvel. Yet Marvel wasn't in much of a negotiating position and would all but go out of business before it got its

Plans were in place for an X-Men movie that would bring together the Marvel comic mutants

movie act fully together. Thus, Warner Bros. pressed ahead with a darker retelling of *Batman*, hiring Tim Burton to direct. It was a massive hit in 1989 but, again, the sequels enjoyed mixed fortunes. *Batman Returns* (1992) is the best-liked of the first run of *Batman* movies, but its box office was notably down on its predecessor. In came director Joel Schumacher for *Batman Forever* in 1995, and the box office was back up, although audience appreciation was down. The fourth film, 1997's *Batman & Robin*, was the lowest-grossing in the series and a critical failure.

An X-Men movie was always going to be a much tougher sell than a Batman or Superman film, with the main characters far less known that the aforementioned iconic heroes. Still, 20th Century Fox finally gave the go-ahead in 1996, hiring Bryan Singer – hot off the back of his Oscar-winning *The Usual Suspects* (and not far off finishing his underrated *Apt Pupil*) – to direct.

It was still a bumpy ride to the screen. The star power in the movie was light, with Patrick Stewart at that stage the highest-profile screen presence, courtesy of his years of service on the TV series *Star Trek: The Next Generation*. Hugh Jackman, who would effectively be playing the lead role of Wolverine, wasn't even on board until three weeks into filming (Dougray Scott, the original choice, had to back out when production clashed with *Mission: Impossible II*, in which he played the villain), and even then Jackman was regarded as an unknown.

Hindsight is easy, but there was little doubt that Fox had taken a massive gamble here. Even so, it wanted the budget trimmed by $5m before cameras rolled, costing the film characters such as Nightcrawler and Beast. But eventually, the show was on the road.

The summer of 2000 had far more traditional blockbusters lined up than a superhero movie: the *Mission: Impossible* sequel, star-driven movies such as *The Perfect Storm*, *Gone in 60 Seconds*, *Charlie's Angels*, *The Patriot* and a breakout by the name of *Gladiator*. *X-Men* was something of a wildcard, but when Steven Spielberg delayed shooting *Minority Report* for Fox (choosing to make *A.I. Artificial Intelligence* first), *X-Men* became – along with *Big Momma's House* – the studio's big summer release.

Fortune certainly favoured it. It arrived in the midst of a middling summer, one where there was nothing else quite like it. Backed by a skilled marketing campaign, the film opened in July 2000 in the US, to generally positive reviews but much higher than expected takings. Despite X-Men being a relatively unknown comic-book brand as far as a mainstream audience was concerned, the film's $57.5m opening weekend eclipsed the similar opening for any *Batman* or *Superman* film. Fox had a new franchise on its hands.

It was determined to cement its position. With Marvel Studios in the financial mire, Fox found itself with the rights to make films based on the Marvel comic-book superheroes Daredevil and Fantastic Four, and it put projects based on those properties onto its slate, as it quickly got moving on an *X-Men* sequel. And as movie studios were edging away from sheer film star power to generate big hits, rivals this time took notice, and with some success.

This had happened before, it should be noted. A year after Warner Bros. released *Batman* in 1989, Disney lined up another comic-book hero, Dick Tracy, and sunk millions into the making and of the promotion for the film – to not enough avail, as its experience of making and promoting the movie would put Disney off tackling a similar project for a long time. Rivals, too, failed to take advantage. A series of relatively lacklustre superhero movies followed, but few were really championing Billy Zane as The Phantom or Alec Baldwin as The Shadow.

This time it was very different. For one thing, the *X-Men* sequel, *X2: X-Men United* (released in 2003), righted many of the wrongs of the original. But also, Marvel had sold the screen rights for *Spider-Man* to Sony, and Sam Raimi's *Spider-Man* (2002) had proved an even

Batman (1989): it took over a decade for another comic-book character to enjoy the success of Tim Burton's ground-breaking blockbuster.

bigger hit by the time *X2* rolled around the following year.

The hits kept coming and the momentum grew. It was the third chance for Hollywood to capitalize on a superhero movie explosion, and this time it worked. Sony's *Spider-Man 2* (2004) remains one of the finest in the genre, and even Fox's *X-Men: The Last Stand* (2006) overcame fan backlash to become the biggest *X-Men* movie at the box office, at least until 2014's *X-Men: Days of Future Past* came around.

In the midst of this, there were two further developments. Warner Bros. finally worked out what it wanted to do with its *Batman* movie franchise, offering it to a young filmmaker called Christopher Nolan, off the back of his stunning breakthrough, *Memento*, and his remake of *Insomnia*. Then Marvel Studios – which by this time had seen Universal bring *Hulk* to the big screen – got itself financially into a position from which it could control more of its own destiny. It

sold the *Iron Man* screen rights to Universal Studios, which in turn passed them on to 20th Century Fox, which in *their* turn passed them on to New Line Cinema (eventually owned by Warner Bros.). None of them could get a script to work and thus the rights reverted back to Marvel. It didn't miss its chance.

Marvel got working on the *Iron Man* project from scratch in late 2005, and the following year hired Jon Favreau to direct. It was Favreau who persuaded the studio to give Robert Downey Jr the lead role. None of the breakout comic-book movies since 2000's *X-Men* had required a star name; also, Robert Downey Jr's career was in a tough place (he had served time in prison in 2000) and so he was a risky choice. Yet by *Iron Man 3*, he'd become such a big name that Marvel was reportedly paying him $50m, all in, for the part.

Marvel had struck gold – *Iron Man* was the breakout hit of summer 2008. Only defeated at the box office by *The Dark Knight*, it overtook

The Avengers, and *Avengers: Age of Ultron*, have been the culmination of Marvel's cinematic universe work.

DEVELOPMENT & PRE-PRODUCTION

Iron Man was in development for many years, before Robert Downey Jr eventually landed the role.

At one stage, 20th Century Fox was planning spin-off movies for the characters of Wolverine and Magneto, in what became the early building blocks of a cinematic universe. Superhero characters crossing over wasn't really a thing in the 2000s, and, to a degree, Fox was ahead of the proverbial game.

The problem was that Fox's attempt didn't go to plan. The release of 2009's *X-Men Origins: Wolverine* was hampered by a workprint of the film leaking online in its entirety weeks ahead of release. Also, the relatively dour movie was seen as a step backward from the far more joyous series. Furthermore, the critical reception to *X-Men: The Last Stand, Fantastic Four* (2005) and *Fantastic Four: Rise of the Silver Surfer* (2007), and the double whammy of *Daredevil* (2003) and tepid spin-off *Elektra* (2004) had dented the studio's confidence. It would take the "soft" reboot, *X-Men: First Class* (2011) – which incorporated elements of the planned, but ultimately abandoned, *X-Men Origins: Magneto* film – to get it motoring again.

Marvel, though, was by 2009 preparing *Iron Man 2* for release the next year, and was teasing more and more what would become 2012's *The Avengers*. When *The Avengers* became one of the first movies ever to break the $1bn mark at the global box office, pretty much every major studio started investigating a cinematic universe of its own.

the US gross of *Indiana Jones and the Kingdom of the Crystal Skull*. Marvel, in turn, started plotting, with a post-credits scene teasing the *Avengers* initiative. Its Marvel cinematic universe was thus underway, and while its next film, *The Incredible Hulk*, would struggle in comparison, the following debut adventures for Thor and Captain America, together with Joss Whedon's *The Avengers*, completed the Marvel turnaround.

The crumbs for that success, though, go all the way back to the summer of 2000: the summer when Fox threw its might behind *X-Men*, in turn creating a film universe that has accommodated *The Wolverine*, *Deadpool*, *Logan* and more. What if it had flopped? Chances are the blockbuster movie world would look very different.

FILMS YOU MAY NOT KNOW WERE BASED ON COMIC BOOKS

Comic-book movies seem to dominate blockbuster cinema in the 2010s, with the schedules bursting with superhero films. But comic books have a lot more up their sleeves than capes and superpowers.

One of the most constant complaints aimed at Hollywood blockbusters seems to be the obsession with comic books. For those who were starved of superhero movies throughout the 1970s and 1980s, the downpour is welcome. But to lump superhero and comic-book movies together overlooks the versatility and breadth in the storytelling found in some comics. Granted, the likes of Batman, Superman, Iron Man and the X-Men debuted in the pages of comics. But then so did stories that became acclaimed films for the likes of David Cronenberg, Tom Hanks and Walt Disney Animation Studios.

American Splendor (2003) is an excellent example. It gives the brilliant Paul Giamatti probably his best screen role (with the exception of *Sideways*). He plays the late Harvey Pekar, in a biopic that skilfully marries up elements of fiction and aspects of Pekar's life. (It's a genuinely wall-breaking biopic, in which the real Pekar is seen ambling in from time to time.)

The film is based on the *American Splendor* series of autobiographical comic books written by Pekar, and on the 1994 graphic novel *Our Cancer Year*, which he penned with his wife, Joyce Brabner, during his

battle with cancer. Writer–directors Shari Springer Berman and Robert Pulcini deserve considerable credit for the way they translate panel to screen. Few biopics, be they based on books, plays or interviews, have the sheer verve that Berman and Pulcini bring to Pekar's story. Pekar passed away in 2010, but he lived long enough to see the film of his life become a justified cult hit.

The late Harvey Pekar, who popped up regularly in the biopic of his life, *American Splendor*.

Road to Perdition remains a visually loyal comic-book adaptation.

A more mainstream example of the high-quality storytelling in comics that became films is the 2002 film **Road to Perdition**, starring Tom Hanks. Hanks hasn't starred in too many movies that garnered a rating of "R" (for "Restricted") from the Motion Picture Association of America, exceptions being *Bachelor Party* (1984) and *The Green Mile* (1999).

Director Sam Mendes picked *Road to Perdition* for his second film, following his Oscar-winning triumph *American Beauty*, with David Self adapting the 1998 source comic book of the same name, which was written by Max Allan Collins and illustrated by Richard Piers Raynor. For this crime drama set in 1931, Mendes eloquently realized the moody, shadowy art of the page on screen. (See also Warren Beatty's *Dick Tracy*, Zack Snyder's *Watchmen* and Robert Rodriguez' *Sin City* for further examples of bringing the style of the page to the screen.) *Road to Perdition* would become a commercial hit and also attract several Oscar nominations.

THE OTHER WAY AROUND

Sometimes in a film you get to see a character who puts together their own comic book, to get through day-to-day life. One of the most under appreciated examples of this is found in 2002's *The Dangerous Lives of Altar Boys*, directed by Peter Care and based on a novel by Chris Fuhrman. Starring Kieran Culkin and Emile Hirsch, it follows a bunch of friends at a Catholic school who put together a comic book that gets them on the wrong side of those in charge, most notably Jodie Foster's Sister Assumpta. It's not the easiest film to find, but it's very much worth seeking out.

David Cronenberg's *A History of Violence* was a lean adaptation of a comic book, stripping the story back to its core.

THERE'S MORE...

Here are a few ore films you may not have realized were originally based on comic books or graphic novels.

WHEN THE WIND BLOWS (1986)
TIMECOP (1994)
MEN IN BLACK (1997)
FROM HELL (2001)
GHOST WORLD (2001)
OLDBOY (2003)
BULLETPROOF MONK (2003)
30 DAYS OF NIGHT (2007)
WANTED (2008)
OBLIVION (2013)
THE DIARY OF A TEENAGE GIRL (2015)

Its origins are little-known, however, and the marketing campaign certainly did little to play them up.

A shout, too, for David Cronenberg's brilliant, tense **A History of Violence**, which Josh Olson adapted from the 1997 graphic novel of the same name, written by John Wagner and illustrated by Vince Locke. The movie was released in 2005 – and earned added fame for reportedly being the last mainstream Hollywood film to get a wide VHS release. There was some controversy in the build-up to the film, when Olson announced his intention to use the graphic novel as a basis.

Viggo Mortensen, who would star in the film, turned the movie down off the back of Olson's original draft, and it was only director Cronenberg hammering the screenplay from around 120 pages down to a lean 72 that led to Mortensen's change of heart. Much of the flashback backstory of the graphic novel is gone, but while *A History of Violence* is rarely regarded as a particularly faithful example of a story going from page to screen, it is a very successful one. The tone and feel were captured, even if chunks of the storytelling were sacrificed.

Comic books and graphic novels (novels with a comic-strip format) have long ventured into areas that mainstream storytelling media have avoided. Unsurprisingly, they have held more and more appeal to filmmakers, be they making outright superhero films or offbeat dramas. It's just that these sources tend not to get the credit and respect they deserve.

HOW *ALIEN: RESURRECTION* LED TO THE *ICE AGE* MOVIES

•••

As we know, ideas for films can come from all sorts of places. Another example of an unusual source of inspiration is the hugely successful *Ice Age* franchise: the roots of these films go back to the 1997 film *Alien: Resurrection*.

When Blue Sky Studios was tasked with creating swimming CGI (computer-generated imagery) xenomorphs for *Alien: Resurrection*, the fourth film in the *Alien* franchise, its animators looked to the natural world for ideas. Aptly for H R Giger's demonic creations, inspiration was found in a Galápagos Islands creature nicknamed by Charles Darwin the "imp of darkness".

"We patterned [the xenomorphs'] movements on reference footage of sea iguanas," Blue Sky's digital effects supervisor for *Alien: Resurrection*, Mitch Kopelman, told *American Cinematographer* magazine in November 1997. "They have this crazy little swim where they tuck their legs under their bodies and use this really long tail to

Alien: Resurrection's stunning underwater sequences were the highlight of a muddled film.

propel themselves." The result was the CGI swimming aliens that pursued Ellen Ripley and co. through the flooded kitchens of the USM *Auriga* in the film.

Alien: Resurrection was Blue Sky's first gig from 20th Century Fox. A VFX (visual effects) house at the time, the studio had spent its first decade building up revenue piecemeal from television adverts and idents (short pieces identifying channels). "When I started at Blue Sky," *Rio* and *Ice Age* director Carlos Saldanha said, "it was a handful of people, a lot of TV commercials, a lot of flying Tylenol pills!"

There were not just Tylenol (headache) pills, but also computer-generated M&Ms and talking coffee beans. Plus there was a CGI electric razor so photorealistic that it tricked the judges at that year's Clio Awards for advertising into thinking it was the real deal, according to Blue Sky co-founder Carl Ludwig.

Disney had given the Blue Sky founders their first experience of producing CGI for the movies. All six founding members had worked together at the now-defunct New York computer tech company MAGI, which had been hired by Disney to create the Light Cycle animations for 1982's *Tron*. After MAGI closed its doors for good in the mid-1980s, those former employees united to start their own company. In 1987, Blue Sky Studios was born.

The studio quickly became recognized for the strength of its character animation. "Every time we did a project, I would try to put more character animation in it," creative vice-president Chris Wedge explained. Whenever it came to cutting together the studio's latest demo reel, Wedge would include only that side of their work, building Blue Sky a reputation as character animators for hire.

Wedge's reputation-building paid off when MTV decided to develop its 1992 live-action-stop-motion short *Joe's Apartment* into a 1996 feature film. The job of creating computer-generated cockroach characters fell to Blue Sky, which had previously made several animated idents for the channel.

Joe's Apartment, a not-often-talked-about MTV production, boasted some of the building blocks of the *Ice Age* series.

That success was the calling card Blue Sky needed to break into CGI work for Hollywood. Commissions followed for Universal's *A Simple Wish* and DreamWorks Pictures' *MouseHunt*, Paramount's *Star Trek: Insurrection* and three 20th Century Fox pictures, *Alien: Resurrection*, *Fight Club* (creating the penguin that tells Edward Norton's character to "slide" in his power-animal vision) and *Titan A.E.*

The huge financial losses brought about by *Titan A.E.* (around $100m according to producer Chris Meledandri) led to the closure of Fox Animation Studios in 2000. By that point, Blue Sky had grown from a company with a staff of six to one of over a hundred. "And when it came time to do the movies," says Chris Wedge, "we were ready."

Not just ready, but bolstered by having won an Academy Award for Wedge's animated 1998 short film *Bunny*. Outwardly the story of an elderly female rabbit irked by a bothersome moth while baking, *Bunny* is a perfectly formed reflection on love and grief.

"*Bunny* came from my desire to tell something that felt very organic, something that felt like the world of stories and fairy tales that I knew as a child," Wedge told us. In the film, he continues, "hopefully enough of [our ideas] were evident that it got Fox's interest going in joining us to make feature films."

In 1999, the year of the Oscar win for *Bunny*, two years after the two companies first collaborated on those swimming xenomorphs for *Alien: Resurrection*, 20th Century Fox bought Blue Sky Studios and made it into its movie animation arm.

The studio's first post-purchase brief? Developing an idea that Fox had been knocking around for a while, the story of a ragtag group of animals trying to survive the Ice Age. And the rest, as they say, is (pre)history.

Ice Age movies, at their peak, were grossing just shy of $1bn worldwide apiece.

RAISE YOUR CAPS

It's not just Blue Sky Studios that got their first screen break in the 1990s. Early movie work by Pixar Studios can be seen in Disney's 1991 classic *Beauty and the Beast*. The majestic swoop across the ballroom as the Beast and Belle dance was generated using Pixar's CAPS technology (CAPS standing for Computer Animation Production System). Even before that, Pixar's CAPS had been used for the striking opening of 1990's *The Rescuers Down Under*, also from Disney, as the camera dashes across a field of flowers. Pixar's first full-length feature, *Toy Story*, would eventually follow, in 1995.

UNMADE *STAR WARS* & *STAR TREK* MOVIES

Getting a *Star Wars* or a *Star Trek* project off the ground must be a bit easier than other projects, right? After all, even badly performing films in the respective franchises rarely take less than nine figures at the box office. Yet some *Star Wars* and *Star Trek* films have died in development hell. Here is a selection of them. (Across films, TV and videogames, there are over 50 in all, and counting.)

STAR TREK: *PLANET OF THE TITANS*

When the original *Star Trek* television series first aired in the 1960s, it wasn't the juggernaut we know it as today. But its repeated showings in syndication on US television helped build its audience. Such was the show's growing popularity that a feature film was being discussed from the early 1970s.

One project that got quite advanced was *Star Trek: Planet of the Titans*, penned by two British writers, Chris Bryant and Allan Scott (the pair had written 1973's *Don't Look Now*). Philip Kaufman (*The Right Stuff*) was signed up to direct, and the plan was to shoot the film in the UK to cut costs. Pre-production work actually began, and the story would have seen the USS *Enterprise* go down a black hole, with the crew then finding themselves at the dawn of humankind.

But *Star Trek: Planet of the Titans* was a troubled enterprise (arf). There were (eventually resolved) difficulties getting the two leads, William Shatner and Leonard Nimoy, to commit to the film. Furthermore, the budget was ballooning and the project was running over schedule. The plug was pulled just weeks before *Star Wars* was released in cinemas for the very first time, back in 1977.

Star Trek: The Motion Picture, the first *Star Trek* film, would follow two years later and be unrelated to *Star Trek: Planet of the Titans*.

STAR WARS: **GEORGE LUCAS'S EPISODES VII–IX**

When J J Abrams and his team were developing what would become 2015's hugely successful *Star Wars: The Force Awakens*, they had the option of tapping into the original sequel trilogy that George Lucas had mapped out. As early as 1980, Lucas had talked about *Star Wars* being a nine-part saga, and he would duly make films one to six.

The story goes that the sequel trilogy would have seen a romance for Luke Skywalker, narrative arcs for his children, and the rebirth of the Republic, although Lucas subsequently distanced himself from those ideas. He had been working on fresh *Star Wars* ideas, but when Disney bought Lucasfilm, it opted to develop its own story arcs instead.

STAR TREK: *THE FIRST ADVENTURE*

Star Trek was set to celebrate its 25th birthday in 1991, and Paramount Pictures intended to mark the occasion with a new feature film. As such, it earmarked *Star Trek: The First Adventure* to head into production once work was completed on *Star Trek V: The Final Frontier*, which William Shatner had directed and which was released in 1989.

Star Trek: The First Adventure would be a film that covered some of the ground that J J Abrams's 2009 *Star Trek* movie reboot would explore, as the action was primarily to be set in the Academy, as we got to see how James T Kirk, "Bones" McCoy and Spock met in the first place. It would have introduced a new core cast, who presumably would have been given the job of taking the movie franchise forward.

But that didn't happen. Although a screenplay was penned and some design work was undertaken, Paramount put *Star Trek: The First Adventure* into turnaround after a year of work. The decision was attributed to a change of management at Paramount, with the new regime wanting something more conventional and less risky for *Star Trek*'s birthday. Thus, it opted to give the original crew one last big-screen adventure, green-lighting the excellent *Star Trek VI: The Undiscovered Country* instead.

━━━━━

THE *STAR WARS* ROBOT FILM

In the aftermath of the success of the original *Star Wars* movie, and with *The Empire Strikes Back* on the way, George Lucas gave an interview back in 1980 to *Prevue* magazine in which he admitted that "I came up with some ideas for a film about robots, with no humans in it".

While an animated television series focusing on droids would follow in due course, this feature plan sounded like a spin-off for R2-D2 and C3-PO. But while modern cinema is rich with spin-off movies and cinematic universes, in the early 1980s it was an era when big sequels were still looked down upon. Lucas would stop talking about his robot movie within months of first mentioning it. Likewise, he mooted a Wookiee movie at around the same time, but that too died a quick death.

The original *Star Trek* crew: their transporter struggled a little to get them to the movies.

SEQUEL TO STAR TREK: NEMESIS

The final big-screen adventure of the *Star Trek: The Next Generation* crew was the tenth *Star Trek* film, *Star Trek: Nemesis*, a not very highly regarded entry in the growing Trek box set. But it did leave some threads behind, and at one stage the intention was to give Jean-Luc Picard (Patrick Stewart) and his crew a final trip around the planets, which would have brought in elements of the *Star Trek: Deep Space Nine* and *Star Trek: Voyager* television series as well.

The plot would have seen Riker (Jonathan Frakes) commanding the USS *Titan*, but getting caught in Romulan space, requiring the assistance of the *Enterprise*, *Voyager* and *Defiant* ships. However, when *Star Trek: Nemesis* floundered at the box office, this particular project was quickly abandoned.

STAR TREK: THE BEGINNING

Realizing that *Star Trek: Nemesis* had brought the adventures of the *Star Trek: The Next Generation* crew to an end, Paramount first looked to reboot *Star Trek* on the big screen in 2005, with *Star Trek: The Beginning*. The film would have focused on an ancestor of William Shatner's James T Kirk leading a small group during the Terran/Romulan War. Erik Jendresen, who worked on the *Band of Brothers* television mini-series, was recruited to write a screenplay.

However, another change at the top of Paramount Pictures put an end to this one. The incoming management went in a different direction, eventually commissioning the successful 2009 big-screen reboot, starring Chris Pine and Zachary Quinto.

Paramount opted to reboot *Star Trek* with new stars Zachary Quinto (left) and Chris Pine (right), rather than make a *Star Trek: Nemesis* sequel.

George Lucas's sale of Lucasfilm to Disney led to the cancelling of *Star Wars* 3D re-releases.

ATTACK OF THE CLONES/REVENGE OF THE SITH 3D RE-RELEASES

In February 2012, before he sold Lucasfilm to Disney in October of that year, George Lucas re-released *Star Wars: Episode I – The Phantom Menace* in cinemas, in 3D. It'd be fair to say that it remains one of the least-liked *Star Wars* film, but Lucas was insistent that he wanted to re-release 3D remasters of each of the movies in order. If there wasn't sufficient interest in Episodes I to III getting re-releases, the subtext seemed to say, then the chances of Episodes IV to VI – the films the fans really wanted to see again on the big screen – appearing were very slim.

As it happened, one of the first things Disney did when it bought Lucasfilm from George Lucas for just over $4bn (and how much of a bargain does that look now?) was to cancel the already booked-in big-screen re-releases of *Attack of the Clones* and *Revenge of the Sith*. Disney suggested that it hadn't ruled out revisiting the idea of 3D re-releases, but that its focus was on the annual roster of new *Star Wars* movies it had planned instead.

On the small screen, one of the *Star Wars* projects that sounded the most promising was a hugely ambitious live-action tv series that George Lucas spent many years developing. His plan was to have two seasons of scripts in place before he got going, and he recruited a team of writers including Ronald D Moore (*Battlestar Galactica*), Chris Chibnall (*Doctor Who*) and Matthew Graham (*Life on Mars, Ashes to Ashes*) to be part of his group of scribes. They duly worked on and off over a period of two years to come up with scripts – Lucas wanted to make all the episodes and then find a broadcaster, once they were done. In some ways, he was foreseeing the Netflix model, in which an entire series is released in one chunk.

It all stopped quite suddenly, though. "We just came to the end of the process," recalled Matthew Graham. "[George] wanted 50 scripts, and we got to the point where there were 50 scripts." But those 50 episodes then stayed in limbo, with the party line being that Lucas was waiting for technology to advance to the point where it'd make the show he wanted to realize affordable.

"I can't remember the time frame. We worked on the show in 2008, 2009, maybe [it] bled a little into 2010," Graham recalled. "I had phone catch-ups with the producers about when they were going to move the production to Australia. Then it all went quiet for six months or ten months or something, then suddenly I heard that Lucasfilm had been sold to Disney." Since that happened, there's been no sign of the project being resurrected, and the 50 scripts remain under lock and key.

ACTORS CAST IN COMIC-BOOK MOVIES (WHO NEVER GOT TO PLAY THE ROLE)

•••

The story of Nicolas Cage's casting as Superman in the 1990s, for the aborted *Superman Lives* (which would have been directed by Tim Burton), has become so infamous that it inspired a fun documentary, *The Death of "Superman Lives": What Happened?* (2015). But Cage is far from the only person to be cast as a significant comic-book character, only to end up not playing the role.

CATWOMAN

For 1992's *Batman Returns*, Annette Bening – off the back of her terrific turn in Stephen Frears's *The Grifters* – won the role of Catwoman, ahead of the likes of Cher and Bridget Fonda. But she had to decline when she discovered she was pregnant. Michelle Pfeiffer would take on the role – although, notoriously, Sean Young lobbied for it (having originally been cast as Vicki Vale in 1989's *Batman*, from which she had to drop out after a riding injury), attempting to track down Tim Burton while wearing her own home-made Catwoman costume.

BATMAN

Following George Clooney and Christian Bale, Armie Hammer was supposed to be the next big-screen Batman. Hammer would eventually come to prominence in *The Social Network* and *The Lone Ranger*, but he was cast as the Dark Knight in director George Miller's ultimately abandoned *Justice League: Mortal*

project. The film had been scheduled for a 2009 release, before the studio pulled the plug.

VULTURE

Michael Keaton has finally brought Vulture to life on the big screen in 2017's *Spider-Man: Homecoming*. However, the role was originally John Malkovich's, as he was cast in it back in 2010 when Sam Raimi – who helmed the first three *Spider-Man* films – was set to make his fourth in the series. But *Spider-Man 4* didn't happen. The rising price of the film, along with strained relations between Raimi and the studio, led to Sony rebooting instead, with the short-lived *The Amazing Spider-Man* series.

WOLVERINE

Not only was Hugh Jackman not the first choice to play Wolverine in the first *X-Men* film, but he wasn't even the first to be cast in the role. That honour had gone to Dougray Scott, who had to bow out of playing the character when *Mission: Impossible II* – in which he was playing the villain – heavily overran (as a consequence of the delays on Tom Cruise's previous film, *Eyes Wide Shut*). Scott thus dropped out of *X-Men*, and Jackman got a fast track to becoming a movie star.

IRON MAN

It's often forgotten how big a gamble the casting of Robert Downey Jr as Iron Man was, with director Jon Favreau going out on a metaphorical limb for the then troubled actor. Had fate taken a different turn, though, Tom Cruise would have donned the red suit. He was set to star in and produce *Iron Man* in the earlier 2000s but dropped out in 2004, noting that "it just didn't feel to me like it was going to work".

"It just didn't feel to me like it was going to work"
Tom Cruise on Iron Man

SPIDER-MAN

For many years, between making *True Lies* and *Avatar* in particular, writer–director James Cameron was wrestling with bringing Spider-Man to the big screen. At the time, the webslinger was caught up in complicated rights disputes, which ultimately prevented him from bringing his take on the character to fruition. He'd even decided on his star, with Michael Biehn all set to reunite with Cameron following their work together on *Aliens* and the first two *Terminator* films. Cameron wanted Arnold Schwarzenegger to play Doctor Octopus, but Arnie would have to content himself with his notable turn as Mr Freeze in 1997's *Batman & Robin*.

Tom Cruise dropped out of playing Iron Man in 2004. Nicolas Cage had been linked with the role, too.

STRANGE OR ILL-ADVISED MOVIE SEQUELS THAT NEVER WERE

Jessica Rabbit kidnapped by Nazis. Kevin Costner rescuing Princess Diana. We look back at a few strange movie sequels that were never made.

E.T. II: NOCTURNAL FEARS

As *E.T. the Extra-Terrestrial* sailed past the $300m mark at the box office in 1982, Spielberg and co-writer Melissa Mathison began putting together a treatment for a sequel called *E.T. II: Nocturnal Fears*. The proposed movie would have flipped the story of E.T. on its head, with alien friendship turning over into alien abduction. It would have brought back Elliott and his siblings, captured by an evil race of aliens who were distant cousins of E.T.'s breed of friendly and gentle scientists.

Disturbingly, Elliott and his brother and sister would have been experimented on and tortured, before E.T. finally swooped in and rescued them. The whole premise sounded rather nightmarish for a family film and, sensing this, Spielberg later ditched the

Steven Spielberg wanted E.T. to stand alone, and thus plans for a follow-up were abandoned.

Ferris Bueller only got to have one day off in the end. A plan for a sequel back in 2007 quickly petered out.

idea, saying it would "do nothing but rob the original of its virginity". Oh, and another reason to be thankful that *E.T. II: Nocturnal Fears* didn't happen: it divulged E.T.'s real name, which, we're told, is Zrek. Nice.

FERRIS BUELLER 2: ANOTHER DAY OFF

Like *E.T. the Extra-Terrestrial*, the film *Ferris Bueller's Day Off* had a style and atmosphere that would have been tricky to replicate in a sequel. Although Matthew Broderick and John Hughes had thrown around ideas for what might happen in a follow-up – Ferris's antics at college or his first job were proposed – they both concluded that it probably wasn't a good idea.

There were reports that a script put together by writer Rick Rapier in 2007 might finally be made into a movie. Called *Ferris Bueller 2: Another Day Off*, it would catch up with Ferris, now wealthy, 40 and hankering for a day off work. For the time being, however, it seems that a sequel to the much-loved 1986 movie is officially on the back-burner.

ROGER RABBIT: THE TOON PLATOON

Anarchic, funny and featuring a ground-breaking mix of live action and 2D animation, *Who Framed Roger Rabbit* was a deserved success for director Robert Zemeckis. Given the sheer number of great characters and ideas his noir comedy fantasy introduced, it's a little surprising, perhaps, that a sequel never appeared.

Yet screenwriter Nat Mauldin actually wrote a prequel called *Roger Rabbit: The Toon Platoon*, in which Jessica is kidnapped by Nazis and Roger discovers that his father is Bugs Bunny. The script was rewritten in the late 1990s, and involved Roger's rise to Broadway stardom rather than his brush with the Third Reich. Alan Menken was commissioned to write five songs for the project, now called *Who Discovered Roger Rabbit*.

Getting the thing animated, however, proved problematic. Test footage, comprising hand-drawn animation, CGI and live action, failed to impress Disney, and with the budget predicted to be somewhere north of $100m, the plug was pulled. For years it seemed as

The Bodyguard: Kevin Costner has very rarely touched sequels, but a possible *The Bodyguard 2* was a rare exception.

though a Roger Rabbit sequel would never happen and it's possible that it never will. In 2013 at San Diego Comic Con, producer Don Hahn said of the various Roger Rabbit sequel scripts that had been floating around Hollywood over the years, "There's none actively in discussion right now".

THE BODYGUARD SEQUEL

The film that marked the acting debut of singer Whitney Houston, and the success of which ensured that her song "I Will Always Love You" was played constantly on the radio, *The Bodyguard* was a big hit, in spite of mixed reviews. Maybe it's inevitable, then, that title hero Kevin Costner attempted to get a sequel off the ground toward the end of the 1990s, when he made a surprising choice of co-star for the film: Princess Diana.

Like Houston in the original, Diana would have played a fictionalized version of herself – in this instance, a vulnerable princess shielded from the press by Costner's gallant Frank Farmer. Princess Diana's untimely death in 1997 meant that she never got to fulfil the chance to become a Hollywood actress.

CLOSE ENCOUNTERS OF THE THIRD KIND SEQUEL: NIGHT SKIES

Steven Spielberg's wish-fulfilment fantasy of UFOs, mashed potato mountains and alien abduction was an unexpectedly huge hit for Columbia Pictures in 1977, and naturally enough, it wanted a sequel. Unenthusiastic about making one, but anxious that a sequel might be made without him (as had happened with *Jaws*), Spielberg began putting together a project called *Night Skies*.

Spielberg's concept for the sequel played up the subtle horror elements of the original *Close Encounters of the Third Kind*, with a story based on a real-life case known as the Kelly–Hopkinsville encounter, in which a family of farmers claimed to have been attacked by a group of little green aliens.

Although the project got far enough through the pre-production stage for the special-effects creator Rick Baker to have come up with various alien and ship designs, Spielberg soon abandoned it. The ideas he came up with would later be reused in *E.T. the Extra-Terrestrial*, *Poltergeist* and *Gremlins*.

DEVELOPMENT & PRE-PRODUCTION

40

MRS. DOUBTFIRE SEQUEL

Unlike Martin Lawrence's *Big Momma's House*, which spawned two further films, Robin Williams's hit comedy *Mrs. Doubtfire* never received a sequel. However, Fox did get as far as commissioning a script for one, with actress Bonnie Hunt on writing duties. The story would have involved Williams dressing up as Mrs. Doubtfire once again, this time so he could spy on his daughter at college. Williams, perhaps sensing that the premise was a bit creepy, turned it down.

Coincidentally, the comedy antics in *Big Mommas: Like Father, Like Son* involved Martin Lawrence and his screen son, Brandon T Jackson, hanging around a girls' school for the performing arts. Yes, it was a bit creepy.

FORREST GUMP SEQUEL

On the face of it, making a sequel to *Forrest Gump* might not have sounded like such a bad idea. Robert Zemeckis's 1994 film was a huge hit, won a raft of Oscars and became one of the most quoted movies of the mid-1990s. If all had gone to plan, we would have heard a lot more of Forrest Gump's gentle aphorisms in a sequel, written by the same scribe as the original, Eric Roth. Like the first film, it would have seen Forrest turn up at unexpected moments in history, though some of the ideas Roth had for a sequel sound far more eyebrow-raising than the scenarios we saw in the original. For one thing, Forrest would have danced with Princess Diana a few years before her car accident, and one scene would have seen Gump hiding in the back of O J Simpson's car as he's pursued by the police. (O J Simpson, as you may recall, was suspected of murdering his wife, Nicole Brown Simpson, and waiter Ron Goldman in June 1994.) At the time of writing, nothing more had surfaced from the project.

SEVEN SEQUEL

For a while, New Line appeared to be intent on making a belated sequel to David Fincher's hit 1995 thriller, *Seven*. A spec script called *Solace* was optioned, which would have been rewritten to accommodate Morgan Freeman's character, William Somerset, from *Seven*.

In spite of a follow-up novel, *Gump & Co.*, being published in 1995, plans for a big-screen *Forrest Gump 2* faded away.

Fourteen years separated *Jurassic Park III* and *Jurassic World*: but a very different fourth movie nearly happened.

This time, the detective would somehow have acquired psychic powers. In the end, New Line saw sense and cut any tenuous links between *Seven* and *Solace*. The movie finally came out in 2015 (although it didn't make it to the US until the end of 2016) with Anthony Hopkins in the lead, by now playing a psychic doctor named John Clancy. With a box office take of about $22m, *Solace* made less than a tenth of *Seven*'s haul 20 years before it.

JURASSIC PARK THIRD SEQUEL

Long-term *Jurassic Park* fans will know that, after Joe Johnston's second sequel emerged in 2001, a fourth entry was planned but remained trapped in development-hell for well over a decade. It took director Colin Trevorrow to finally bring us, in 2015, *Jurassic World*, which became a huge hit for Universal.

Long before *Jurassic World* rebooted the franchise, a procession of writers and directors were attached to a sequel, including *The Departed* screenwriter William Monahan and *The Crazies* director Breck Eisner. Around the year 2004, John Sayles – who'd previously

been involved with such monster movies as *Piranha*, *The Howling* and *Alligator* – turned in his draft of a script entitled *Jurassic Park IV*, and it's one of the few that have managed to slip out into public view.

That script's premise is something *Jurassic World* would later hint at: the use of behaviourally controlled dinosaurs by a private military company. The story is told from the perspective of an unemployed mercenary named Nick, who winds up at a Swiss castle run by an evil company called the Grendel Corporation. Nick is pressed into becoming a trainer for the militarized dinosaurs; in one scene, the toothy critters are used in a *The Expendables*-type mission that involves rescuing a kidnapped ten-year-old kid from a warehouse full of bad guys. Another mission involves assassinating a drug boss at his luxurious (and heavily guarded) mansion. Sayles's *Jurassic Park IV* script doesn't really feel like a *Jurassic Park* sequel at all – more a straight-to-video action movie that happens to have dinosaurs in it.

THE MOVIE SEQUELS YOU MIGHT NOT KNOW EXISTED

Sequels are pivotal to the bottom line of Hollywood studios now, but in times gone by they were sneered at or sent straight to video. In fact, there's a whole subset of movie sequels that you may simply have never heard of.

At the time of writing, there were no less than seven sequels to the 1992 surprise hit *Beethoven*. Naturally, in that time the core cast changed a lot, but as long as there was a shaggy Saint Bernard dog to stick on the DVD cover, then films such as *Beethoven's Big Break* (2008) and *Beethoven's Christmas Adventure* (2011) could somehow get through the system.

Beethoven is not alone in being pillaged for cheap straight-to-DVD sequels. The *American Pie* series enjoyed four cinematic movies, and four spin-offs – *American Pie Presents: The Naked Mile*, for instance. While even a huge hit like *Home Alone* (1990) eventually descended to a

Few audiences are better catered for than fans of *Beethoven* sequels. They breed faster than the dogs themselves.

The Birds II: let's just go ahead and say it's hardly up to the level of the original film.

reboot of sorts in the 2012 television movie *Home Alone: The Holiday Heist*. Yet for every *Kindergarten Cop 2* or *Ace Ventura: Pet Detective Jr.* (yep, it's a thing), there's a follow-up that wasn't intended to be hidden in a bargain bucket at a corner shop.

Take something like **The Sting II**. The 1973 original movie was awarded seven Academy Awards, including Best Picture, and Universal – at a time when sequels were very much a rarity – didn't rush into a follow-up. It took a decade, in fact, before *The Sting II* came about, with the aid of original screenwriter David S Ward (who would later become the creative force behind the *Major League* movies). Paul Newman and Robert Redford wisely gave *The Sting II* a miss, as did most audiences, with Jackie Gleason and Oliver Reed instead taking on the roles of con artists. In the words of *People* magazine, the film is "a real-life con game involving the ticket buyer". Ouch.

The Sting II isn't the only sequel to a classic.

For some bizarre reason, 31 years after the release of Alfred Hitchcock's outstanding 1963 thriller *The Birds*, the Showtime network debuted a made-for-TV sequel, *The Birds II: Land's End*. Even more bizarrely, the star of the original – Tippi Hedren – agreed to appear in the movie, but in a different role. She would subsequently declare that the film "embarrasses me horribly" in a 2002 interview with *Chiller Theater* magazine. Director Rick Rosenthal didn't wait that long, insisting his name be taken off the final cut of *The Bird's II: Land's End*, which is instead credited to "Alan Smithee" (for a long time a credit regularly used by directors who wanted to dissociate themselves from a film).

One person who did reprise the same role in a sequel to an acclaimed original was Ruth Gordon, who had won the Academy Award for Best Supporting Actress for playing Minnie Castevet in 1968's *Rosemary's Baby*. Staggeringly, a sequel followed in 1976 by the name of **Look What's Happened to Rosemary's Baby**. Few took up the offer of the film's title, however. Again, this was a television movie, and just to, er, add to its authenticity, it had utterly ignored the follow-up book, *Son of Rosemary*, from author Ira Levin.

———

A more modern example is the excellent 1993 film Addams Family Values. When it failed to match the box office of 1991's The Addams Family, Paramount Pictures opted not to pursue a third film. But one still happened, in 1998: Addams Family Reunion. Appreciating that Raúl Juliá, one of the stars of the first two films, had tragically passed away, Paramount opted to replace pretty much the entire cast, with Tim Curry and Daryl Hannah taking over from Raúl Juliá and Anjelica Huston in the lead roles. Huston and Christopher Lloyd were offered the chance to return, but they wisely opted to wash their hair instead. Only Carel Struycken as Lurch and Christopher Hart as Thing returned. A TV series followed later in the same year, in turn replacing virtually all of the replacements for the cast that had been replaced.

One reviewer at Amazon summed it up: the film "was never given a DVD release, and quite rightly so".

Tim Curry and Daryl Hannah try, and fail, to recreate the Addams Family magic.

EVERY ONE OF THESE FILMS ACTUALLY EXISTS:

AMERICAN PSYCHO 2
("ANGRIER. DEADLIER. SEXIER.")

BAMBI II

BRING IT ON: FIGHT TO THE FINISH

CRUEL INTENTIONS 3

JARHEAD 2: FIELD OF FIRE

THE JERK TOO

LEGALLY BLONDES

MARLEY & ME: THE PUPPY YEARS

MEAN GIRLS 2

MEATBALLS 4

THE NEVERENDING STORY III

ROAD HOUSE 2: LAST CALL

S. DARKO

SINGLE WHITE FEMALE 2: THE PSYCHO

SMOKEY AND THE BANDIT PART 3

SON OF THE MASK

TOOTH FAIRY 2

TREMORS 5: BLOODLINES

WARGAMES: THE DEAD CODE

Son of the Mask: no caption could possibly get across how bad it is.

HOW A HE-MAN SEQUEL & A SPIDER-MAN MOVIE BECAME A JEAN-CLAUDE VAN DAMME HIT

•••

It's not uncommon that ideas for one film eventually end up in another. The Indiana Jones follow-ups, for instance, are not short of moments that were once considered for other chapters of that ongoing story. But the Jean-Claude Van Damme hit *Cyborg* was a stranger hybrid of ideas than usual...

A BATTLE FOUGHT IN THE STARS, NOW...COMES TO EARTH.

DOLPH LUNDGREN   FRANK LANGELLA

MASTERS
OF THE
UNIVERSE
The Live-Action Motion Picture

(*Above*) *Masters of the Universe* was expected to be a big hit. It wasn't, but it's still fun.

(*Left*) *Cyborg* includes key JCVD ingredients: fighting, lack of shirt, rain.

Cannon Films was in trouble by 1987. Its boom years, which lasted from the late 1970s to the mid-1980s, were largely thanks to an eclectic and hurriedly-made collection of B-movies: Chuck Norris action pictures, Charles Bronson revenge flicks and lots of things with the word "ninja" in the title. Thanks to its outsider status and anything-for-a-buck approach to filmmaking, Cannon Films became a major name in Hollywood, the grinning faces of its brusque founders – producers Menahem Golan and Yoram Globus – frequently appearing in TV news reports and Tinseltown trade papers.

In the mid-1980s, however, Golan and Globus began to change their strategy. While they would still make Charles Bronson and Chuck Norris films, they decided to break into the Hollywood big league with movies based on popular toys and comic-book characters. Unfortunately, Cannon's fast-and-loose approach to filmmaking didn't really gel with the requirements of a major summer film. They'd made expensive deals for the rights to make a *Superman* sequel, a Spider-Man movie and an adaptation of Mattel's toy line, He-Man, but Cannon could ill afford to pay for the production values those films demanded.

Cannon's approach to making films was to sell them before they were made. They'd attach a star and put together a poster, and use that package to attract financial backing. It was a tactic that worked perfectly well for the kinds of low-budget films Cannon was previously used to making (around the $1m–$2m range), but less so for something like *Superman IV: The Quest for Peace*, which, partly because of repeated budget cuts, wound up an embarrassing flop.

Cannon's He-Man movie, *Masters of the Universe*, was being made around the same time as *Superman IV*, and, not unreasonably, the studio expected big things. At one time, He-Man toys were flying off shelves all over America, and the tie-in animated series was a TV hit. The same financial headaches that plagued *Superman IV*, however, also hampered *Masters of the Universe*. Cuts were made everywhere to save cash, and director Gary Goddard later revealed in interviews that, while they were filming the final fight between Dolph Lundgren's He-Man and Frank Langella's Skeletor, the producers were pulling the plug as the cameras were actually rolling. Like *Superman IV*, *Masters of the Universe* would ultimately fail to turn much of a profit.

Nevertheless, Cannon took the bold step of announcing a *Masters of the Universe* sequel in 1987. Lundgren's flat refusal to reprise the role of He-Man didn't deter the producers, either; they simply hired muscle-bound surfer and model Laird Hamilton to take his place. The He-Man sequel also had a new director:

Albert Pyun, who had recently agreed to make Cannon's *Spider-Man* movie.

By late 1988, production had begun on *Masters of the Universe 2* and *Spider-Man*, with sets and costumes all put together ready for filming. The idea was that Pyun would direct both films simultaneously, starting with two weeks' production on *Spider-Man*, in which Pyun would shoot the scenes where Peter Parker receives his fateful spider bite. Then Pyun would shoot six weeks of *Masters of the Universe 2*, thus giving the actor playing Peter Parker enough time to bulk up to play Spider-Man before filming on that movie resumed.

Anyone wondering whether we'd missed an early comic-book movie classic with Cannon's *Spider-Man* should rest assured. As Pyun admits himself, producer Menahem Golan didn't really "understand" Spider-Man as conceived by Marvel; instead, he imagined the character as a literal human–spider hybrid with eight hairy arms.

Cannon's plans for Spider-Man and He-Man were scuttled, ultimately, by the studio's ongoing cash flow problems; when cheques made out to Marvel and Mattel bounced, relations between the studio and the rights holders began to falter. According to *Masters of the Universe* director Gary Goddard, He-Man toy manufacturer Mattel may have withdrawn the rights to *Masters of the Universe 2* after seeing the low-budget follow-up Cannon was planning to make. "Mattel saw the script, or perhaps the storyboards," Goddard said in a 2010 Q&A, "and pulled the licence."

All told, Cannon spent approximately $2m on both *Masters of the Universe 2* and *Spider-Man* and had little more to show for it than a collection of sets and costumes. Determined to give this latest black cloud a silver lining, Cannon turned to Pyun, and within the space of a single weekend a project called *Slinger* – and later retitled *Cyborg* – was born.

Pyun wrote a script that could incorporate the various abandoned sets and costumes into a dark, post-apocalyptic sci-fi fantasy. He envisioned a future where humanity was on the brink of being wiped out by a deadly virus, and where the only hope of a cure lies inside the head of a female cyborg.

In his haste to get a story on paper, Pyun named all the characters after guitars and amplifiers – Gibson Rickenbacker, Fender Tremolo, and so on. At the behest of the formidable Menahem Golan, upcoming martial-arts star Jean-Claude Van Damme was cast as Gibson – a canny choice as it turned out, since Van Damme was on the cusp of breaking through in the late 1980s. *Cyborg* would ultimately be released between two of Van Damme's early hits: 1988's *Bloodsport* and 1989's *Kickboxer*, both released by Cannon.

Jean-Claude Van Damme's career breakthroughs in the late 1980s proved fortuitous for Cannon Films.

It should be pointed out that Pyun never really intended to make the straight martial-arts movie that Cannon wanted. He envisioned something darker and more full-blooded, a kind of rock opera shot in black-and-white and with minimal dialogue. Understandably, Cannon pushed for a more crowd-pleasing action film instead.

Shooting on *Cyborg* took place over 23 days with a budget of just $500,000. The production was far from plain-sailing. Van Damme had to spend up to four hours in makeup while fake scars were applied. An early scene where Gibson is crucified resulted in Van Damme being strung up in the baking North Carolina sun for 7½ hours. Worst of all, actor Jackson "Rock" Pinckney, who played one of the "pirate" henchmen alongside villain Fender Tremolo (Vincent Klyn), was badly injured during a fight scene and, despite surgery, lost the sight in his left eye. Four years later, Pinckney took Van Damme to court and was awarded $485,000 in damages.

When filming was complete, Pyun assembled a black-and-white rough-cut of *Cyborg* for Cannon's producers to look at. "I fell in love with the [black-and-white] look and screened a heavy metal temp stereo mix and played back at 90db during the screening," Pyun later told *Forces of Geek*. "As you can imagine, the screening did not go well."

Pyun duly went back and made a less outlandish edit, with colour and less deafening rock music. This cut passed muster with Cannon, but not with test audiences. By then, *Bloodsport* had come out, and they were expecting more of the Van Damme they'd seen in that film: oiled-up and high-kicking, not, as seen at one point in the film, crucified.

The resulting cut – overseen by Cannon and not Pyun – may have been far from the director's moody intentions, but it proved to be a decent-sized hit. It made a shade over $10m at the box office, and its return on investment

Vincent Klyn in *Cyborg*.

was far better than the more expensive, comic-book fare that Cannon had dabbled in a few years earlier. *Cyborg* became a lasting cult film, too, thanks in no small part to its solid action, unusual mix of styles and superbly nasty performance from villain Vincent Klyn.

It says a lot that a 25-year-old, low-budget action film, cobbled together from the ashes of two much bigger productions, is still warmly remembered and enjoyed by B-movie connoisseurs. As well as a cult movie, *Cyborg* is a snapshot of a singular moment in filmmaking history and of the last throes of an equally unique studio. Cannon fell apart after *Cyborg's* release in 1989, brought low by a series of expensive ventures that didn't take off. Ironically, it was when Cannon returned to its off-the-cuff approach to filmmaking that it garnered one of the most lucrative movies of its final years. Had Cannon made more films like *Cyborg* and fewer films like *Superman IV*, its fate might have been very different.

WHY THE 1970s WERE SO GOOD FOR GANGSTER MOVIES

•••

**Each decade has a film genre that particularly comes to prominence.
So why were the 1970s so rich in gangster films?**

"There's only one thing that gets orders and gives orders, and this is it," says gangster Tony Camonte, motioning to a Tommy gun in 1932's *Scarface*. "It's a typewriter. I'm gonna write my name all over this town with it, in big letters!"

Loosely based on the exploits of real-life mobster Al Capone, *Scarface*'s story of Camonte's violent rise and fall fascinated audiences and horrified American censors. The film's producers, Howard Hawks and Richard Rosson, had attempted to head off accusations that their movie glorified gang violence, but the powers behind the Motion Picture Production Code took an increasingly dim view of crime movies in the 1930s, and cracked down on stories told from the perspective of criminals. In the middle of the decade, for example, the Code Administration handed down a directive that expressly forbade movie-makers from fictionalizing the story of bank robber John Dillinger.

Everything changed in the late 1960s, when the Production Code, which had begun to look out of step with the bold and explicit movies flowing into the US from Europe and elsewhere, was finally put to rest. The result was a new-found freedom for a generation of filmmakers: as described in Peter Biskind's book *Easy Riders, Raging Bulls*, such directors as Martin Scorsese, Francis Ford Coppola and Dennis Hopper were free to tell stories about criminals, gangsters and other wayward characters on the fringes of society.

Bonnie and Clyde, released in 1967, is an example of a movie that could never have been made under the old Hollywood order. Directed by Arthur Penn, and starring Faye Dunaway and Warren Beatty, it is the fictionalized story of two young bank robbers in the Great Depression. Controversial for its level of violence, *Bonnie and Clyde*, like *Scarface* 35 years earlier, was a hit with audiences; younger critics, such as Pauline Kael and Roger Ebert, were also hip to its counter-culture sensibility. As the 1960s flipped over into the 1970s, change was in the air: there was a sense that the movies Hollywood was making were out of touch with the new landscape of TV, the

Faye Dunaway in *Bonnie and Clyde*. Tame by modern-day standards, hugely controversial in 1967.

Vietnam War and the Civil Rights Movement. Hollywood may have wanted to make big, glossy movies like *Doctor Dolittle* in 1967, but what audiences were responding to were films rooted in the gritty and the everyday: *Bonnie and Clyde*, *Blow-Up* and *The Graduate*, all made in 1966–7, were far more successful than the hugely expensive *Doctor Dolittle*.

By the early 1970s, the stage was set for the return of the gangster movie – a genre that for decades was regarded as the preserve of B-movie moguls like Roger Corman (his 1967 *The St. Valentine's Day Massacre*, for exmaple, was about the infamous 1929 gangland killing in Chicago.) Director Francis Ford Coppola had initially turned down the chance to direct an adaptation of Mario Puzo's novel *The Godfather* for this very reason; he eventually took the job because he was in debt and, ironically, Paramount had made him an offer he couldn't refuse. Released in 1972, *The Godfather* was nothing short of a phenomenon, making close to $250m worldwide and briefly becoming the highest-grossing film of all time. In an era in which the US President himself was revealed to have shaky morals (the Watergate scandal first began to rise around Richard Nixon's feet in 1972), Coppola's operatic story of a young man's rise to power proved magnetic.

The result was a new era of classic gangster and crime films. The year 1973 alone included Martin Scorsese's *Mean Streets*, about a bunch of young guys trying to hustle their way up the Manhattan Mafia food chain; John Milius's *Dillinger*, which starred Warren Oates as the bank robber of the title; and *Black Caesar*, directed by Larry Cohen and featuring a soundtrack by James Brown. The following year, Coppola made *The Godfather Part II*, which attracted even more acclaim than its predecessor. These movies and others like

The Godfather: a film with scenes expertly spoofed by two animated movies – *Zootopia* (*Zootropolis* in some countries) and *Rugrats in Paris* – both aimed at audiences not old enough to watch Coppola's classic.

them, such as Sydney Pollack's *The Yakuza* (1975), were tough and explicitly violent in ways that filmmakers wouldn't have dared consider even in the pre-Code days (prior to 1934 and the enforcement of the Production Code). For a time, cinema was alive with outlaws and hoodlums.

Directors were now free to tell stories about wayward characters on the fringes of society

The rise of blockbusters driven by special effects such as *Jaws*, *Star Wars* and *Close Encounters of the Third Kind* in the second half of the 1970s meant that no other crime film would make the same impact as *The Godfather* – not even its sequel. But today the best gangster movies remain timeless, which might explain why they were still being made in the 1980s and '90s and into the new millennium. Whether we like them or not, we're drawn to characters with their own moral code, iron will and cold, violent ambition.

WHY THE 1980s WERE SO GOOD FOR FANTASY MOVIES

•••

The fantasy movie genre ruled the box office in the 1980s. Well, that and *Top Gun*. Join us as we uncover some of the treats of the decade.

Of the ten top-grossing films of the 1980s, only two weren't fantasies (and seeing as they involved either Eddie Murphy being thrown through a plate-glass window or Tom Cruise flying an F-14A Tomcat upside down, you couldn't exactly call them gritty realism). Featuring no aliens, ghosts, mystical artefacts, Jedi, superheroes or time-travelling DeLoreans, *Beverly Hills Cop* and *Top Gun* stood alone as the two non-fantasy 1980s hits in the top ten.

It was the inverse story in the 1970s. Of the box office big-hitters in that decade, only *Star Wars: A New Hope* and *The Exorcist* had fantasy elements. Next to those on the list appeared crime dramas, spy thrillers, disaster movies, musicals, a comedy, a romance, a monster flick and a boxing story. It was an altogether more varied and more adult selection.

Go back a further ten years and it was a similarly eclectic mix – the best performers of the 1960s were Disney animations, musicals, psychological thrillers, epics, relationship dramas, spy flicks, a Western…no single genre or audience dominated.

Optics, artistry and technology put fantasy and sci-fi universes within reach

What then, made the popularity of the fantasy genre explode during the 1980s? The first answer is technology. Solid computer-generated imagery, as showcased at the beginning of the decade in Disney's *Tron*, wasn't widely used until the 1990s, but developments in computing made VFX (visual effects) achievable when it had hitherto not been possible. A combination of optics, artistry and technology put fantasy and sci-fi universes within reach.

It wasn't just filmmakers who had access to new tech; so did movie audiences. The popularity of domestic video recorders grew throughout the decade. The introduction of priced-to-buy instead of priced-to-rent VHS cassettes, trailblazed by the heavily discounted 1982 release of *Star Trek II: The Wrath of Khan*, created the home release market. As well as cutting themselves a paycheck for licensing films to television, studios could now bypass cinemas and sell their product direct to audiences.

The home release market cemented high-grossing box office numbers for successes and made sleeper hits of box office failures. In 1982 *Conan the Barbarian*, starring Arnold

Schwarzenegger, raked in cash on VHS, while kids' fantasies *Return to Oz* and *Labyrinth* built up cult followings on tape despite flopping on cinema release.

This new revenue source was vital for the major studios, whose struggles with the competition from television in the previous decades had made them increasingly risk-averse. Perhaps cynically, the *New Yorker* critic Pauline Kael suggested, in her 1980 article "Why Are Movies So Bad? Or, The Numbers", that the conglomerate-run studios of the day were helmed by executives "whose interest in movies rarely extends beyond the immediate selling possibilities; they could be selling neckties just as well as movies". Blockbuster *Jaws* in 1975, followed by 1977's *Star Wars* and 1982's *E.T. the Extra-Terrestrial*, had shown studios which "neckties" sold big, so what followed were more and more cut from the same cloth: sequels to recent hits and effects-driven movies in imitation of them.

After Steven Spielberg and George Lucas, fantasy and sci-fi no longer meant B-movie schlock. They meant money.

Between the mid-1970s and mid-1980s, the majors' collective release average dropped. Attempting to avoid commercial risks and reproduce past successes, studios made fewer films with less variety. A desire to sell overseas contributed to this homogeneity. Movies designed to appeal to global audiences aim to avoid local specificity in geography or politics – how better to achieve that than by making them about mythical battles between good and evil set in fantasy lands?

Narrowing focus didn't guarantee commercial success for studios. Make a space opera and sometimes you get *Star Wars*, sometimes you get a financial failure like 1984's *Dune*. Of the rash of swords-and-sorcery clones released in the early 1980s

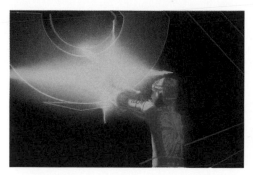

Tron had an impact not just on films, but on a legion of computer games too.

(*Clash of the Titans*, *The Beastmaster*, *Conan the Barbarian*, *Krull*...) there wasn't a theatrical hit among them.

Those stories may have gone out of fashion but action and increasingly sophisticated special effects didn't. They were the legacy the 1980s fantasy era left to 1990s cinema. *Conan the Barbarian* stuck around but ditched the loincloth and broadsword for a leather jacket and an Uzi 9mm. Robert Zemeckis, director of the *Back to the Future* trilogy, used what he'd learned in Hill Valley (the films' setting) to insert *Forrest Gump* into American history. Lucasfilm's visual effects company ILM swapped the X-wings and Wookiees of *Star Wars* for the Velociraptors and T-Rex of *Jurassic Park*. And James Cameron went back under the *The Abyss*'s waters to dredge up an unsinkable ship.

FIVE MUST-SEE 1980s FANTASY MOVIES

THE DARK CRYSTAL (1982)
THE NEVERENDING STORY (1984)
HIGHLANDER (1986)
BIG TROUBLE IN LITTLE CHINA (1986)
THE PRINCESS BRIDE (1987)

WHY THE 1990s WERE SO GOOD FOR SCIENCE FICTION

•••

As much as science fiction had been a cinema fixture for decades, the 1990s saw a fresh confidence in the genre. More to the point, it was a confidence that was matched by audience interest. The after-effects of the original *Star Wars* trilogy were dimming, and since the mid-1980s few new standalone sci-fi movies had broken through. *RoboCop* and *Bill & Ted's Excellent Adventure* were perhaps the most notable, but both would build their audience by word of mouth, reaping the rewards with their respective video releases.

Yet 1990 kicked off with an ambitious science fiction blockbuster, slap bang in the middle of summer. Just a year after *Batman* had stormed the box office, suggesting superheroes may finally be arriving in earnest, it was Paul Verhoeven's ultra-violent *Total Recall* – the second of his three notable sci-fi blockbusters (following *RoboCop* and preceding 1997's *Starship Troopers*) – that would outgross the likes of *Dick Tracy* and *Back to the Future Part III*. It was buoyed up, of course, by the star power of Arnold Schwarzenegger – a year later, his film career would peak

1992's *Freejack* featured a rare movie appearance from Mick Jagger, in the lead role.

with *Terminator 2: Judgment Day*. Two hugely expensive, intelligent science fiction blockbusters in two consecutive summers.

Science fiction, like horror, tends to be cyclical, but in this case audiences seemed open for more, and major film stars and directors were happy to oblige. Steven Spielberg's *Jurassic Park*, of course, ruled the summer in 1993, while Sylvester Stallone backed *Demolition Man*, Kevin Costner chose *Waterworld*, Bruce Willis picked *The Fifth Element* and *Armageddon*, Dustin Hoffman chose *Sphere* (not very wisely, as it happened), while even Mick Jagger popped up in *Freejack*. Will Smith, meanwhile, would find his blockbuster movie career effectively launched by the likes of *Independence Day* and *Men in Black*. Director Roland Emmerich, who

Schwarzenegger followed up 1990's *Total Recall* (pictured) with 1991's *Terminator 2: Judgment Day*. They're two of his biggest ever hits.

made *Independence Day*, had previously come to prominence through 1990's *Moon 44* and 1994's *Stargate*.

And this was all part of the difference. When *Star Wars* first hit big, science fiction – at least in its mainstream form – was still looked down upon. To a degree, at least artistically, it still is. Note how close *Inception* and *Gravity* have come to taking home a Best Picture Oscar, only for the Academy to opt for a more traditional choice instead (*The King's Speech* and the excellent *12 Years a Slave* respectively). Like comedy, science fiction and major film prizes – outside of technical categories – rarely mix. What the 1990s brought about, though, was the children of *Star Wars* getting their hands on major movies. The people who were inspired by George Lucas's galaxy were the emerging filmmakers. Furthermore, audiences backed big sci-fi movies.

The other key difference between the 1990s and previous decades lay with technical breakthroughs. The visual effects industry came of age in the 1990s. At the cutting edge, the aforementioned *Terminator 2: Judgment Day* and *Jurassic Park* were breaking heavy ground, and many films would follow their path in the years that followed. Crucially, too, further down the effects line, previously out-

of-reach visuals were becoming affordable to low- and mid-budget productions. Though not a sci-fi film, the generally forgotten biopic *The Babe*, starring John Goodman, broke ground in using computers to generate a full crowd of spectators, without the expense of paying thousands of extras. Sequences that were previously impossible were now within the grasp of filmmakers and were sometimes even saving them a bit of change as well.

The decade was rounded off with a science fiction film whose impact is still being felt in modern cinema. The Wachowskis' 1999 breakthrough hit *The Matrix* drew influence from Hong Kong cinema and harnessed computer effects in an innovative way, to present a blockbuster that was genuinely unlike anything Hollywood was making at the time. The imitators soon followed, but it's notable that the 1990s final science fiction hits (*Star Wars: Episode I – The Phantom Menace* being 1999's biggest film) were the ones less reliant on a movie star – with due respect to Keanu Reeves and Ewan McGregor – but more on visuals, effects and brand names. Blockbuster cinema has never really gone back from that, and nor has science fiction retreated back into the doldrums.

SMALL 1990s SCI-FI FILMS WORTH SEEKING OUT

HARDWARE (1990)
SCREAMERS (1995)
STRANGE DAYS (1995)
GHOST IN THE SHELL (1995)
GATTACA (1997)
CONTACT (1997)
DARK CITY (1998)
EXISTENZ (1999)
GALAXY QUEST (1999)

WHAT THE 2000s DID FOR TEEN MOVIES

•••

The years 2000–2009 were some of the most fruitful times for the teen movie. Here's why.

In 2001, in Joel Gallen's *Not Another Teen Movie*, moviegoers met the students of John Hughes High. There was arty weirdo Janey, her besotted and quirkily dressed pal Ricky, square-jawed student president Jake, queen bee cheerleader Priscilla, sexy exchange student Areola, sensitive, beanie-wearing Les (given to finding beauty in floating plastic bags) and three dorky freshmen on a quest to lose their virginity. Not to forget Mr T as the wise, advice-dispensing janitor. A whirlwind of gross-out gags and makeovers, the school year at John Hughes High lasted a single

Napoleon Dynamite was a breakout hit in 2004, returning nearly $50m in the US, off a $400,000 production budget.

week, had just one class – weird science – and revolved around three events: a party, a football game and a prom.

It's easy to assume that the arrival of *Not Another Teen Movie* spoof might have sounded the death knell for the high school flick. After all, isn't parody the end stage of any genre? Not necessarily. Just ask James Bond, who survived spoofs from 1967's *Casino Royale* to 1997's *Austin Powers* and still rakes it in today. Or Sherlock Holmes, the first pastiche of whom was published while Sir Arthur Conan Doyle was still writing.

Parody doesn't signal the end of a genre, it signals saturation. After a purple patch in the late 1990s, by 2001 the movie market was flooded with teen films. From classic literature retold in a high school setting (*10 Things I Hate About You*, based on *The Taming of the Shrew*; *Clueless*, based on *Emma*; *She's All That*, based on *Pygmalion*; and *Cruel Intentions*, based on *Dangerous Liaisons*) through comedies (*Jawbreaker*, *Can't Hardly Wait* and *American Pie*) to postmodern slasher horrors (*Scream* and *Cherry Falls*), teenagers had rarely been more frequently on the big screen and their disposable income never better targeted.

The growth of the multiplex through the 1990s had made cinemas into a teen destination of choice once again. There was significant cash to be made from adolescent audiences, as Universal discovered when, from a budget of just $11m, sex comedy *American Pie* grossed over $200m worldwide and spawned a trio of lucrative sequels.

All of this meant that by the time *Not Another Teen Movie* arrived, there was no lack of material to skewer. Gallen's spoof had two decades of frat films, teen romcoms and gross-out comedies to draw upon. It merged references to the class-conflict romances and home-made prom dresses of John Hughes films with jabs at 1990s masturbation gags and cheerleading sports movies.

If parody doesn't spell the end for a film genre, it does ring in the changes. Having a jeering finger pointed at its pitfalls and habits forces a genre to evolve. The first evolution is irony. (Post-2000, if a filmmaker had a character strut slo-mo down a high school corridor to a slinky pop tune, it was either an homage – *Easy A*, *Jennifer's Body* – or a gag – *Mean Girls*, *Superbad*, *21 Jump Street*.) The second evolution? Innovation.

Body-swap comedies and dance flicks were the decade's early mutations. The *Step Up* franchise proved a global hit, only fizzling

out at the box office with its fifth instalment. Another song-and-dance franchise, Disney's *High School Musical*, made wheelbarrows of cash by targeting tweens.

Around the mainstream were stranger films that were less easy to categorize as teen movies. *Donnie Darko* and *Napoleon Dynamite* had high school settings but didn't follow the pre-2000 rulebook. Like *Ghost World*, *Youth in Revolt* and *Submarine*, they were off-kilter teen flicks that owed more to indie cinema than *Porky's* or *Fast Times at Ridgemont High*.

The major trend in the teen movies of the 2000s, though, was for less innovation and more derivation. Behold the YA book-to-movie adaptation. *The Lord of the Rings* trilogy and the *Harry Potter* films kick-started a fantasy resurgence that paved the way for Catherine Hardwicke's 2008 moody juggernaut *Twilight*.

After *Twilight*'s Bella and Edward came the flood. YA adaptations competed for the film's crown until a successor eventually arrived in the form of *The Hunger Games*. By the end of the *Harry Potter* decade, studios had learned that adaptation franchises ruled and, thanks to Sam Raimi's *Spider-Man* trilogy, that there was no more direct route to a teenage wallet than through the pages of a comic book.

> ## *Disney's High School Musical made wheelbarrows of cash by targeting tweens*

FIVE MUST-SEE 2000S TEEN MOVIES

DONNIE DARKO (2001)
BEND IT LIKE BECKHAM (2002)
MEAN GIRLS (2004)
NAPOLEON DYNAMITE (2004)
SUPERBAD (2007)

UNDERRATED MOVIES OF OSCAR-WINNING FILM DIRECTORS

Cinema can sometimes be broken down into films you want to watch and films you feel you should watch. When a director wins an Oscar for a certain movie, that tends to be the one to which people subsequently gravitate. Yet there are some perhaps less awards-worthy, yet often very enjoyable, features to be found reading down the resumés of Oscar-winning directors.

MARTIN SCORSESE

Won for: *The Departed*
But check out: *The King of Comedy*

Generally regarded, and rightfully so, as one of his finest films, Martin Scorsese's *The King of Comedy* casts Robert De Niro as aspiring stand-up comedian Rupert Pupkin, who joins forces with Sandra Bernhard's Masha for a scheme that looks, well, a little doomed. A black comedy, it failed miserably at the box office on its original release, yet its reputation has grown since then.

The constantly overlooked De Niro-Scorsese masterpiece, *The King of Comedy*.

STEVEN SPIELBERG

Won for: *Schindler's List, Saving Private Ryan*
But check out: *The Adventures of Tintin: The Secret of the Unicorn*

A modest hit on its release, Steven Spielberg's Tintin movie isn't a vintage piece of work from the bearded megaphone-wielder, but it's a lot more fun than it seems to be given credit for. (The odd visual style doesn't do it too many favours, sadly.) It also features a wildly exciting chase sequence that's almost at the standard of peak *Indiana Jones*.

DANNY BOYLE

Won for: *Slumdog Millionaire*
But check out: *Millions*

Director Danny Boyle's adaptation of Frank Cottrell Boyce's novel *Millions* was marketed as the first film from the director – who at that point was best known for *Shallow Grave* and *Trainspotting* – that you could take children to see. Wise advice, too. It's a smart comedy drama starring James Nesbitt, about a young boy who happens upon a big bag of money. Sadly, it flew under most people's radar.

ANG LEE

Won for: *Life of Pi*
But check out: *The Wedding Banquet*
Although Ang Lee's bold green *Hulk* movie never really got the respect and recognition it deserved, his 1993 breakthrough *The Wedding Banquet* is still the film that's worth digging the deepest to find. A joyous comedy drama, it tells of a gay man who marries a woman to help her get a green card and to help him keep his parents happy. Predictably, all doesn't go to plan.

Clint Eastwood's light and fluffy *Space Cowboys*.

KATHYRN BIGELOW

Won for: *The Hurt Locker*
But check out: *Blue Steel*
There's rightly a lot of love out there for Bigelow's 1987 vampire film *Near Dark*, but a bit more light deserves to be shone on her 1990 cop thriller *Blue Steel*. In an era where few women were getting lead roles in studio pictures – well, outside of romcoms – Bigelow gave Jamie Lee Curtis the lead role of rookie cop Megan Turner, and the ensuing battle to bring down a psychopath remains taut cinema.

Jamie Lee Curtis is outstanding in 1990's *Blue Steel*.

CLINT EASTWOOD

Won for: *Unforgiven, Million Dollar Baby*
But check out: *Space Cowboys*
Lots to choose from here, but Eastwood's able touch for directing comedy is given a workout with the fun, yet often forgotten *Space Cowboys*. The film is leaner than the not-too-dissimilar *Armageddon*, and has a similarly troubled final act, but Eastwood is wise enough to keep the attention on his leads – himself, James Garner, Tommy Lee Jones and Donald Sutherland – who are spectacularly good fun as NASA's oldest astronauts.

PETER JACKSON

Won for: *The Lord of the Rings: The Return of the King*
But check out: *The Frighteners*
Arriving after his peak schlocky horror feature *Braindead* and his breakthrough serious feature *Heavenly Creatures*, *The Frighteners* is a wildly entertaining horror comedy, starring Michael J Fox. Boasting an excellent Danny Elfman score, it's a film that ripples with confidence. This would be the last standalone movie Jackson made before he embarked on his Middle Earth and *King Kong* endeavours. A real treat, too.

THE 1990s SPEC-SCRIPT GOLD RUSH

•••

Shane Black, 28 years old, poses for a photograph outside his Los Angeles bungalow, dubbed the Pad O'Guys. It's 1990, and Black's name has appeared all over the Hollywood trade press thanks to his latest script sale: an action thriller called *The Last Boy Scout*. Black sold it for $1.75m – said to be the highest price ever paid for a screenplay at that time. So here's Shane Black, scruffy, barefoot on the concrete paving slabs outside his house, next to a trio of metal dustbins, their lids strangely missing.

The photo of Black was displayed full-page as the opening splash in a feature in *New York* magazine about young Hollywood screenwriters selling scripts and becoming millionaires almost overnight. Black had unwittingly become the poster boy for a generation of young screenwriters who had grown wealthy thanks to a burgeoning market for spec scripts (speculative screenplays); Black's peers also included Brian Helgeland, Rick Jaffa and Joe Eszterhas (see page 64), all of whom had sold or would sell scripts for at least $1m in the 1990s. And where there's money, journalists usually find a story.

Black's style of writing certainly had a youthful, sensationalist swagger about it. The script that really got him noticed was *Lethal Weapon*, a buddy-cop thriller which sold for $250,000 and emerged as a $120m worldwide hit in 1987. With its pithy dialogue, intense jabs of action and amusing asides, Black's script wasn't just a dry blueprint for a movie, but a piece of writing with a clear and distinct voice.

Lethal Weapon was a huge hit, and launched an entire wave of thrillers with odd-couple pairings, guns and one-liners (Warner made *Lethal Weapon 2* in 1989; Black's screenplay for that film was rejected for being too dark.)

When Black's agents began hawking his next script, *The Last Boy Scout*, around Hollywood, it resulted in a feeding frenzy, with studios including Fox, TriStar and Carolco all placing increasingly absurd bids. Black eventually chose Warner's offer, even though it was lower, because of his prior work with Joel Silver ("he gets my ideas," Black said at the time).

Unusually high though Black's paycheck for *The Last Boy Scout* was, the bidding war surrounding his script was by no means a one-off. David Chappe's thriller *Gale Force* was purchased by Carolco in 1989 for $500,000. Brian Helgeland and Manny Coto sold a sci-fi thriller called *The Ticking Man* for

Perhaps the best Bruce Willis-headlined action movie of the 1990s, *The Last Boy Scout* made as many headlines for the cost of its screenplay as it did for the film itself.

$1.2m the following year. Neither of those films were ever, ultimately, made.

Two things caused the script market to heat up in the early 1990s. One was the increasing competition among studios for high-concept film ideas following a damaging writers' strike in 1988. The other force came from the talent agencies who marketed those scripts; a 2013 *Vanity Fair* article puts the surge in prices down to the ingenuity of one Alan Gasmer. Gasmer was an agent at William Morris, one of the most prestigious talent agencies in Hollywood. Rather than simply place a new script on the market and wait to see the offers roll in, Gasmer cleverly set a time limit: he'd put a screenplay up for sale on a Monday and close the bidding on a Friday, causing a sense of urgency and a flurry of bids as couriers delivered scripts to studios and producers raced to call in with their offers. In a good week, the buzz surrounding a script would become self-perpetuating: in 1990 alone, 14 scripts were each sold for $1m or more.

In 1990 alone, 14 scripts were each sold for $1m or more

Interest in the Hollywood clamour for spec scripts regularly made headlines as the prices climbed ever higher. Just when the industry had digested the $1.75m that Black received for *The Last Boy Scout*, Joe Eszterhas nearly doubled that figure with his erotic thriller screenplay *Basic Instinct*, which he sold to Carolco for $3m. Eszterhas sold his treatment for the erotic thriller *Jade* for $2.5m in 1992.

Then Shane Black returned with his latest thriller, *The Long Kiss Goodnight*, and stunned just about everybody when he sold it to New Line for $4.5m in 1994. Once again, Black's name was associated with a small club of obscenely well-paid, usually white male screenwriters. But this time at least one member of the Hollywood press responded not with stunned fascination, but with outright disgust.

"I've got to hand it to you, Shane, you know how to beat the system," Peter Bart wrote in a ranting piece for *Variety* entitled "Script Fee Vomits Upward For Mayhem Meister".

Bart's scathing open letter seemed to express something hinted at in that 1990 image of Black standing barefoot next to his open bins: that the scripts sold in the era's bidding gold rush were violent, lowbrow fodder dashed off in a few hours and flogged for a fortune.

The Long Kiss Goodnight didn't mark the end of the script gold rush, but it did mark a major turning point. If Bart and other commentators patrolling Hollywood wanted the movie to fail, they eventually got their wish, in a fashion – directed by Renny Harlin and released in 1996, *The Long Kiss Goodnight* made a so-so $89m from a $65m investment.

Two films written by white-hot erotic thriller doyen Joe Eszterhas also stumbled: *Showgirls* was a critically derided failure in

Jade (pictured) and *Showgirls* both flopped, and loudly, with Joe Eszterhas's writing career never reaching the same prominence again.

The Long Kiss Goodnight's box office returns dampened down expectations of spec-script projects.

1995, while *Jade*, directed by William Friedkin, saw similarly slim returns on its $50m budget the same year.

Scripts continued to sell for eye-watering amounts well into the 2000s, with writer-director M Night Shyamalan making headlines with his sky-high deals for *The Sixth Sense*, *Unbreakable* and *Signs*. Nevertheless, the market changed as the 21st century dawned, with the number of spec sales falling and studios relying increasingly on existing properties like Marvel and DC comics to sell movies rather than high concepts. *Vanity Fair* also suggests that the internet effectively ended the panicked phone calls and ferocious bidding wars of the 1990s, when scripts were either shuttled around by couriers or, at the height of the screenwriter's power, read by appointment at an agent's office.

Then again, there's also something of a mythical quality to the spec-script boom of the 1990s. Even at its peak, the number of screenwriters who became millionaires from their craft was absolutely tiny – one 2007 report estimated that of the 8,000 or so Writers Guild of America union members, only half of them received an income from their work.

Even the image of the cocksure, arrogant young writer knocking out action scripts and making millions was essentially a mirage. Shane Black may have looked like a rough-and-ready chancer, but the image didn't match the writer who, in private, often spent months working on his screenplays and, to this day, holds a clear affection for detective fiction and the craft of writing.

This, perhaps, is the other story lying behind all those nine-figure script sales: the tendency for money to cloud the creative waters. Black may have earned well over $4m for *The Long Kiss Goodnight*, but the indirect result was that he didn't have another script produced for nearly a decade; his retreat didn't end until he returned with *Kiss Kiss Bang Bang* in 2005, produced by his old producer-partner Joel Silver. *Kiss Kiss Bang Bang* revived both Black's career and that of the film's star, Robert Downey Jr, and the pair reunited again for *Iron Man 3* in 2013 – a hit that propelled Black back into the Hollywood big league.

That Black's 2016 buddy thriller *The Nice Guys* wasn't a huge commercial success shows how much the industry has changed over the past 25 years or so. But while the spec-script gold rush is over, there is a positive outcome: whereas *The Long Kiss Goodnight* was dismissed by one critic as vomit inducing, *The Nice Guys* earned widespread praise. No longer obscured by the headline-grabbing nine-figure paychecks, the real value of Black's screenwriting can finally speak for itself.

THE MAN WHO SOLD $26M OF MOVIE SCRIPTS

How many screenwriters get their name prominently on a movie poster? Unless they're already published authors – such as Gillian Flynn with *Gone Girl* – precious few. Which makes the story of Joe Eszterhas all the more remarkable…

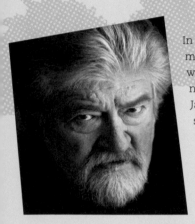

In the hierarchy of movie making, the writer is nowhere near the top. As James Moran, screenwriter of films such as *Tower Block* and *Severance*, once said, "In the movies, the writer is slightly less important than the tea boy." This is borne out by the fact that once a screenplay has been delivered, it's generally knocked around by a combination of actors, the director, studio executives, producers and the weather. In television, screenwriters tend to have an ongoing influence over a project; in cinema – less so.

Which makes the story of Joe Eszterhas all the more remarkable. Not only did Eszterhas, in the late 1980s and 1990s, sell his work for previously unheard-of amounts of money, but his name also became big enough in its own right to get some prominence on promotional posters. Not to the same degree as the name of, say, Tom Cruise or Tom Hanks, as he's likely to admit himself – but

in an era in which 35 different screenwriters were left squabbling over a credit for writing *The Flintstones* movie (true story), a superstar screenwriter with genuine clout was a rarity.

Eszterhas had achieved some success in the 1980s. He penned the original *Flashdance*, taking home a reported $275,000 for his troubles. The hit thriller *Jagged Edge* followed, and a further half a million dollars was his. But the breakthrough film was an erotic thriller that he wrote, by the name of *Love Hurts*. Eszterhas manufactured his own bidding war, sending the script to every production outlet of note in Hollywood. Then at 10am on a given day, bids were encouraged. Within hours, Eszterhas had $3m to his name for his

Basic Instinct made Sharon Stone (*right*) a star and made Joe Eszterhas (*above*) three million bucks.

work. Oh, and the movie would change its name to *Basic Instinct*.

Like many of his scripts, the final cut of *Basic Instinct* would differ slightly from the original screenplay. Notoriously, the scene where the camera leers up Sharon Stone's skirt to discover a lack of underwear was the construct of director Paul Verhoeven. But that, and the controversy over the film as a whole, helped fuel a major box-office – and subsequent video – hit, with $352m banked from cinema takings alone.

For Eszterhas, his already quite successful writing career was transformed overnight. That, combined with his prolific, furious rate of work, left him perfectly placed to reap the dividends of the suddenly red-hot spec-script market (see page 60).

In the years that followed, Eszterhas would sell over $20m worth of further screenplays, the vast majority of which made it into feature films. He was accused of mining similar material – erotic thrillers were said to be his bread and butter, with some justification – and films such as *Sliver* certainly seemed to follow the *Basic Instinct* template. Yet still the cheques came in.

That said, he would overstretch himself, as he confessed in his excellent memoir, *Hollywood Animal*. His last high-profile movie, *Burn Hollywood Burn*, became a star-laden, notorious box office disaster, winning countless awards from the annual Golden Raspberry Award Foundation. He wrote, "I had become too big for my own britches. Here I was writing a ruthless satire of the industry itself, a savage piece which even used as many real names and situations as legally possible." Critics hated it, the public avoided it, and his high-profile career fizzled out at seemingly double-quick speed.

It didn't really, of course; he just moved away from doing as many movies. He wrote his aforementioned memoir and penned

a separate book about rediscovering his Catholic faith. He was set to make a film with Mel Gibson back in 2011, and he told the story of that unsuccessful and extremely rocky subsequent collaboration in the incendiary short book *Heaven and Mel*.

As he headed into his 70s in the mid-2010s, Eszterhas assumed a lower profile, channelling his writing into his own website. But still: with over $2bn of box-office revenues attributed to the 16 movies made that bear his name, he can enjoy the proceeds of a career in which he became, for a good few years, the closest the screenwriting community has had to a movie star of its own. There's certainly not been one since.

THE 11 BIG DEALS

BASIC INSTINCT
Selling price: $3m
Film made? Yes

SACRED COWS
Selling price: $500,000, rising to $750,000 if made
Film made? No

ORIGINAL SIN
Selling price: $1.25m rising to $1.5m
Film made? No

SLIVER
Selling price: $1m
Film made? Yes

RELIABLE SOURCES
Selling price: $2m rising to $4m
Film made? No

JADE
Selling price: $4m
Film made? Yes

SHOWGIRLS
Selling price: $3.7m
Film made? Yes

ONE NIGHT STAND
Selling price: $4m
Film made? Yes

MALE PATTERN BALDNESS
Selling price: $2m
Film made? No

FOREPLAY
Selling price: $1m
Film made? No

GANGLAND
Selling price: $1.3m
Film made? No

MOVIE SCRIPTS THAT CHANGED CONSIDERABLY FROM THEIR ORIGINAL DRAFTS

•••

From action films to thrillers, here are eight scripts that were changed drastically after their original drafts.

CON AIR (1997)

Starring a drawling Nic Cage, *Con Air* will probably be remembered as one of the most screamingly over-the-top action movies of the 1990s. But according to director Simon West, it was originally written not as a high-octane action flick but as an offbeat drama-thriller.

"The original script was much smaller than the eventual film," West told us back in 2013. "It was a character piece, really, by Scott Rosenberg, who did *Things to Do in Denver When You're Dead* and *Beautiful Girls*, which were very small little indie films with great characters. Jerry [Bruckheimer] liked it, obviously, and I liked it just because of the characters and their names, like Cyrus the Virus and Diamond Dog and things like that. I thought, well, I can do something with this."

Con Air was therefore rewritten to suit producer Jerry Bruckheimer's personal brand of wide-screen destruction, with several actors adding their own contributions. That southern drawl? That was Nic Cage's idea.

> **"I'm not going to shoot you between the eyes. I'm going to shoot you between the balls!"**

COMMANDO (1985)

"This was about a guy who'd been an Israeli soldier, who'd actually turned his back on violence," recalled screenwriter Jeph Loeb of his original *Commando* screenplay. "That's not the movie they made."

Indeed it wasn't. Released in 1985, *Commando* was a post-*Terminator* action vehicle for the hulking Arnold Schwarzenegger, who played an ex-soldier all too willing to get the guns out when his daughter is kidnapped.

Loeb and co-writer Matthew Weisman initially had Kiss rocker Gene Simmons in mind, but Nick Nolte was also considered when Simmons turned it down.

Everything changed when Schwarzenegger was chosen, at which point action-hotshot writer Steven E de Souza was brought in to give the script a reworking. The result was a garish and eminently quotable machine gun opera which probably lacked some of the light and shade Loeb and Weisman intended, but at least contained such choice lines as, "John, I'm not going to shoot you between the eyes. I'm going to shoot you between the balls!" Poetry.

BRAINSCAN (1994)

Released at a time when virtual reality helmets were all over the media, *Brainscan* is an amiably silly horror film about a video game that turns an unwitting teenager (played by Edward Furlong) into a murderer. In fact, it may have been even darker in an earlier draft. According to T Ryder Smith, who played the Freddy Krueger-like villain Trickster, his character was originally written as little more than a face on a screen. It was when director John Flynn saw Smith at an audition that he decided to give Trickster a more prominent role.

"I didn't know at the time that they were in the process of expanding the character into a three-dimensional being, and that the discussion was about how much makeup might be needed," Smith said of his audition. "I still thought I was going to be pretty much just an off-screen voice."

Given that *Brainscan* was an early script from Andrew Kevin Walker – who would go on to write such dark odysseys as *Seven* and *8mm* – it's probably fair to say that the film could have been very different had Trickster been a more subtle presence.

LIVE FREE OR DIE HARD/ DIE HARD 4.0 (2007)

You may not have heard of WW3.com, but you'll probably have heard of the film it ultimately became: *Live Free or Die Hard* (released as *Die Hard 4.0* outside North America). Like all the *Die Hard* sequels, with the exception of the fifth, it wasn't originally a John McClane adventure; screenwriter David Marconi wrote it as a standalone cyber-thriller, its premise taken from a *Wired* magazine article called "A Farewell to Arms". That script was hot property in the late 1990s

– *Variety* magazine even reported that WW3.com was scheduled as a major summer film for 1999. But then the 9/11 attacks happened, and the entire project was quietly set aside. Years later, the WW3.com screenplay was dusted off and reworked as a *Die Hard* sequel by Mark Bomback. Inevitably, the nature of the screenplay changed in the hands of a different writer, but the result was another hit for the venerable franchise.

PRETTY WOMAN (1990)

It's strange to think that a frothy romantic comedy could be made out of a sombre drama about prostitution, but that's exactly what happened with *Pretty Woman* – a $460m hit that was for years Disney's most profitable live-action movie. Screenwriter J F Lawton originally wrote *Pretty Woman* in the late 1980s as $3,000, a drama about a 22-year-old LA prostitute's doomed relationship with a wealthy businessman from New York.

Needless to say, the film was lightened up a bit when Touchstone Pictures took it on; in fact, Lawton's rewrite was even considered to be a bit *too* light, according to a piece in *Vanity Fair* magazine. The screenplay was rewritten by other, unnamed writers, who brightened up the tone and changed the downbeat ending. But like the writer of

Julia Roberts in *Pretty Woman*: a film that was supposed to be a dark drama about prostitution.

WW3.com, Lawton is simply thankful that his story got to the screen in the first place. "The fact that Disney came in and wanted to do it as a big-budget movie with a major director was a great thing," Lawton later enthused.

LAST ACTION HERO (1993)

This, surely, is one of the weirdest screenwriting stories of the 1990s. Two Hollywood outsiders, Zak Penn and Adam Leff, wrote a screenplay designed as a parody of mainstream action movies – the kind of stuff written by Shane Black. That screenplay was soon picked up as an expensive vehicle for Arnold Schwarzenegger. And who did the studio bring in to rewrite it? You guessed it – Shane Black.

"With *Last Action Hero*, we watched what was a genuine love note to movies – that was the way it was written, by two guys outside the industry – turned into this giant superstar wank," Zak Penn said. "It was actually pretty informative and interesting to watch."

Carrie Fisher, William Goldman and David Arnott were also brought in to provide their own polish to the script. But far from being the biggest hit of 1993's summer season, *Last Action Hero* was instead swallowed alive by a film called *Jurassic Park*. For Penn, attending the premiere and seeing the heavily altered version of his story was a curious experience. "As we watched the movie, my parents were turning to me and saying, 'Did you write all these fart jokes?'" Penn recalled. "And I said, 'I promise, I didn't.'"

JADE (1995)

An erotic thriller written by Joe Eszterhas (*Basic Instinct*) and directed by William Friedkin probably sounded like a sure-fire success at the time, but *Jade* ultimately proved to be a financial and critical disappointment. According to Eszterhas, the major reason for

the film's failure was Friedkin's alterations to his script. In his book *Hollywood Animal*, Eszterhas relates his reaction to an early scene described by a respected film critic as "totally out of character and pretty dumb". "When I read the review I got nauseous," Eszterhas wrote. "Because I agreed with [the critic] Dolores Barclay. It was one of the scenes that was not in my script, that Billy Friedkin had inserted."

Eszterhas goes on to write that reviewers consistently picked fault with the screenplay, which, he maintains, Friedkin "destroyed" and "butchered". Friedkin has himself admitted that he had pretty much rewritten the entire script.

THEY (2002)

About a group of people terrorized by mysterious beings that visit in the night, *They* came and went without much of a fuss in 2002. But the original screenplay, written by Brendan Hood, had a far bolder, more sci-fi-infused premise. In it, a group of college students discover that humans are being used as unwitting organ donors for a hidden race of "organic machines".

"I came up with the idea that there were a bunch of monsters out there – organic machines who were basically a fusion of metal and flesh that would prey upon human beings and use them for replacement body parts and skin," Hood told the film-industry website JoBlo.com. "These creatures existed in our world, but had somehow never been detected for two reasons – they had the God-like ability to alter reality and the power to erase people's memories."

Just about all of that was ejected as the screenplay passed through the hands of other writers – and of the producers, who clearly had their own idea of which way the story should go. *They* wound up becoming a rather generic supernatural horror.

THE COMIC-BOOK MOVIE THAT WAS MADE NEVER TO BE SEEN

•••

Between 2005 and 2015, three different *Fantastic Four* films – based on the characters known as "Marvel's first family" – made it to the big screen. It would be fair to say that none of them is particularly loved, with the 2015 film in particular being given a very rough ride. Remarkably, then, the film that is most faithful to the work of creators Stan Lee and Jack Kirby is one that was never officially released. Meet 1994's *The Fantastic Four*.

Put together by a legitimate hero of low-budget movie making, Roger Corman, *The Fantastic Four* was almost an urban legend in the pre-internet days. Made for an astonishingly low $2m and shot on the cheap in 21 days, it never saw any kind of official release but circulated heavily on the comic-convention bootleg circuit. Nowadays, it's much easier to find.

The film came about when a relatively small German studio, Neue Constantin, was able to secure the rights to the *Fantastic Four* for approximately $250,000 in 1986. Marvel movies were two decades away from becoming very big things.

In the post-*Batman* 1989 climate, superhero movies were looking more attractive to big studios. Marvel were hoping to land a substantial payday for an option from a larger studio once Constantin's rights lapsed on 31 December 1992. However, Constantin had

The Fantastic Four: for a film made to fulfil – quickly – a contractual obligation, the 1994 take on Marvel Comics' superhero team Fantastic Four has achieved real notoriety.

Doctor Doom: the 1990s movie villain keenest on waving his hands around to dramatic effect.

no intention of letting that option lapse, and as long as they were in production before the deadline, the rights would remain theirs. Constantin's Bernd Eichinger went to the one man they knew could make an ambitious sci-fi movie in a hurry and on a tiny budget: Roger Corman. Production began on 28 December 1992, with just three days to spare before Marvel would get the rights back.

Corman didn't direct *The Fantastic Four*, however. That unenviable task fell to Oley Sassone, who helped see the project through a whirlwind four-week shoot on a budget reported to have been as low as $1m. Even the Dolph Lundgren *Punisher* flick had $11m to work with, and that didn't involve an orange rock monster or a guy who could stretch.

The Fantastic Four presents a pretty faithful origin story for both the team and the key villain, Doctor Doom, updated only slightly to remove the early 1960s space race and Cold War concerns. It's the most faithful version

of the Doom character seen in live action, looking like his comic-book counterpart, although arguably in need of some work to make his dialogue more audible. To make up for the fact that you can't see his face, Joseph Culp's Doom gesticulates wildly, emphasizing every point with a wave of his hand or the point of a finger, like Darth Vader after some mime lessons and a few drinks.

To keep the budget under control, Johnny Storm (Jay Underwood) doesn't go full Human Torch until the film's final moments, when crude animation is used to show him racing a laser beam into space (don't ask). The Invisible Woman's powers were certainly the easiest to do, but Rebecca Staab's scenes are marred by the fact that Sue Storm is mostly busy being love-struck by Reed Richards (Alex Hyde-White), whose stretching power is only deployed sparingly, via endearingly crude practical effects.

The Thing, though, is a pretty impressive creation. It was designed by John Vulich and

Everett Burrell, who created the zombie effects for the 1990 *Night of the Living Dead* remake. They based the Thing's design on the version drawn by John Byrne during his legendary run as writer and artist on the comics.

For all its charms, *The Fantastic Four* still isn't a very good movie. Yet it is remarkable not only in its fidelity to the source material, but also in the absolute sincerity with which it approaches such an impossible task considering its budget. The Stan Lee and Jack Kirby comics to which this tries so very hard to pay tribute were time- and dimension-hopping stories of the highest adventure. The movie may not have succeeded, but, then again, other attempts with 50–100 times the budget also fell short of the mark.

The Fantastic Four was scheduled to open in September 1993, but it wasn't to be. A January 1994 opening was floated but never materialized either. Those fans who were curious could rent a VHS copy of another Corman production, *Carnosaur*, to see a trailer. But the film then vanished. It had done its contractual job.

As recently as 2005, Roger Corman denied even owning a print of the movie. Reportedly, Marvel Studios founder Avi Arad purchased the film from Eichinger "for a couple of million dollars in cash and burned it" (his own words, courtesy of *Los Angeles* magazine). He clearly didn't do a good-enough job, given how easy it is to find the film now.

However, as Stan Lee himself said, "It was never supposed to be seen by any living human beings," something Eichinger has repeatedly denied. A documentary, *Doomed: The Untold Story*, has since been made, ensuring that the story of a film designed to fulfil a contractual requirement continues to be the most interesting *Fantastic Four* movie ever made.

The Fantastic Four you never (legally) saw...

HOW MODERN FAMILY FILMS HAVE DITCHED THE "CHOSEN ONE"

•••

Innovation is rife in family movies, and in putting together films for younger audiences, the likes of *The LEGO Movie* and *Monsters University* have been taking a few more narrative risks.

The year 2013 saw the release of a film, *Monsters University*, that sold a message antithetical to the upbeat "you can do it if you really try!". "Sometimes you can't do it," said this film, "even if you really, really, really try."

It's not as bleak a caution as it might seem. An imaginative scenario in which the hero fails, but adapts, teaches a useful lesson. Wishing upon a star, working your socks off, thinking you can…in real life none of that guarantees a result.

Monsters University tells the story of Mike Wazowski, a young monster with dreams of being a professional Scarer. Years of hard work led Mike to study Scaring at the titular college, only for him to discover that he simply didn't have it in him. All the hard work in the world couldn't replace what he was missing: the natural quality of being scary.

Monsters University isn't the only modern family film to reject traditional victory narratives in favour of more realistic life lessons. The excellent

Kung Fu Panda franchise and *The LEGO Movie* both subvert the concept of the prophesied hero. They don't do this by making the lead a "nobody" (from *Star Wars* to *Harry Potter*, nobodies turning out to be somebodies has long been the shape of family film). Instead, they subvert the concept by swapping destiny and determinism for choice and motivation. Prophecy shmophecy, say these kids' pictures; heroes aren't born, they're made. Moreover, they're self-made.

It's not about simply denying reality. The message of *Kung Fu Panda*'s hero Po (*left*) isn't the tempting idea that anyone – fit, fat, agile or klutz – can achieve anything, but that our strength isn't bestowed from outside; we have to recognize it in ourselves and make what use of it we can. Po's idiosyncratic fighting abilities – the layer of fat that can resist nerve blasts, the heft to belly-bounce his enemy into the sky, the motivating factor of much-loved food – aren't despite

The *Kung Fu Panda* trilogy is centred on Po, a character with deliberate limitations.

Monsters University: one of a collection of Pixar films that's, at heart, a little more down to earth.

his size, but thanks to it. Now, the message to young audiences isn't that you can do anything if you believe in it enough, but to recognize your strengths and apply them.

The LEGO Movie is a neat illustration. Its everyman lead, Emmet Brickowski, is initially taken for prophesied hero The Special, a "chosen one" destined to save the world, the ultimate Master Builder. The problem with Emmet being chosen as the ultimate creator is that he's not really the creative type.

In itself, that's a twist on the kids' movie tradition. From *The NeverEnding Story* to *A Bug's Life* and more, we're used to seeing the oddball creative first being ridiculed for, and then saving the day with, their boundless imagination. Unlike the heroes of 1980s kids' fantasies (*Labyrinth*, *Willow*, *Return to Oz*), Emmet isn't a marginalized dreamer but the most regular of Joes. The few ideas Emmet does have are acknowledged to be terrible, and largely remain so throughout the film.

What Emmet *can* do is follow instructions. In a reversal of the "mock the dreamer/hey, the dreamer saved us!" pattern, Emmet is

scorned for lacking imagination, but then his lack of imagination helps to save the day. The ability to work as part of a team within a structure that's bigger than its individual parts is Emmet's superpower.

In much the same way, the eponymous lead in Aardman Animation's *Arthur Christmas*, a golden-hearted but nervous youngest son, doesn't overcome his anxiety, but instead learns how to use it to his advantage. Arthur coins the phrase "Do it with worry!" as his somewhat awkward mantra near the end of the film, finding strength in his "weakness". Like *Kung Fu Panda*'s Po, Arthur doesn't defeat his idiosyncrasy but learns to thrive by acknowledging it.

It's an uplifting message. If there are no "chosen ones", then we all have the choice of becoming a hero. We can celebrate our strengths and work with others to save the day without waiting for a superhero to come along and save it for us. In that way, modern family movies aren't teaching kids how to fulfil their destinies, but how to forge them.

THE CHANGING PRICE OF BLOCKBUSTER MOVIES

•••

In 1990, a $70m price tag for a film was regarded as shocking and exorbitant. Within two years? It would seem like an economical bargain.

When 1990's *Die Hard 2: Die Harder* was deep into production, Hollywood executives were worried. 20th Century Fox had moved quickly to arrange a follow-up to 1988's surprise hit *Die Hard* (a film now rightly regarded as a modern classic), and Bruce Willis was back on location reprising his most famous role, that of John McClane, by November 1989.

The shoot would be a troubled one. Filming continued until April 1990 – just three months before the movie was due in cinemas – and

True story: Black & Decker sued for $150,000 when one of its products was cut out of *Die Hard 2*.

the problems were piling up. Director Renny Harlin (who stepped in for the original's director, John McTiernan, who was committed to making *The Hunt for Red October*) and his team had banked on their location being suitably snowy when it came to film key outdoor sequences. It wasn't. In fact, when the required snow didn't naturally appear, the production had to change locations, and then bring in costly artificial snow for snowstorm sequences. With Willis attracting a higher salary second time around, and with the schedule allowing little margin for error, costs ballooned. The final negative bill – before distribution and marketing costs – was in the region of $70m–$75m (more than double the cost of the original).

Many people were openly wondering how such an expensive film could ever make money, but in this instance Fox won its gamble. A $239m box office return and a sizable video hit returned ample sums to its coffers. And by the time *Terminator 2: Judgment Day* stormed into cinemas the year after, costing $100m just to make (see page 120), *Die Hard 2* looked like a smashing deal.

However, as the 1980s moved into the 1990s, the rules on how much money a film could take were beginning to shift. Traditionally, costs had been kept (relatively) under control. The massive 1989 blockbuster *Batman* cost around $35m to make and was seen as expensive. That same year, *Ghostbusters II* was regarded as a costly (if not

Air Force One reused some of the plane set from 1996's *Executive Decision*. Still cost a fortune to make, though.

unsuccessful) sequel, with a $25m production budget. It would be fair to say that Fox's *Die Hard 2* had started to rewrite the rules.

Through the 1990s, more would do so, as year by year studios spent big on their tent-pole productions. Take the hits of 1994, most of which got the green light in the aftermath of *Terminator 2*'s huge success. *True Lies* was the most expensive (see page 120), but *Forrest Gump* – a risky drama at the time it was greenlit – cost $55m, *Clear and Present Danger* was up to $62m and *Interview with the Vampire* was $60m. Go forward to 1997, and the costs continued to balloon. Sony spent $90m on *Men in Black*, Harrison Ford ate up a good chunk of *Air Force One*'s $85m bill, and the excellent *Contact* cost Warner Bros. a cool $90.

Within a couple more years, the average price of a blockbuster movie was over $100m. What's more, by the mid-2000s, the top-end cost was soaring seemingly uncontrollably. Universal spent over $200m on Peter Jackson's *King Kong* remake. The sum of $210m got pumped into *X-Men: The Last Stand*.

The sequels to *Pirates of the Caribbean* were routinely costing over $250m, and the money spent on them was being sucked out of small productions.

By 2006, a relatively effects-free film such as *The Da Vinci Code* was costing $125m, while what should have been a fairly straightforward comedy remake – *The Pink Panther* – was budgeted at $80m. But why?

At heart, it is because the movie industry got bigger. In particular, Hollywood enjoyed a spectacular injection of money from the DVD revolution. Although videos, and video rentals, had been lucrative, DVD was transformative. Now, it became the norm to own films outright, and while some studios fought it, DVD brought with it the ultimate abolition of the "rental window". Until that time, a film was released in cinemas, then on video to rent, and a few months later to buy. Now, the DVD was there to buy from day one of its home release, as is the norm today. More people started buying more films and were paying more money to do so.

> ### *By the mid-2000s, the top-end cost was soaring seemingly uncontrollably*

The *Transformers* films headed to China for extra funding, and extra box office.

Furthermore, studio back catalogues suddenly became ripe for picking. Up until this point, some films of old had been given video releases or were sold in packages to television networks around the world. But now, an individual DVD release of, say, a relatively unknown 30-year-old film was viable. At its peak – before streaming and illegal downloading burst the bubble somewhat – dozens of new DVD releases were heading into stores weekly.

The other big expansion, and one that continues today, was the box office market. Previously, a film's success was mainly judged on its American box office takings. But as worldwide distribution expanded and became more aggressive, that was no longer the case. A film such as *Ice Age: Continental Drift* took an incredible $877m at the global box office in 2012, with $161m of that coming from the US.

In recent years, it has been the opening up of the Chinese market that has offered new riches. Hollywood productions are so keen to woo Chinese cinemagoers – and get past tight restrictions on film release in China – that they're shooting footage in the country itself. *Iron Man 3* notoriously featured a nonsensical

extra scene for its Chinese release, adding in a character played by Wang Xueqi (a big star in China). It secured a release in China, adding over $100m to the film's takings.

Michael Bay's derided *Transformers: Age of Extinction* (2014) went further, filming key sequences in China, and seeing its falling US takings greatly mitigated by the incredible $320m contributed by Chinese audiences. China thus became the most lucrative market for *Transformers* films in one fell swoop.

The eventual bottom line is that by 2016, summer tentpole movies – while not individually as expensive as *Pirates of the Caribbean* sequels – were predominantly costing a lot of money. The price of *Captain America: Civil War* was about $250m. *Fantastic Beasts and Where to Find Them* came to $180m. Even one of the cheaper ones, *Jason Bourne*, still cost Universal $120m.

With markets still emerging, and more riches to chase, a total levelling off of movie budget prices doesn't appear imminent. And with a $2bn box office gross becoming a prize for the very biggest productions, there remains no shortage of studios willing to gamble hard on having the next big thing.

WHY HAVE COSTS SHOT UP SO MUCH?

It's hard to single out just one reason why a film should cost $50m one year, and $75m the next, but there are obvious contributing factors. Financial inflation of prices is one, as is the rising cost of talent. The days of a $20m upfront salary for an actor may be all but gone, but lucrative back-end deals are not unknown. For example, Sandra Bullock made headlines in 2014 when the *Hollywood Reporter* revealed that she had negotiated a 15 per cent cut of the box office of *Gravity*, in which she was starring. The film's success meant she would probably pocket at least $70m.

Likewise, the costs of visual effects have ballooned, not least because there's still something of a technological arms race as each blockbuster tries to outdo the others. Prices, too, of behind-the-camera talent have escalated, advertising has become more expensive and press tours need to go to more places. In short, as the potential money coming in has increased, so has the willingness to spend a bit more on a movie in the first place.

THE DEATH OF MID-BUDGET MOVIES

In 2016, Warner Bros. CEO Kevin Tsujihara noted that the top 10 blockbuster movies at the box office in 2013 accounted for 25 per cent of all business. In justifying his company's move to a more franchise-driven model, with fewer, more expensive films, he noted that in 2016 the top 10 films would seize 30 per cent of box office takings. It made sense, he reckoned, to bet big and go for a bigger slice of that money.

This approach has not been unusual, with Disney, for one, making far fewer theatrical releases, and very few non-franchise ones. In the early to mid-1990s, Disney was pursuing an approach that would put a new film in cinemas pretty much every week. By 2016, its big-screen output was all but dominated by some animated releases (from both Walt Disney Animation Studios and Pixar), two or three Marvel titles, a live-action fairy-tale retelling and a *Star Wars* feature. Its appetite for riskier, mid-budget fare had diminished – as had everyone's.

Paramount, for instance, used to base its release strategy on middling-budget films (around the $30m–$60m mark), being rewarded with hits such as *Kiss the Girls* and *Double Jeopardy*. Even when the films floundered at the box office (as the hugely underrated *Changing Lanes* did), the financial exposure wasn't too bad.

Now Paramount and the other studios aim big, but, conversely, smaller production outfits have moved in and breathed new life into mid-budget films. The likes of *The Accountant*, *The Girl on the Train*, *Jack Reacher: Never Go Back*, *Arrival* and *Bridget Jones's Baby*, for instance, all secured good box office returns in 2016. What's more, they each cost $30m–$50m to make.

MID-BUDGET IS IMPORTANT

Such productions span the gap between huge films and micro-budget ventures. They allow greater scope, with a bit of financial wiggle-room for greater risk-taking. Because most studios have abandoned such films, it seems important that everyone else does not.

PRODUCTION

HOW TINY DETAILS MADE A HUGE *STAR WARS* UNIVERSE

•••

Star Wars revolutionized blockbuster cinema, in terms of both visual and special effects. But it deserves more credit for the little details of the original trilogy, which brought a whole new universe to the screen.

The spaceship roars onto the screen, a huge bulk, pale against the inky depths of space. It's an Imperial Star Destroyer, its surface bristling with an incalculable number of spiky outcroppings. As its multiple engines rumble into view, we can only guess at its size.

Except, of course, the Star Destroyer isn't really a colossal battle cruiser, but a scale miniature, one of dozens expertly crafted by a team of artists and builders at Industrial Light and Magic (ILM). Those spiky outcroppings, which hint at all kinds of mysterious scientific applications, are in reality tiny pieces of plastic, cunningly applied to the model to suggest a craft of unfeasible size.

The *Millennium Falcon* flees a colossal Imperial Star Destroyer – note the incredible detail on the ships' surfaces.

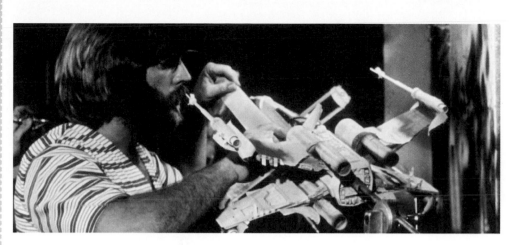

An ILM model maker puts the finishing touches to an X-wing for 1977's *Star Wars*.

Special effects artist John Dykstra, then aged just 29, led the team responsible for building the huge array of exotic craft in *Star Wars*. Stretched for both time and budget, they came up with all sorts of ingenious ways of making futuristic and believable-looking ships using materials readily at hand. One of the techniques Dykstra's team used was "kitbashing": they took small pieces from dozens of model kits and applied them to their scale miniatures in ways that made them unrecognizable to all but the most eagle-eyed. Parts from World War II flak cannons, battleships, fighter planes, tanks and submarines all made it onto the ships and vehicles in *Star Wars* and its sequels, from the Star Destroyer to Han Solo's *Millennium Falcon*.

Among the ILM artists working on *Star Wars*, the finest details on the movie's spacecraft were dubbed "greebles" or "greeblies" – the network of tiny tubes and mechanical-looking parts that break up the surface of a miniature and give it the feeling of a real, working machine. According to Frank Burton, who was a department head on *The Empire Strikes Back*, "Greeblie is a word George Lucas coined on *Star Wars* for something you can't otherwise define."

Where did the ingenious idea of adding them come from? Visual effects artist and production designer Fon Davis, who has worked with some of the industry greats at ILM since the mid-1990s, has a remarkable list of movies to his credit. He has worked as a model maker on the 1997 reissues of the original *Star Wars* trilogy, the *Star Wars* prequels, *Starship Troopers* and *Guardians of the Galaxy* to name a few.

So did George Lucas really coin the term greeble or greeblie? "It's possible," Davis said. "It came out of his group – it was the Industrial Light and Magic model makers that started calling them greebles."

George Lucas takes a close look at the Death Star model used for 1983's *Return of the Jedi*.

In 2001: A Space Odyssey, Douglas Trumbull used kit parts to create realistic-looking spaceships, such as Discovery One.

In creating the effects for Star Wars, John Dykstra and his team were building on the pioneering advances in effects that had come before, most famously in Stanley Kubrick's seminal 2001: A Space Odyssey, released in 1968. The extraordinarily inventive Douglas Trumbull (who directed another sci-fi classic, Silent Running) worked on that film for several years, devising all kinds of ground-breaking models and sequences that would ultimately win the film a Best Visual Effects Oscar.

Brian Johnson, who was handed Academy Awards for his work on Alien (1979) and The Empire Strikes Back (1980), recalls using kitbashing techniques to create some of the miniature effects for 2001: A Space Odyssey – and even suggests that the technique may predate that film.

"Derek [Meddings, special effects designer] and I certainly did use plastic kittery in large quantities," Johnson told Space1999.org, "and I am sure Douglas [Trumbull] used kit parts before 2001. We both knew what to do when we modified the Moon Bus."

Fon Davis agrees: "2001: A Space Odyssey was probably the first huge milestone in terms of greeble details. What it comes from is very practical. There's always budgets and schedules, right? So the need for greebles has more to do with budgets and schedules than anything else."

Creating fine details from pre-existing kit parts is therefore a practical and quick means of allowing a model maker to create a miniature quickly, without spending hours – or potentially weeks – individually conceiving and crafting those details by hand. There can be a practical aspect to applying greebles to a spacecraft, too. Take the Millennium Falcon, for example – that incredible detailing you can see running around the side of the ship in the original trilogy? That's there, in large part, to disguise a seam where the top of the miniature can be lifted off between takes.

The use of parts from model kits not only speeds up the building process, but also provides the audience with a subconscious link between the real world and the fantastical one on the screen. The use of utilitarian-looking bits and pieces, reworked and put together in new ways on a miniature, creates a subtle bond between the military vehicles most of us are familiar with and the more outlandish mecha dreamed up by George Lucas and his artists.

So of all the parts used for greebles in Star Wars, why are so many of them taken from military model kits? Because military kits are less recognizable to most of us than the pieces from a car – the kind of vehicle most of us see every day.

"Car model kits, as it turns out, don't have a lot of great greeble details, even in the motor," Davis explains. "That's because it's too recognizable as pieces from an automobile. If you use a military kit, it's less recognizable to the general public. But if you use something like an automobile part, you can see coilovers, or air filters, or fan belts."

Model kits proved so useful to ILM's model-making department that it had an entire room stocked with model kits and other useful parts.

"We had a room that on one side had all Evergreen products, which were also very popular with model makers, and then on the other side of the room just a shelf of model kits," Davis recalls. "We had set budgets for all these [miniatures], so we would try to find model kits that cost the least amount of money but had the most useful parts."

Some of those parts were regularly used in the *Star Wars* franchise and other effects sequences created at ILM. Adam Savage, who used to work at ILM as a model maker and now co-presents the popular TV show *MythBusters*, jokes about something he calls the universal greeblie in a video posted on Tested.com.

"There's this German [cannon] that has all these little beautiful parts that went into almost every spaceship," Savage says. "There's this little dome with four pips that we called the universal greeblie [...] The universal greeblie – the UG – was on, I think, every single Industrial Light and Magic model almost ever."

According to Fon Davis, the kit to which Savage is referring is the Krupp K5 rail cannon, a scale replica of a particularly deadly piece of ordnance from World War II sometimes nicknamed the Leopold.

The CGI boom of the 1990s might have led you to believe that things like kitbashing, greebles and miniature building in general have fallen out of favour. Far from it. The *Star Wars* prequels, released between 1999

and 2005, made extensive use of miniature effects ("We actually did more miniatures for the prequels than were done on the original series – a lot of people don't know that," Davis says). In more recent years, Davis and his team at effects company Fonco have built the miniatures for such hits as Neill Blomkamp's *Elysium* and Christopher Nolan's *Interstellar*.

In fact, not only is model building still a major part of the visual effects industry, but Fon Davis is now busier than ever. "I hear it all the time," laughs Davis. "People are like, 'Don't you ever miss [model making]?' And I'm like, 'What are you talking about? I never stopped working!'"

Even the advent of 3D printing hasn't replaced those kitbashing techniques pioneered in the 1960s and 1970s – nor has it seen off the humble greeble. "We do pretty much 3D-print 24 hours a day for all the projects we're working on," Davis says, "but we still have a hallway in the model shop filled with model kits. Any time you can get something off the shelf, it's going to be less expensive and take less time."

The approach to creating visual effects may have changed over the decades but, once again, creating the illusion of a huge, believable universe will all come down to those fine, greeblie details.

The iconic *Millennium Falcon* uses all kinds of parts from military model kits to create its richly textured surface.

FILMS RUMOURED TO BE GHOST-DIRECTED

•••

Just because the end credits of a movie tell you the name of the person who directed the film, it doesn't mean that's what they actually did. Here are but a few movies whose true authorship is still shrouded in mystery.

Had the budget stretched far enough, the tome you hold in your hands might have been put together by a crack team of ghostwriters, allowing us to sit back with a long coffee while others did all the work. No such luck, sadly. Ghost-authoring in books, though, is a fairly common business, with celebrity autobiographies rarely written by the person whose face is on the cover.

Curiously, it occasionally happens in film directing, too, that the person whose name is listed as director on a given film wasn't actually the person who did the directing. Just to be clear: these aren't instances of directors taking their names off a movie, because of

Tombstone, where Kurt Russell was said to be calling the shots in more ways than one.

studio interference or such gubbins. Instead, they retained credit, while someone else effectively ghost-directed the movie.

Rarely is there a definitive declaration that this is what's happened, incidentally. But here are cases where it has been suggested that the film's main director wasn't the one listed on its IMDb page.

TOMBSTONE
Named director: **George P Cosmatos**
Rumoured ghost director: **Kurt Russell**
We've a lot of time for *Tombstone*, a fun, blood-splattered ensemble western that thoroughly trumped Kevin Costner's competing project, the slower, more deliberate, three-hour *Wyatt Earp*, at the box office. *Tombstone* also had the better facial hair. It was originally set to be directed by Kevin Jarre, who penned the screenplay to the movie and shot some of the scenes featuring Charlton Heston. But when Jarre was fired from the project, in came George P Cosmatos, a man with the likes of the Sylvester Stallone vehicle *Cobra* to his name. Cosmatos was shipped in at the very last minute, arriving on set a day after he was given the job of directing the

film. It was already behind schedule, and the script urgently needed cutting down. Chaos threatened to ensue, with the film's star, Kurt Russell, credited with keeping the show going. More than that, though, he argues that he directed the film. As Russell told *True West* magazine back in 2006, he said to Cosmatos, "I'm going to give you a shot list every night, and that's what's going to be." He added that "I'd go to George's room, give him the shot list for the next day, that was the deal. 'George, I don't want any arguments. This is what it is.'" What's more, Russell argued that a similar thing had happened on *Rambo: First Blood Part II* – that Cosmatos was listed as director, but Stallone called the shots.

One thing Russell definitely didn't get to do with *Tombstone*, incidentally, was edit the picture. His schedule didn't allow it.

RETURN OF THE JEDI
Named director: Richard Marquand
Rumoured ghost director: **George Lucas**
Of his original trilogy of *Star Wars* films, George Lucas is only credited as being the director of one of them. In fact, his director's credit for *Star Wars* (1977), which has become known as *Star Wars: Episode IV – A New Hope*, would be his last until the first of the prequel trilogy, the, er, "much-loved" *Star Wars: Episode I – The Phantom Menace* (1999).

However, in the intervening two decades, Lucas oversaw many projects as a writer and a producer. And in the case of the third *Star Wars* film, *Return of the Jedi* (1983), there's a school of thought that he pretty much directed the film.

Lucas ceded the chair to his film school professor, Irvin Kershner, for the second in the original trilogy, *The Empire Strikes Back* (1980). While the film shot in Europe, Lucas had to be in America to oversee problems with his burgeoning Lucasfilm company. He had a few frustrations with some of what

Kershner did, although Lucas did offer him the chance to direct *Return of the Jedi*. A worn-out Kershner declined.

Instead, Lucas settled on the relatively unknown Welsh director Richard Marquand, who would go on to helm the hit thriller *Jagged Edge*. Notably, though, *Return of the Jedi* was filmed in America, and Lucas was present on set for a lot of the time. As it happened, he was right next to Marquand, wanting specific shots, which the director – who died in 1987 at the age of just 49 – duly provided. This gave Lucas the material he needed to shape *Return of the Jedi* in the editing room, and that's what is said to have happened.

Marquand was certainly present, and few debate that he had his say. But also, there remains a festering – often denied – suspicion that George Lucas was calling more of the shots…

SUPER MARIO BROS.
Named directors: Annabel Jankel, Rocky Morton
Rumoured ghost directors: **Dean Semler, Roland Joffé**
The late, great Bob Hoskins didn't have to think twice when he was asked by the *Guardian* newspaper in 2007 about the films he'd made but didn't care for. "The worst thing I ever did? *Super Mario Bros.* It was a f--kin' nightmare. It had a husband-and-wife team directing, whose arrogance had been mistaken for talent. After so many weeks their own agent told them to get off the set! F--kin' nightmare. F--kin' idiots."

From that, it's best to conclude that Hoskins wasn't a fan of the 1993 movie's take on the popular videogame characters. He wasn't alone: *Super Mario Bros.* is regarded as one of the worst blockbuster movies of the 1990s.

The husband-and-wife team to whom Hoskins refers were Annabel Jankel and Rocky Morton, who had shot to prominence for creating the 1980s television sensation

Max Headroom. But they struggled to adapt to helming a feature film. To give but one account, John Leguizamo – who co-starred in the movie – recorded in his memoir accounts of their frequent arguments. And he noted that "after a while, Annabel and Rocky turned a lot of the crew against them", adding that the crew "made T-shirts with all the kinds of dismissive comments the directors made. People wore them on the set." Ouch.

The duo didn't make it to the end of production, with producer Roland Joffé and director of photography Dean Semler stepping in. Neither got credit for their work, but as an actor on the production, Mark Jeffrey Miller noted back in 2010, once Jankel and Morton had left, "Everyone was much happier".

The pair haven't directed a movie since. And few people have had much that was nice to say about their sole big-screen effort.

TANGO & CASH

Named director: Andrei Konchalovsky
Rumoured directors: Albert Magnoli,
Stuart Baird

They barely make 'em like 1989's *Tango & Cash* any more, a violent, hugely enjoyable, star-driven action adventure. But heck, this was one troubled production.

The final cut of the film is credited to Russian director Andrei Konchalovsky, who

The late Bob Hoskins disliked *Super Mario Bros.* even more than most of its audience.

had moved to the US in the early 1980s and rightly earned acclaim for films such as *Runaway Train* (1985). *Tango & Cash* would be the highest-profile project of his directorial career, but he didn't see it through to the end. With nearly three months' worth of filming completed, he left after a disagreement with producer Jon Peters about the film's ending. By that time, cinematographer Barry Sonnenfeld had also got his marching orders. Within a decade, Sonnenfeld would be a sought-after Hollywood director in his own right, courtesy of the likes of the *Men in Black* trilogy, *The Addams Family* and *Addams Family Values*.

Tango & Cash needed fresh blood, however, and it first got it in the shape of Peter MacDonald, a second unit director and executive producer on the project. He held the fort until in came Albert Magnoli. He filmed the movie's action sequences for its denouement, before the footage was handed over to Stuart Baird (who would go on to direct the entertaining *Executive Decision*, among others) in the edit suite.

There, the film was overhauled once more, again without Konchalovsky's input. Baird was credited with piecing the movie back together and creating a workable final cut. The film would do well at the box office and continues to enjoy an audience to this day.

POLTERGEIST

Steven Spielberg was unable to direct 1982's horror hit *Poltergeist*, because of a clause in his contract that meant he couldn't helm another film until he'd done with his then-current project, *E.T. the Extra-Terrestrial*. He handed over directing duties on *Poltergeist* to Tobe Hooper (best known for the original *The Texas Chainsaw Massacre*, of course). Hooper's name was on the end credits, but suspicions soon arose that Spielberg had actually ghost-directed the picture. A comment attributed to Spielberg in the

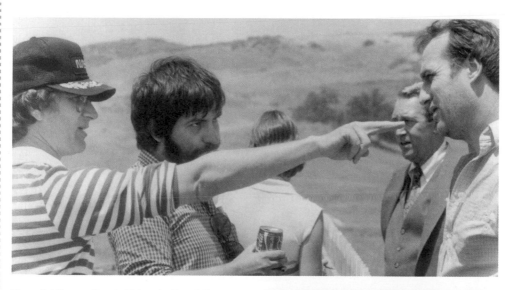

Steven Spielberg on the set of *Poltergeist*. He and director Tobe Hooper were close collaborators on the project.

Los Angeles Times around the time of the release added a few extra background noises. "If a question was asked and an answer wasn't immediately forthcoming, I'd jump in and say what we could do. Tobe would nod agreement, and that became the process of collaboration," he said.

That comment caused such ripples that the Directors Guild of America decided to investigate, to see if Hooper's credit was being undermined. Nothing happened there, though.

The question of who actually directed *Poltergeist* continues to rumble, but the heart of it seems to be two collaborators working together. To what degree perhaps lies at the heart of the mystery. Spielberg reportedly storyboarded the movie, and he was present on set for the vast bulk of the filming. Hooper was and remained the on-set director, and the two of them worked closely on the film. Although Hooper conceded in 2000 that Spielberg did some pick-up shots for the movie, he maintains that he shot the bulk of the film, and he remains its credited director.

LOCKOUT

More common than a "ghost director" is for the director to be locked out of the editing process.

Best friends Kevin Costner and director Kevin Reynolds came together on *Robin Hood: Prince of Thieves* (1991) and *Waterworld* (1995). For both, Reynolds was absent when the final cut was locked down. Interestingly, extended cuts of both films have since appeared.

●●●

Going back further, before he made *The French Connection* and *The Exorcist*, William Friedkin shot what would become 1968's *The Night They Raided Minsky's*. A commitment to his next project, an adaptation of Harold Pinter's *The Birthday Party*, meant that Friedkin was barely around for the post-production phase. Instead, the film was edited and fundamentally improved and changed by Ralph Rosenblum, as Rosenblum charts in some detail in his excellent book *When the Shooting Stops… the Cutting Begins*.

FILMS THAT CHANGED DIRECTOR, ONCE FILMING HAD STARTED

...

It was just weeks into production, and Universal Pictures wasn't happy with *Spartacus*. The film had been shooting for three weeks under the stewardship of the original director, Anthony Mann, and the executives weren't impressed. Mann was fired in February 1959. Stanley Kubrick would be hired (and would battle with the film's star, Kirk Douglas), and an all-time classic movie would be the result.

In fact, *Spartacus* was more of an exception to the rule of what could be expected to happen following a change of director. (Kirk Douglas's excellent memoir, *I Am Spartacus*, deals with the story in more depth.) Sometimes, after cameras have started rolling, a director might quit, they might be fired or other circumstances might take hold – but whatever the cause, a change of director is a major upheaval, and often one with consequences.

WARGAMES (1983)

The much-loved Matthew Broderick-headlined story of a young computer hacker taking the world to the brink of nuclear war was steered to the screen in the end by director John Badham. But he was a late replacement. Badham got the nod after the original director, Martin Brest, got his marching orders. (He would instead go on to make *Beverly Hills Cop*.) The footage that was coming through wasn't fun enough, reckoned the studio, and the tone of the film (about nuclear destruction!) was too downbeat. Badham quickly retooled the movie, lightening it, and the film would ultimately be rewarded with much cash, and Oscar nominations.

THE OUTLAW JOSEY WALES (1976)

A terrific western this, with Clint Eastwood on excellent form in the title role. In the end, Eastwood would also direct the movie, but that wasn't the original plan. When filming began, it was Philip Kaufman (*The Right Stuff*) directing, having also co-written the screenplay. But problems soon arose. Kaufman's directorial style was notoriously precise, whereas Eastwood tends to prepare lots and then shoot quickly. Rumours arose, too, of the pair sharing affection for Sondra Locke. (Shortly after filming, Locke and

Clint Eastwood and Sondra Locke on the set of *The Outlaw Josey Wales*.

Eastwood would be in a relationship, which lasted until the late 1980s.)

Whatever the eventual reason, Kaufman was removed from the film, and Eastwood would direct, to much acclaim. Kaufman, meanwhile, would move on to his acclaimed remake of *Invasion of the Body Snatchers*.

EXORCIST: THE BEGINNING (2004)

A pretty bizarre story this. *Exorcist: The Beginning* was envisaged as a prequel to 1973's classic *The Exorcist*, with *Birdman of Alcatraz*'s director John Frankenheimer set to steer the spooky ship. Frankenheimer had to depart, though, and would pass away not long after. In his place came Paul Schrader (an established director, but perhaps still best known for writing the screenplay to *Taxi Driver*). Schrader duly shot the movie and delivered his final cut – which the producers hated.

They hated it, in fact, to the point where Morgan Creek Productions decided to

Footage shot by original director Anthony Mann remains in the final cut of Stanley Kubrick's *Spartacus*.

It would be fair to call 2004's *Exorcist* movie "troubled".

overhaul the project. Even though filming was technically done, it hired *Die Hard 2* director Renny Harlin to come in and deliver a more conventional cut. He did, with his film notably different from Schrader's. Not that it mattered, as *Exorcist: The Beginning* was savaged on release.

But word was growing of Schrader's version, not least from the man himself. Morgan Creek therefore gave him a small amount of extra money, and Schrader would finish off his own version, which duly became known as *Dominion: Prequel to the Exorcist*. The critical reaction slightly improved, but it still didn't seem to shift too many box sets.

JUMPIN' JACK FLASH (1986)

A breakthrough movie for Whoopi Goldberg, *Jumpin' Jack Flash* is a lively and enjoyable spy comedy, which would mark the feature directorial debut of Penny Marshall (who would go on to make *Big*, *A League of Their Own* and *Awakenings*). Marshall described the experience as "hell", remarking, "It was insane. It was quite an experience, an amazing learning experience. I had a lot to learn and this was one way to do it."

It sure was – for Marshall had been drafted onto the film after filming had been going on for *six weeks*, which meant that for nearly a third of the film's shooting time Howard Zieff (*Private Benjamin*) was in charge. He left for

reasons that were never disclosed, although the production was said to be a troubled one. Marshall quickly learned on the job, and while the reviews were hardly glowing, the box office was decent enough. A profit was made, and Marshall would jump onto making arguably her best film – 1988's *Big* – shortly after.

HEAT (1986)

Not *that* one – not the 1995 classic crime thriller starring Robert De Niro and Al Pacino. This one is the 1986 film, starring Burt Reynolds, which was subsequently remade as the pretty decent *Wild Card*, starring the more than decent Jason Statham.

The 1986 *Heat* was a very troubled beast. By the time it landed on cinema screens, it had gone through five changes of director, according to its screenwriter, William Goldman. Here are the ones we know about.

First up, the late Robert Altman (*The Player*) was in charge for precisely one day of shooting, quitting when his Canadian cameraman, Pierre Mignot, was denied a visa to work in the US. By day two, Altman had been replaced by Dick Richards, who would ultimately get final credit on the movie. Mind you, he and Reynolds apparently didn't share the best working relationship, and tittle-tattle (well, tittle-tattle and a $25m lawsuit) suggests it ended up in a fight.

Richards departed, and Jerry Jameson took on the job next, apparently shooting around 30 per cent of the film. But then (still following this?) Dick Richards was lured back – before he was off to hospital, courtesy of a fall from a camera crane, so somebody came in to finish the movie off. The film shot, in total, for just over a month. In 2000, William Goldman published the book *Which Lie Did I Tell?* and even then, nearly 15 years on, he had to be cautious as to what he wrote, because, he reflects, "to my knowledge, lawsuits are still flying".

SUPERNOVA (2000)

This sci-fi horror had been a project in gestation for the best part of a decade when Walter Hill – a man with films such as *48 Hrs.* and *The Warriors* on his resumé – came on board. *Supernova* had originally been set to be directed by Geoffrey Wright, but "creative differences" led to Wright's departure just two weeks before filming was due to begin. In stepped Jack Sholder – though not for long. Finally, Hill came in, and shot his take on the movie. Despite complaining that the budget was halved midway through, he battled on to complete a cut. Then MGM, the studio funding the film, screened an unfinished version of *Supernova* for a test audience.

The response? Ouch. Hill quit in the aftermath, having objected to screening an unfinished movie in the first place. So, back came Sholder, who re-edited the film, and shot yet more material for the movie. Notably, he also removed a good chunk of Hill's footage. Sholder's version was then also test-screened, with better results than Hill's cut.

In the midst of all of this, new management came in at MGM, and they wanted Hill back. Hill promptly asked for $5m to shoot new material to fix the film, and MGM baulked at that. Instead, it hired the director of *The Godfather*, Francis Ford Coppola, who was on the board of the studio at the time. He spent around $1m re-editing the film – including adding a love scene, by superimposing the faces of James Spader and Angela Bassett onto other figures – but that didn't improve matters either. MGM, by this stage, cut its losses, and the film was let loose to hideous reviews at the start of 2000. If you look in the credits for the name of director Walter Hill, you won't find it. Instead, the film was apparently directed by "Thomas Lee". Only Thomas Lee doesn't exist. He's a pseudonym for Hill, who took his name off the movie.

Supernova: search the credits, and director Walter Hill's name will not be found...

GONE WITH *THE WIZARD OF OZ*

Some of the most beloved films have been hit by changes of director behind the scenes. *The Wizard of Oz*, for instance, is regarded as a flat-out classic now, but it managed to get through a director or two. Norman Taurog was first and was navigating the yellow brick road when filming began. Richard Thorpe then came in for two weeks, shooting the scene in which Dorothy meets the Scarecrow. After Thorpe, George Cukor took the reins for a little while, and Victor Fleming – of *Gone with the Wind* fame – was up next. But even he didn't make it to the final day of shooting, with King Vidor picking up the last few shots.

Gone with the Wind, meanwhile, started filming with George Cukor, who got the push after three weeks. Then, straight from *The Wizard of Oz* set came Victor Fleming. Fleming, again, didn't get to the finish line, collapsing from exhaustion three months after starting on the film. Sam Wood would complete production from the director's chair.

THE BLOCKBUSTER MOVIE WITH 35 SCREENWRITERS

•••

In 1994 *The Flintstones* changed the way writing credits were arbitrated on movies – but only after 35 screenwriters had been put through the mill.

Few people have fond memories of 1994's *The Flintstones* movie. Some warm to it, but despite all the box office dollars that it pulled in on its original release, the film was critically savaged. Yet, in the build-up to the movie's release, there was something else quite remarkable about it: the sheer number of writers fighting to be credited on the project.

Having umpteen writers on a film is nothing new, of course (*Catwoman* had up to 28 people working on it). The dark arts of the Writers Guild of America, which arbitrates over who gets final credit on a film, are unknown to all those but the people within the organization's inner sanctum. However, it quickly became clear that some serious work would be needed

The Flintstones: a story of how 35 writers came up with one of the worst blockbuster screenplays of the 1990s.

to get the number of credited screenwriters on *The Flintstones* down to a number that would fit on the bottom of the poster.

Thus, when the movie was released, the final credit went to Steven E de Souza, Jim Jennewein and Tom S Parker. That said, some early cinema standees (the term for lobby stands promoting the film), before the final credits were locked down, were listing seven or eight writers.

The origins of *The Flintstones* movie actually date back to 1985, when de Souza (best known for the mighty *Die Hard*) was hired to pen a screenplay, with the idea being that Richard Donner would direct. De Souza's screenplay didn't fit what the studio wanted, however, and in came Mitch Markowitz, who penned a script, but Richard Donner wasn't keen on it. Donner, in all, would oversee five scripts, with eight writers involved, before departing.

Next on the scene was Steven Spielberg's Amblin Entertainment, who snapped up the rights for themselves in the late 1980s. Eventually, Brian Levant, who was a passionate fan of the original series and who was riding high off the back of his then recent hit *Beethoven*, was hired to direct. He arrived to a blank slate, as Spielberg had rejected the scripts that had been written up to that point.

Levant's background was primarily television, but one of his first moves was to hire Gary Ross (who would go on to direct *Pleasantville* and the first *The Hunger Games* movie) to put together a draft. Levant didn't like what he read, and eventually he moved toward a television "writers' room" approach to shaping the script. (This was then rare in movies but has become more common ever since Paramount used a writers' room to map out the future of *Transformers* movies.)

A team of eight writers came up with a new draft, delivering it in early 1993. But that, too, failed to get the film its green light. Levant arranged a further four round-table sessions of a similar ilk, adding different writers each time. At one stage, *City Slickers* and *Parenthood* co-writers Lowell Ganz and Babaloo Mandel came in to do two days' work on the movie, pocketing $100,000 for their trouble.

Reports vary on just how many writers in all worked on the project, but the common consensus tends to sit between 32 and 35. Only one of them was a woman, Dava Savel (who was writing, or would write, episodes of the television series *Ellen* and *Will & Grace*, moving on to producing the latter show). At the time, she told *Entertainment Weekly*, "I have no idea if I have one line in there. Can you believe it?"

When it came time to submit final credits, the *Chicago Sun-Times* reported in January 1994 that Universal was looking to name nine

Having umpteen writers on a film is nothing new... Catwoman had up to 28 people working on it

people. Story credit was set to go to Michael Wilson, and screenplay credit to Brian Levant, Al Aidekman, Cindy Begel, Lloyd Garver, David Silverman, Stephen Sustarsic, Nancy Steen and Neil Thompson. But this jarred with the Writers Guild of America. Its members were keen to impose a ceiling of three writers, or writing teams, as a maximum number who could be credited on a movie. Levant's original eight withdrew from the arbitration process.

By then, it was widely known just how many pens had contributed to *The Flintstones'* script, and it'd be a regularly cited fact in reviews of the film. (Think along the lines of "35 people couldn't even think of one funny joke". Now rinse and repeat.) Even then, one of the three who did ultimately receive credit, Jim Jennewein, wasn't happy. "We had no contact with the script after Levant came," he said. "Everyone thinks drama needs a single unifying voice, and I think the same holds true for comedy. Screenwriting is a real craft, and movies are different from TV." This was, it should be noted, before the days of HBO's acclaimed scripted dramas.

The Writers Guild would refine its arbitration rules in the wake of the muddle with *The Flintstones*, limiting credits to those deemed to have contributed a set amount to the final screenplay for a movie. After all, each credit on a movie costs a studio money down the line, with writers generally entitled to residuals.

As for the film itself? Critics be damned: it earned over $340m at the global box office, at a time when that was deemed a tidy sum. But while director Brian Levant would return to direct the prequel movie *The Flintstones in Viva Rock Vegas* over half a decade later, the cast was changed. And a mere four writers would be credited with penning that one.

THE TIMELINE OF A MODERN FILM

It takes a long time to make a movie – but why? What is the process and why does it take so many years to make one feature? Here's how the production of 2012 film *The Hunger Games* breaks down...

MARCH 2009

Production company Color Force snaps up the film rights to *The Hunger Games* novel, reportedly for $200,000. It enters into a deal with Lionsgate to back the picture, which has a working budget of $88m (cheap, by Hollywood standards).

MOST OF 2009–SUMMER 2010

Work begins on the screenplay for the film. The first draft is written by the book's author, Suzanne Collins, subsequently working with screenwriter Billy Ray.

Lionsgate gambled heavily on *The Hunger Games*, trimming the budgets of its other productions to ensure it could do the film version justice.

SEPTEMBER 2010

Lionsgate enters negotiations with Gary Ross to direct the film. He signs on the dotted line by the end of the month. He works with Suzanne Collins to continue to shape the script. Writing and early design work continue.

MARCH 2011

Lionsgate confirms that it has auditioned around 30 people for the lead role of Katniss Everdeen, announcing Jennifer Lawrence in the part on 16 March 2011. (Lawrence was filming 2012's *X-Men: First Class* at the time and took three days to accept the part, dropping out of her proposed role in Oliver Stone's film *Savages*.) Also, pre-production work begins in earnest, preparing sets, costumes and more for the proposed near-four-month shoot of the film.

APRIL–MAY 2011

Casting work continues, until, by the end of May, key cast members Donald Sutherland, Woody Harrelson, Toby Jones, Stanley Tucci and Lenny Kravitz are signed up.

The success of *The Hunger Games* turned Jennifer Lawrence into a movie star.

MAY 2011

Filming begins in North Carolina. The state would host the vast bulk of the production (and the three sequels). The first publicity shot of Jennifer Lawrence as Katniss appears on the cover of *Entertainment Weekly* magazine.

AUGUST 2011

Lionsgate announces the release date for the next movie in the series, *The Hunger Games: Catching Fire*, even before the first film is complete. Scripting work gets under way. The first clip of *The Hunger Games* movie is introduced – in a pre-recorded segment – by Jennifer Lawrence at the MTV Video Music Awards on 28 August.

SEPTEMBER 2011

On 15 September, principal photography on *The Hunger Games* is completed. With a tight release date to hit, the filmmakers head to the edit suite to put their cut together.

OCTOBER 2011

The cast are back on location for some reshoot work, getting material that has been identified as required following the first rough assembly of material from the movie.

NOVEMBER 2011

The first official trailer for the movie is released on 14 November 2011. The film is still deep in post-production.

FEBRUARY 2012

With the film still not quite complete, advance ticket sales open on 22 February, four weeks ahead of the movie's release. The final cut is locked down by the end of the month.

MARCH 2012

Premiere takes place on 12 March in Los Angeles, ahead of the global cinema release at the end of the month. It goes on to gross nearly $700m from box offices worldwide.

TIME AND MOTION PICTURES

The Hunger Games is one of the speedier examples, taking just over three years, from signing the deal, through adapting the book, to releasing the movie. Most big animated films take at least four years, although generally only the last year of that is spent physically animating the story. Likewise, it's not uncommon for big films to linger in "development hell" for years. *Men in Black 3*, to pluck one example, was first proposed during the filming of *Men in Black II* in 2002, yet wouldn't appear for another decade.

THE THINGS MOVIE ACTION HEROES GET UP TO ON THEIR DAYS OFF

When asked what he did between acting jobs, Robert Duvall once said, "Hobbies, hobbies and more hobbies." The question is, what do other action heroes get up to when they're not shooting bad guys, blowing up trucks or rescuing their daughters from Val Verde? Things like these...

JOHN MATRIX – *COMMANDO*

Retired US army colonel John Matrix (Arnold Schwarzenegger) may be a battle-hardened warrior, but he has a softer, cuddlier side, too. In the seminal 1985 anti-war drama *Commando*, we see what domestic bliss looks like to a walking gun cabinet like Matrix: he lives in a large wood-built house in the middle of nowhere, and likes to relax by carrying an enormous tree trunk around its rambling grounds.

By the time we see Matrix and his daughter Jenny feeding a deer together, we almost start to wonder whether what we're watching isn't really an action hero's day off at all, but an early promo video for Arnold Schwarzenegger's Governor of California campaign.

The important thing to note is that, like just about everyone else on this list, Matrix likes to do tough, outdoorsy-type things: chopping down trees, carrying chainsaws and logs one-handed, and so forth. At no point do we see him fluffing cushions or vacuuming the dog or watching daytime talk shows.

Arnie: your go-to guy for carrying around enormous tree trunks, when he's not fishing that is.

JOHN RAMBO – *RAMBO III*

Following the events of *First Blood* and *Rambo: First Blood Part II*, former Vietnam War veteran John Rambo has had more than his fill of war. In *Rambo III* (1988), he is now living a quiet life in Thailand, spending much of his time helping monks do up their ailing monastery. But while Rambo has turned his back on machine guns and hand grenades, he can't quite resist the allure of sweaty one-on-one

Useful pub quiz trivia: the character of Rambo (seen here in the 2008 film of the same name) was originally supposed to die at the end of his first film, *First Blood*. Spoiler alert: he didn't.

action, so when he's not playing handyman at the local monastery, he's engaging in illegal fights in a dingy warehouse.

Like John Matrix, John Rambo reminds us through his hobbies that he's both a warrior and a gentle soul at heart. Rambo may be a master of topless stick fighting, but he's also sensitive enough to enjoy repairing Far Eastern religious buildings.

JOHN RAMBO – *RAMBO*

After using his combat skills to help out the Taliban in *Rambo III* (a move he might now regret), John headed back to Thailand and lay low for 20 years. If you've been wondering what hobbies Rambo got up to in the two decades between adventures, *Rambo* (2008) provides the answer: he made a living from giving people rides in his boat and catching wild serpents for a local snake show. Again, these aren't the kinds of hobbies ordinary mortals commonly indulge in. Fear not, though: Rambo is still in touch with the artistic side he displayed in *Rambo III*. But where most people might take up a bit of Sunday painting or gardening, Rambo likes to sullenly sharpen huge knives in his workshop.

NICK CHERENKO – *THE MECHANIK*

In this 2005 action epic, Dolph Lundgren plays Nick Cherenko, a hitman turned mechanic. Dolph therefore offers a range of services you won't find anywhere else in action cinema: he'll check your handbrake tension and wheel alignment, and then afterwards rescue your daughter from a gang of sex traffickers in St Petersburg.

J J MCQUADE – *LONE WOLF MCQUADE*

A chap with a name like J J McQuade isn't likely to be into badminton and pigeon fancying, especially when he's played by Chuck Norris. When McQuade, a Marine turned Texas Ranger, isn't shooting Mexican bandits and getting into tussles with evil arms dealers in this 1983 film, he enjoys relaxing in his caravan park with his pet wolf.

For McQuade, relaxing means taking his shirt off and discharging firearms in the afternoon sun. When the appeal of that starts to wane, he'll kick his own shed until it collapses. What McQuade's neighbours in the next caravan make of this, we've no idea.

FILMS THAT FELL APART MID-PRODUCTION

•••

On page 101, we're going to take a look at what happens to
a film when one of its key stars dies after filming begins.
But there are other reasons why films are shut down
mid-production – usually involving money.

In October 2011, director David Twohy was set to drive into work to continue filming the third film in a series that had kicked off with the excellent *Pitch Black* and stumbled with *The Chronicles of Riddick*. The new film, *Riddick*, was seen as a way to kick-start the series again (its profile had been raised by impressive tie-in video games), aided by Vin Diesel's star rising again thanks to the growing success of the *Fast & Furious* series.

Riddick was still a sizeable risk, in spite of Diesel's stature. The previous film had cost $105m to make, and had been expected to be a big summer hit in 2004. Yet it had returned just $115m in worldwide cinema takings and wouldn't see green ink until long into its DVD and home formats life. *Riddick* was a project put together on a much tighter budget of $38m, but, even then, raising that finance had proved tricky, and holding it in place even trickier. Thus, on that day in October 2011, the TMZ website reported that the cast and crew were physically locked out of the Montreal studio where the film was being shot. The problem? Reports of bills being unpaid and "some serious cash flow issues" led to the locks being changed at said facility. A month later the

A studio may decide to cut its losses should it lose confidence in a project

debts were paid off, fresh funds were found, and the movie was able to be completed. (It would gross roughly the same as its predecessor, but would be more profitable.)

Other films, however, were not as fortunate. Back in 2015, Bruce Willis and Sir Ben Kingsley were both working on a thriller called *Wake*. Ten days of filming had been completed by the end of February, before the project was shut down, as it had run out of cash. The production company behind the movie, Benaroya Pictures, was confident it could get things up and running again. It announced its plan to reassemble the cast and crew in Cleveland come the end of March. But in this case, it wasn't to be. The new start date came and went, and by early April both Willis and director John Pogue had quit the film. Not a frame of footage has been filmed since, and the ten days of material remains locked in a vault/stored on a flash disk somewhere. Vague noises were made about trying to resurrect *Wake* at some point in the future, but its fate seems to sit on the wrong side of rosy.

Money is usually at the heart of such shutdowns, but also, a studio may decide to cut its losses should it lose confidence in a project. Back in 2008, *Pirates of the Caribbean* director Gore Verbinski was deep into pre-production on a big-screen adaptation of the hit video game BioShock. "We started building sets," he recalled. "We just started building them, and pre-vizzing some sequences." But Universal Pictures, which was going to have to spend the best part of $200m to bring the film to the big screen, wanted a softer, family-friendly, PG-13/12A rating for the movie. "I just couldn't manage it," Verbinski mourned, noting for a start the game's reliance on injections, which would deny it anything close to a family-friendly rating. The plug was pulled, and Verbinski went on to make *The Lone Ranger* for Disney instead.

Legalities are another obstacle that have a habit of derailing movies. Director Gil Junger is the man who helmed the much-loved *10 Things I Hate About You* (1999), a film that gave leading roles to Julia Stiles and the late Heath Ledger. Back in 2012, it was announced that he was to make a spiritual successor – if not a sequel – called *10 Things I Hate About Life*. Financing was duly raised, and Evan Rachel Wood was cast in the lead role. Filming commenced in late 2012, but the film was shut down four weeks later. Depending on which account you believe, it was caused by a lack

of money, the pregnancy of Evan Rachel Wood or the latter walking off the project. A hotly contested lawsuit was filed over a year later, after a planned restart date for the production came and went. The bottom line: the film stalled – in spite of a full trailer appearing – and to get it going again would require someone able either to lure Evan Rachel Wood back or to pay for the whole thing to be done from scratch. Neither seems likely.

The granddaddy of the abandoned movie is *The Man Who Killed Don Quixote*, director Terry Gilliam's attempt to bring the story of Don Quixote to film. It's a saga that has spanned decades. By the time he raised a $32m budget and found himself on location in Spain, back in September 2000, it had already taken ten years of work just to get that far. That he had managed to find his money without one cent from Hollywood was little short of a miracle. Yet the production would be infamously cursed.

On day one of shooting, Gilliam found that his location was next to a deafening NATO air base, meaning that captured audio couldn't be used. No matter – the next day, the weather turned, heavy rain and hail descended, and the footage from the previous 24 hours was rendered useless anyway. Problems continued for a few more days, and then Gilliam's lead, the French actor Jean Rochefort, injured his back. He was forced to drop out of the film, and a week later the plug was pulled.

The tale is recounted in detail and style in the outstanding 2002 feature documentary *Lost in La Mancha*. Regular attempts have been made since by Gilliam to revive the project, with glimmers of light for its future and finally, in 2017, he got back on set, reunited with his *Brazil* star Jonathan Pryce for his second attempt to film *Don Quixote*. Notably, Gilliam also allowed a documentary crew to follow him again, just to be on the safe side.

The ill-fated first attempt by Terry Gilliam to film *The Man Who Killed Don Quixote*.

Given that animated films tend to take three to four years to bring to the screen, it's perhaps inevitable that they often face a choppier path, and many movies bite the dust deep into development and even production. DreamWorks Animation, for instance, had been working on a sequel to its 2013 hit *The Croods* for several years, before pulling the plug in 2016. The problem? It couldn't crack the story it wanted to tell (and DreamWorks Animation had just been sold to Universal).

Several other DreamWorks projects met a similar fate when the studio's slate of projects started failing to hit in the mid-2010s. Films such as *B.O.O.: Bureau of Otherworldly Operations* and *Mumbai Musical* were given release dates, and then quietly removed from the schedules, the former in spite of being deep into animation.

Even the seemingly bulletproof Pixar once announced a project that it subsequently scrapped. *Newt* was to tell the story of the last remaining male and female blue-footed newts on the planet, who had to get on to save their species. This one was, as Pixar co-boss Ed Catmull would concede, partly a victim of an experiment within the company that saw the production team located "two blocks away from our main campus to minimize their contact with those who might encourage them to adopt the status quo". The problem? By the time the broader Pixar team got to the film, the issues within it were too deep-rooted to resolve. The plug was thus pulled, with some of the artwork subsequently leaking onto the internet.

In spite of its success, a sequel to *The Croods* was abandoned.

WHAT HAPPENS WHEN A STAR DIES IN THE MIDDLE OF FILMING?

It doesn't happen often, but given that some films take the best part of a year to shoot, every now and then a production has to find a way to cope with the death of one of its stars. Sometimes that proves simply impossible.

Nine years after his death, the final movie of actor **River Phoenix**, *Dark Blood*, finally premiered at the Netherlands Film Festival. Said premiere took place in September 2012. Phoenix's life had ended tragically early, back in October 1993, when he died of a drug overdose at the age of just 23. At that time,

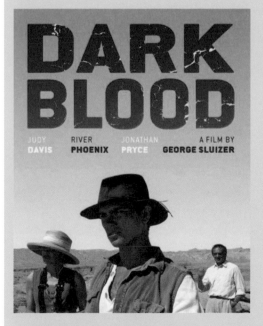

Dark Blood remains unfinished, yet a cobbled together version was ultimately screened.

he'd finished work on the comedy drama *The Thing Called Love* (1993), which had just been promoted and released in America. But when tragedy struck, he was in the midst of the shoot of *Dark Blood*, the new film from the director of *The Vanishing*, George Sluizer.

In fact, he was more than mid-shoot. Around four-fifths of the movie was in the can, and a few weeks of shooting on a Los Angeles sound stage was all that was left to go. Yet crucially for the film, those three weeks included pivotal material for the story, in particular hinging on Phoenix's character. After much discussion between the people paying for the film, and those insuring it, *Dark Blood* was abandoned three weeks after Phoenix's death, as it had been decided that it couldn't be finished without his involvement.

Unbeknown to those insurers and financiers, what was shot of the film was then squirrelled away on the quiet by its director. Sluizer kept the cans of footage himself, news that only came to light in 2011, when it was revealed that he was intending to complete the movie nearly two decades later. This he duly did, using voice-over narration to fill in the gaps, and effectively rendering what was originally set to be a dark thriller into something more of a curiosity (and which was generally reviewed as such). The film never

The late Paul Walker, whose work in *Fast & Furious 7* was completed via digital trickery, with help from his brothers.

got a wide release and, following the death of Sluizer in 2014, is unlikely to do so now.

What is especially notable about *Dark Blood* is that the film was effectively abandoned. Today, in the digital age, trickery, doubles and existing footage would probably be used to cover up scenes that hadn't been shot before the death of the actor concerned – the show would, basically, go on.

The highest-profile recent example was arguably 2015's *Fast & Furious 7*, aka *Furious 7* (although *The Imaginarium of Doctor Parnassus* that lost Heath Ledger mid-production is no less prominent). At the halfway point of the production, one of its leading actors, **Paul Walker**, died in a horrific car accident. He was just 40 years old. For the studio behind the movie, Universal, this was no modestly budgeted thriller. Universal was sinking the best part of $200m just into *making* the film, and the movie was scheduled for a prime

summer 2014 release. It didn't help that the studio's schedule that summer was already looking quite sparse.

The logistical problems that Universal faced, in both honouring Paul Walker and completing its film, were enormous. Walker's character was, and is, crucial to the story (and the franchise as a whole), and there was much filming left to do.

Eventually, the studio shut down the film for four months while director James Wan and his team worked out what they had, what they needed and how they could get it. The release date moved back nearly a year. Eventually, it took sizable script reworking, computer trickery and Walker's brothers – Caleb and Cody – to help plug the missing scenes. The final cut is, understandably, a little uneven. But it sure found its audience. On release – inarguably fuelled a little by the publicity surrounding Walker's death – it went on to gross a $1.5bn worldwide. That made it, at the time, one of the five biggest films of all time.

Oliver Reed died in 1999 in Malta, where the core shoot of *Gladiator* (2000) was based.

It's not hard to think that, even ten years previously, the work needed to retool *Fast & Furious 7* and simply complete the film would have been prohibitively expensive. Now, though, filmmakers have, not to their pleasure, found workarounds.

For instance, **Philip Seymour Hoffman's** death at the age of 46 in February 2014 left behind very much an unfinished career, and also his work in the last two films of the series *The Hunger Games*. Hoffman's role in *The Hunger Games: Mockingjay Part 1* was pretty much completed, but he had two significant scenes left to shoot for 2015's *The Hunger Games: Mockingjay Part 2*. These were ultimately rewritten, and digital trickery was also required, which meant that the film was finally released 21 months after his death.

Also notably, **Oliver Reed** gave his best screen performance in some time, in Ridley Scott's Oscar-winner *Gladiator*. But Reed never got to see the end result: he died on the film's Maltese shoot, and, again, computers were duly deployed.

In each of these examples, filmmakers were faced with a near-impossible decision as to whether to continue. In such instances, a combination of the needs of commerce and the wishes of surviving family and friends usually drives a project to completion.

BRANDON LEE

The first time that computer technology really came into its own in finishing a movie following the death of its lead star was arguably 1994's *The Crow*. Director Alex Proyas's movie was deep into production when, on 31 March 1993, a firearm accident claimed the life of lead actor Brandon Lee. The son of Bruce Lee, he was pronounced dead later that day.

Lee had two days of shooting left, and the producers eventually opted to press ahead with completing the picture. It took a 50 per cent increase in the film's budget to do so (no small matter, given the cost of the production), and Lee's stunt double, Chad Stahelski (who would go on to direct the *John Wick* movies two decades later) was used to finish key scenes. Brandon Lee's face was then digitally superimposed on Stahelski's in post-production. The film turned into a surprise box office hit, and a new reboot is on the way.

The late Brandon Lee, whose promising film career was cut tragically short. *The Crow* franchise has never satisfactorily replaced him.

THE PERILS OF PRODUCT PLACEMENT

•••

To help pay for a movie, and bring in a bit more revenue to the bottom line, movie studios are helping themselves to the proceeds of product placement. But it has not always gone to plan.

Oliver Stone's hugely controversial 1994 movie *Natural Born Killers* generated no shortage of headlines upon release. But it also woke those outside the film industry to the less beneficial aspects of product placement.

Product placement, after all, has been a good ruse in the entertainment industry

CONTAINS OVER AN HOUR OF HAUNTING BONUS FOOTAGE, ADDITIONAL SCENES AND LOST PERFORMANCES!

Not Coca-Cola's favourite movie...

for decades, and in more recent times has significantly helped to offset spiralling film budgets. For example, when announcing the launch of the animation house Illumination Entertainment, its CEO, Chris Meledandri, could boast that over a hundred tie-in deals had already been done ahead of the release of its first two films, *Despicable Me* and *Hop*. The 2013 film *Man of Steel*, meanwhile, reportedly attracted $160m in "commercial partnerships". In 2014, according to figures from PQ Media, product placement was already worth over $10bn a year across film and television. And movie studios want their slice.

Back in 1994, however, the approach to product placement was a lot more laissez-faire. Thus, in the midst of *Natural Born Killers* (a movie based on a screenplay by Quentin Tarantino, but a film he pretty much disowned), the Warner Bros. film melts into a deliberately jarring sitcom sequence, featuring the late Rodney Dangerfield as the father of Juliette Lewis's character, Mallory.

It's an incredibly uneasy moment, with this nasty, unpleasant man's actions set against a television laughter track. It then promptly cuts to an advert for Coca-Cola. Audiences at the time may well have been bemused by this; executives at Coca-Cola were incandescent.

In the words of Oliver Stone on the DVD commentary track for the film, they were "furious". Meanwhile, one of *Natural Born Killers*' producers, Jane Hamsher, penned a book by the name of *Killer Instinct*, where she revealed how she and fellow producer Don Murphy got permission to use the television advert. It was simple: they asked. The Coca-Cola Company, without checking the details, said yes. As the Associated Press reported in August 1994, "Coca-Cola thought that the spot was to be used in a scene in which Tommy Lee Jones watched the Super Bowl on television. Instead, the commercial is interspersed with images such as a headless, bloody body. The spots were used three times in the movie, intercut with brutal images of mayhem."

A subsequent proclamation from the company said, with an admiral flair for understatement, that "we're concerned that our commercial is being used in a way we didn't intend and weren't aware of". The Coca-Cola Company duly changed the way it handled product placement, and other big companies – keen not to be exposed in the same way – swiftly followed suit. It got to a point where, in 2000, Coca-Cola sponsored a short-lived Warner Bros. TV show called *Young Americans*. Such was the influence it could exert that a scene had to be reshot when a Pepsi machine was spotted in the background.

The irony is that, as major brands have become more alert to the power and influence of placing their products in movies, so said placements have become even more jarring and disruptive (albeit with less blood and murder).

For a key sequence in *Percy Jackson & the Olympians: The Lightning Thief* (2010), for instance, our young bunch of heroes are battling the mythical figure of Medusa. As everyone knows, you can't stare at Medusa or you'll turn to stone, and so to see where she is you need a handy mirror. Or, in the case of the first Percy Jackson film, the

Even in Greek legends, it pays to check your iPod…

reflection on the back of a blatantly used iPod, with the Apple logo in full view. It's not alone, either. By the time 2005's *Fantastic Four* movie has finished, a shopping channel's worth of brands has been showcased, including, notoriously, a key scene played out in front of a Burger King billboard. It's enough to put you off your Butterkist popcorn (available now from all good stores).

MAC AND ME

It would be remiss not to salute one of the early forerunners of product placement, *Mac and Me*. Described as "more of a TV commercial than a movie" by critic Leonard Maltin, the 1988 film features cans of Coca-Cola in pretty much every scene, a dancing sequence in McDonald's, liberal scatterings of Skittles, and even Ronald McDonald turning up at one point. The movie's reputation remains awful, but it's a gloriously fascinating bit of fun, if taken in the right spirit (and with the right fast-food products in front of you).

INCREDIBLY ARDUOUS FILM PRODUCTIONS

Script rewrites. Exacting directors. Terrible twists of fate. We look back through the ages to bring you some truly nightmarish film shoots.

THE WIZARD OF OZ (1939)

The glittering quality of MGM's *The Wizard of Oz*, now rightly regarded as a classic, gives little clue to its fraught production process. Although Victor Fleming is widely credited as director, five other directors were involved at various points in its making. Similarly, no fewer than 17 writers had an uncredited hand in its script, among them the poet Ogden Nash.

The script was finally completed in late 1938 and shooting commenced. It was chaos.

Directors were hired and then quickly relieved of duty. Tin Man actor Buddy Ebsen had to be replaced because he suffered a severe reaction to his aluminium-powder make-up, and was replaced by Jack Haley. Margaret Hamilton, who played the Wicked Witch of the West, was burned during the filming of a Munchkinland scene. Miraculously, *The Wizard of Oz*'s production difficulties were never apparent on the big screen.

DOCTOR DOLITTLE (1967)

One of our favourite anecdotes from the musical adaptation of *Doctor Dolittle* involved the decision to build a huge artificial dam in the UK village of Castle Combe in Wiltshire. The construction deeply annoyed local residents – as did the film production's insistence that TV aerials had to be removed from several houses in the area. One day, the famous explorer Ranulph Fiennes (then still in the SAS) decided to blow up the artificial dam with flares and plastic explosive. According to the *Guardian* newspaper, Fiennes was fined £500.

AMERICAN GRAFFITI (1973)

Compared with George Lucas's ambitious sci-fi outings, a drama about 1960s teenagers would appear to be relatively simple to

Rex Harrison, and his legendary singing voice, from 1967's *Dr Dolittle*.

make. This did not prove to be the case, as the film fell behind schedule, a member of the production team was arrested for growing marijuana, and a shooting permit was withdrawn by San Rafael City Council just two days into filming. Actor Paul Le Mat suffered an allergic reaction to a walnut and ended up in hospital. Richard Dreyfuss's head was cut open when Le Mat threw him into a swimming pool. Harrison Ford was arrested during a barroom brawl. Someone set fire to George Lucas's hotel room. From this nightmare emerged one of the most acclaimed films of 1973, and without *American Graffiti* – with the clout its success afforded Lucas and the confidence it gave him – it's arguable that *Star Wars* would never have been his next film.

William Friedkin's *Sorcerer* made a bit of a job of getting across a bridge.

JAWS (1975)

As we'll see from other entries in this list, shooting a film at sea is a potential nightmare. In fact, any would-be filmmakers would be strongly advised to avoid seawater altogether. As Steven Spielberg's adaptation of the hit Peter Benchley novel *Jaws* spun out of budget owing to mechanical problems with Bruce, the film's fake shark, various crew members redubbed the movie "Flaws". Actor Richard Dreyfuss later said of the production, "We started the film without a script, without a cast and without a shark."

SORCERER (1977)

William Friedkin never did make things easy for himself. In his 1977 thriller *Sorcerer*, about a group of men shepherding a truckload of nitroglycerine across South America, the director had a gigantic bridge constructed over a river at a huge cost, only for the riverbed to dry up. Friedkin then relocated the shoot to Mexico, where he had the bridge rebuilt over the Papaloapan River. This, too, ran dry before filming could commence. All told, this 12-minute sequence cost the production $3m to execute – a considerable amount for the time. According to star Roy Scheider, *Sorcerer* "made *Jaws* look like a picnic".

APOCALYPSE NOW (1979)

This film production was so nightmarish that it earned its own documentary, *Hearts of Darkness*. Aiming for absolute realism, Francis Ford Coppola shot his war epic in the Philippines, a location chosen for its visual similarity to Vietnam. A shoot initially expected to last for five months swelled to more than a year. During that time, there were storms and script rewrites, and leading man Martin Sheen (who had replaced Harvey Keitel within the first week of shooting suffered a nearly fatal heart attack. "We were in the jungle. We had too much money. We had too much equipment. And little by little, we went insane" was how Coppola summed up the infamously messy production.

HEAVEN'S GATE (1980)

Like *Apocalypse Now*, the film *Heaven's Gate* spiralled out of financial control, with fatal consequences for the studio that tried to pay for it, United Artists. As the production burned through hundreds of thousands of dollars per day, Michael Cimino shot over a million feet of footage. Rumours began to spread of drug use, unnecessary numbers of takes and Cimino insisting that they wait for a particular type of cloud to float into view for one of his shots. A notorious flop on release, *Heaven's Gate* has since been reassessed in some quarters as a flawed work of genius.

James Cameron's *The Abyss* relied heavily on underwater footage.

FITZCARRALDO (1982)

One of the most difficult productions in film history, *Fitzcarraldo* was Werner Herzog's ambitious, slightly insane story of real-life rubber baron Carlos Fitzcarrald. The film was shot in various parts of South America, and one of its most famous scenes involved the dragging of a gigantic steamship up a hill. Herzog stubbornly rejected the possibility of creating the scene using miniature effects, and instead shot it for real, with a 320-ton steamer and dozens of extras.

ISHTAR (1987)

To get an idea of how grim the shoot on the financially doomed comedy *Ishtar* was, consider this: one sequence involved star Dustin Hoffman lying on the sand as vultures descended around him. In order to make the vultures come down on cue, director Elaine May and her crew placed scraps of meat on Hoffman's body, just out of shot. "Are these vultures going to know where the raw meat ends and I start?" Hoffman nervously asked. May shot the scene 50 times.

THE ABYSS (1989)

James Cameron's *The Abyss* was big, ambitious and very, very expensive. This was largely due to its huge number of underwater scenes, which were filmed in an abandoned nuclear power plant in South Carolina. The submersible oil rig took a total of 18 months to build, and the budget for the sets alone ran to around $2m. Of the difficult production, actor Michael Biehn said, "One day we were all in our dressing rooms and people began throwing couches out the windows and smashing the walls. We just had to get our frustrations out."

WATERWORLD (1995)

Often summed up as *Mad Max* at sea, *Waterworld*'s aquatic locations proved an expensive headache for everyone concerned. Back in the 1990s, digitally matting out unwanted bits of shoreline or stray boats in the distance wasn't an option, so Kevin Reynolds and his filmmakers had to construct the film's artificial island far out at sea.

"Logistically, it's crazy," director Reynolds said. "Each day you shoot on the atoll with all those extras, we had to transport those people from dry land out to the location and so you're getting hundreds of people through wardrobe and everything, and you're putting them on boats, transporting them out to the atoll, and trying to get everybody in position to do a shot. And then when you break for lunch, you have to put everybody on boats and take them back in to feed them."

THE ISLAND OF DR. MOREAU (1996)

In the early 1990s, director Richard Stanley embarked on his dream project: an adaptation of H G Wells's classic novel *The Island of Dr. Moreau*. But just three days after filming commenced in Australia, Stanley was fired. The more experienced director John Frankenheimer was brought in as a replacement – but still the problems with the film's increasingly diva-ish stars continued. In the aftermath, Frankenheimer made a solemn vow: "There are two things I will never, ever do in my whole life. The first is that I will never climb Mount Everest. The second is that I will never work with Val Kilmer ever again."

TITANIC (1997)

James Cameron's formidable directorial presence on *Titanic* (another film involving huge amounts of water) was well documented; Christopher Godwin of *The Times* described Cameron as a "300-decibel screamer, a modern-day Captain Bligh with a megaphone and walkie-talkie, swooping down into people's faces on a 162ft crane".

The shoot reached its grim low point when a disgruntled member of the crew spiked the lobster soup with a hallucinogenic drug. Cameron and more than 50 other people were rushed to hospital. This and other mishaps led the film to overshoot its intended production schedule of 138 days, and its already gigantic budget began to mount. The cost to Fox's coffers was high, but the film, unlike its title ship, proved to be unsinkable at the box office.

Titanic: a film so demanding, its crew were spiked with drugs.

BIG PROBLEMS ON THE SETS OF MODERN MOVIES

•••

Apocalypse Now's incredibly troubled production was so significant that it in turn led to an equally wonderful documentary on the making of the film itself (see page 107). But while few modern movies have had to go through quite so much, many have battled against significant, unexpected on-set difficulties just to get made.

When you think of a troubled film production, a *Police Academy* sequel is rarely a place many choose to start. But as if to prove that even heavily maligned, seemingly straightforward projects can find themselves in incredibly dangerous situations, it's worth taking a look at the unloved *Police Academy: Mission to Moscow* (1994).

It's hard to find anyone who'd take a bullet, or even a quick jab in the arm, for the film. Even its parent studio, Warner Bros., pretty much gave up on it, giving it little publicity and only a small release, and being rewarded with $130,000 – yep, you read that right – in box office takings.

A tough reward that, for those who took the trip to Russia for location work in 1993. The cast had been trimmed down by this point for budgetary reasons, and as they arrived in Moscow a constitutional crisis was erupting. The production found itself in the midst of ten days of street fighting in Moscow, and if you look carefully, should you choose to watch the film, you can see evidence of the tank shells and bullets fired.

> *"We had one flight a week from the mainland, and there were times we ran out of food"*

The crew had to be nimble, quickly picking up shots around the violence that had broken out alongside them. Producer Paul Maslansky, for instance, told the *Los Angeles Times* in October 1993 that they turned up for filming at Moscow's airport one morning, only "we were told we can't shoot because of the state of emergency". A subsequent scene in a cemetery was shot as victims of the violence were being buried. "It was a bit dodgy today," Maslansky admitted. "We got in and out as quickly as possible." The cast and crew wrapped up on schedule, leaving Russia after a month on location.

A far better film is the fourth entry in the *Mad Max* movie series, *Mad Max: Fury Road*. The acclaimed – and heavily Oscar-nominated – 2015 film took a long time to get so far. Pre-production work had originally begun in 1997, and after several aborted attempts to get the film moving in the early 2000s, Tom Hardy was cast in 2010, with the aim being to start filming toward the end of the year. It would be closer to the end of 2011 that the starter gun

Rounded up to the nearest $1m, *Police Academy: Mission to Moscow* grossed $1m.

would be fired, with the plan being to shoot the movie in the Broken Hill area of New South Wales, Australia. It had taken a fair effort from legislators to get the production there in the first place, bringing with it a significant boost to the local economy.

The ten years of drought that Broken Hill had endured gave the area just the kind of desert look that director George Miller was seeking for this movie. But then, out of the blue, it started to rain. And rain. And rain. By the time the water had fallen, the area had started to transform, as the *Sydney Daily Telegraph* described it, into "a sea of blooming wild flowers". Late in the day, Miller and his team opted to relocate production to Namibia in Africa, a decision that incurred criticism by local politicians of George Souris, the New South Wales arts minister at the time. But as Souris's spokesman protested, "We can't control the weather." Quite.

At least the *Mad Max: Fury Road* team could regroup and bolt on extra time as a consequence of their production change. But the sets of 1995's *Waterworld* were primarily afloat (see page 108), and during shooting it was reported that one of the key sets had actually sunk, with filming work still to be done. "There's a myth about that," director Kevin Reynolds cautioned. "People think it's the giant atoll set, and in fact it was not… it was a smaller set," one far less pivotal as it turned out. It still sank, though. In addition, the production had to battle high winds that were causing other sets to float off course.

Mind you, Reynolds would insist that his previous film, 1994's *Rapa-Nui*, had been even tougher. For that one, they shot the movie on Easter Island. "We had one flight a week from the mainland, and there were times we ran out of food to feed people…it was very bad," he remembered.

That said, shooting on, with and around water brings its own perils. The exhaustive production of 1997's *Titanic* is notable in that it could inspire a film of its own. On the one hand, there were injuries, delays and technical issues, and on the other hand there was a director, James Cameron, who didn't suffer fools particularly gladly (see page 109).

Charlize Theron in *Aeon Flux*.

For Harrison Ford, shooting couldn't continue for some time after his notorious accident on the set of 2015's *Star Wars: The Force Awakens*. Ford broke his leg when a metal door on the set of the *Millennium Falcon* landed on him – a court was subsequently told that the actor could have died as a consequence of the incident. A fine of over £1.5m was handed down to the production company, and the immediate impact on the film was for the production schedule to be overhauled. The film shut down completely for two weeks, and two months later Ford would resume full filming duties, albeit with some shots now from the waist up to hide his injury.

There was a slight element of déjà vu for Ford. During filming on 1984's *Indiana Jones and the Temple of Doom*, he damaged a disc in his back, requiring fairly quick surgery. That kept him out of action for around six weeks, and as a consequence far more shots than planned in the movie are actually of Ford's stunt double, Vic Armstrong.

Charlize Theron trumped that, though. Performing backflips while shooting 2005's *Aeon Flux*, she landed on her neck, nearly paralysing herself. Instead, she herniated a disc close to her spinal cord, and production had to shut down for eight weeks while she recuperated. She now leaves more stunt work to the stunt professionals.

An even longer delay hit the third and final movie in *The Maze Runner* series, *Maze Runner: The Death Cure*. 20th Century Fox, and director Wes Ball, had left just a year between the first and second films, and quickly got working on the third, setting a release of February 2017 for the movie. Filming duly began in Canada in March 2016, but just four days into production, disaster struck. In an on-set accident, the film's leading man, Dylan O'Brien, suffered multiple serious injuries, said to include "concussion, facial fracture and lacerations". Filming was shut down for two months at first, before it was realized that O'Brien's injuries were more significant than previously thought. Instead, filming didn't resume until early 2017 – nearly a year after the accident – ahead of the film's new 2018 release date.

There was no time for delay when filming 1991's *The Addams Family*, though. The film's bumpy journey to the screen had already seen it sold by Orion Pictures to Paramount midway through filming, as the former fought – ultimately unsuccessfully – to stave off its money worries. The filmmakers were told that particular piece of news by a journalist. It happened as the film was running some 20 per cent over budget, courtesy of a series of incidents and freshly written material that needed to be woven in.

Most notably, Barry Sonnenfeld – who would go on to direct the *Men in Black* trilogy – was making his movie directorial debut. He'd previously worked as director of photography on films such as *Big* and *Miller's Crossing*, but the jump to the director's chair proved a stressful one. Three weeks into filming, he told *Empire* magazine, "I was standing behind a chair when I started to feel this tremendous pressure in my chest, as if someone was blowing up a balloon inside me. Before I knew what was happening, I got very dizzy and tried to sit down and – wham! – I'd passed out."

He quickly regained consciousness, weeping as he did. Producer Scott Rudin moved quickly and started asking people to go home for the day. But it was Sonnenfeld who kept this particular vehicle on the road. "I remember begging Scott, please let me get up and get going again. If we have to stop every time I faint or start to cry, we'll never get this movie done." The film would be completed, and Sonnenfeld would direct its excellent sequel, too.

NARROW ESCAPES

On the set of the 2013 caper *Now You See Me*, Isla Fisher was in a water chamber for an escape scene. She got stuck and started banging on the side of the glass. The problem was, that's what her character was supposed to do. It was nearly three minutes before she was freed.

•••

While filming Mel Gibson's *The Passion of the Christ*, assistant director Jan Michelini – like Jim Caviezel (see page 203) – was struck by lightning. Twice. He survived to tell the tale.

•••

On the sixth day of filming *Dirty Dancing*, the rehearsal space was burgled, roads to the hotel the crew were staying at were flooded, the set decorator fell off his ladder and was injured, the wardrobe assistant broke her toe, and three of the crew were hit with food poisoning. Oh, and a van from the props department was destroyed in an accident.

•••

Ben Stiller had to get treatment against rabies, when he was bitten on the chin by a ferret while filming 2004's *Along Came Polly*.

•••

Gerard Butler was shooting a stripping scene for 2007's *P.S. I Love You* when his suspender strap snapped off and smacked his co-star, Hilary Swank, in the head. She needed stitches.

•••

Shooting 2011's *The Eagle*, Channing Tatum was on location in a freezing river. To keep warm, he and the rest of the cast had a cocktail of boiled water and river water poured into their suits. The problem? Someone forgot Tatum's river water, and poured boiling water into his suit. The skin off the top of his penis was reportedly burned off as a result.

•••

Watch *The Last Samurai* carefully, and in its climactic battle sequence a horse kicks one of the extras in his nether regions. Full credit to him: he carries on.

That ferret looks friendly, right? Er...

THE 1998 BLOCKBUSTER THAT WAS TURNED AROUND IN SIX MONTHS

•••

With digital filmmaking, digital editing and digital distribution, a film such as 2015's James Bond adventure Spectre can just about start filming 11 months before release and still make it to cinemas on release day. But when releasing a film involved shipping cans of film around the world, such a fast turnaround was near impossible – which made the six months between the start of production and the eventual release of *Lethal Weapon 4* staggering.

The sequel had been in development since 1992's successful *Lethal Weapon 3*, but it became fast-tracked when Warner Bros. found itself without a key blockbuster for the summer of July 1998. (It had been banking on the ill-fated and ultimately abandoned *Superman Lives*, which was set to star Nicolas Cage.) Mel Gibson, Danny Glover and director Richard Donner duly signed up, and physical production started on 8 January 1998.

It's worth noting that *Lethal Weapon 4* was a big action blockbuster, with sizable big-money scenes. The sheer logistics were mind-boggling. The film opens in a street scene as a man with a flamethrower wreaks havoc. It involved outdoor shooting (in more than one sense), complex action sequences and trying to capture the fast movements of Jet Li on film (which sounds like a trivial challenge, but turned out to be anything but). It also had Danny Glover stripping down to his undercrackers. These things need planning.

To add to the problem, the script was never really finished. The screenplay was ultimately credited to Channing Gibson, with story credit going to Jonathan Lemkin, Alfred Gough and Miles Millar. But the truth seems to be that there was never a locked down script as such, even as the film galloped into the edit suite.

Channing Gibson was on hand for the duration of the production, and hasty changes were regularly made. The first draft of the screenplay, for instance, didn't include the returning Leo Getz (played by Joe Pesci) or the character of Butters, played by Chris Rock. They both ended up being written into the film, when the availability of both actors was confirmed late in the day. Furthermore, the ending hadn't been written when Donner unpacked his cameras for the first time on the movie (a similar problem faced by 1995's *Die Hard with a Vengeance*, although that production had a bit more time to sort itself out). It's one reason why the ultimate demise of Jet Li's character in the movie feels so weak.

The late Jeffrey Boam, who co-wrote *Lethal Weapon 3*, was also involved in a script for the new sequel (coming up with an original draft that ultimately wasn't used) and would subsequently argue that *Lethal Weapon 4*'s central plot of counterfeiting Chinese money was low stakes for a movie of this scale. The movie *The A-Team*, released over a decade later, would centre on a similar idea. Furthermore, it was only after *Lethal Weapon 4* got its green light that the Triads were added to the movie as part of its antagonists.

It perhaps goes without saying that *Lethal Weapon 4* was a frantic shoot, with little in the way of time to waste. But as with most Richard Donner productions (given his reputation for friendly filmsets), it was seemingly a calmer one than you might think. That said, it still ran close to the proverbial finishing line.

The last frame of footage wasn't in the can until just 33 days before the film's release date. Factor in that 2015's *Mad Max: Fury Road*'s post-production period allowed three months just to *sort through* the footage, let alone edit it, and you get a flavour of just how testing things were. Add in too that prints had to be struck and physically distributed (again, digital distribution techniques would have helped enormously) and this put an enormous strain on editor Frank J Urioste and his team.

Urioste edited the entire movie on an Avid system, the first time he'd ever put together a movie on a digital setup in its entirety (such equipment is now standard on productions). In short, he probably had less than four weeks to assemble a finished cut of the film to Donner's liking. Granted, editing was ongoing while the film was being shot, but still: it was an exhaustive challenge to get the film done on such a schedule.

The final cut of *Lethal Weapon 4* is generally regarded as a bit of a jumble, and with good reason. It plays a lot better as an outright comedy than as an action film, and given the speed at which it was spliced together, there's clearly not been a lot of time put into tightening the picture up.

Still, Warner Bros.. comfortably won its gamble. Upon release, the reviews were generally quite decent. Few were championing the film as a highpoint of the series, yet nonetheless it was an entertaining, almost old-fashioned way to spend two hours at the movies. This was the summer of effects-fest *Armageddon*, of Spielberg's raw *Saving Private Ryan* and of the prescient *The Truman Show*. An old-fashioned buddy cop comedy? It could be seen as such if most of the 1990s hadn't happened.

Lethal Weapon 4 would generate $285m at the worldwide box office at a point where that was considered an awful lot of money. Contrast that with the likes of 2012's (admittedly expensive to make) *John Carter* and 2016's *Alice Through the Looking Glass*, which brought in similar amounts and are both considered franchise killers.

That said, a *Lethal Weapon 5* never happened, in part due to the well-documented personal problems surrounding Mel Gibson. But also, cinema moved on. *Lethal Weapon* now plies its trade as a TV series, one that is a long way in tone from the dark, brilliant movie that started off the series.

The action sequences were not the strength of the rushed *Lethal Weapon 4*.

HOW THE 1990s CHANGED BLOCKBUSTER CINEMA

●●●

It was the 1970s that ignited blockbuster movies as we know them, thanks to the gigantic success of *Jaws* and *Star Wars*. But two decades later, with the introduction of a few dinosaurs, the rule book changed dramatically.

In 1991, the box office battle for summer supremacy was, on paper at least, a three-horse race. Bruce Willis had his first project as co-screenwriter, *Hudson Hawk*, locked and loaded. Kevin Costner was, er, "perfecting his unusual British accent" for *Robin Hood: Prince of Thieves*. Meanwhile, Arnold Schwarzenegger was set to hit a commercial career peak with the eagerly waited *Terminator 2: Judgment Day* (the first film ever to cost more than $100m simply to *make*).

Kevin Costner in *Robin Hood: Prince of Thieves*. This, and 1992's *The Bodyguard*, saw Costner at the height of his movie star powers.

While *Hudson Hawk* would go on to become a notable box office disappointment (albeit one more fun than it's usually given credit for), *Robin Hood: Prince of Thieves* and *Terminator 2: Judgment Day* hit big, cementing the two leads, Costner and Schwarzenegger, as the biggest movie stars on the planet. The star system was surely in safe hands.

Yet by the end of the decade, both had fallen. Schwarzenegger's *End of Days*, his first film since he'd undergone open heart surgery once he'd wrapped 1997's *Batman & Robin*, finished as the 33rd-biggest film of the year in the US. Down to 57th was Costner's third baseball-themed movie, *For Love of the Game*, his career having failed to recover from the battering he took for his second directorial effort, *The Postman*, in 1997.

By 1999, a lot of things for movies were different, and the decade as a whole saw the erosion of the traditional movie star. Thus, while 1999 had hits that were movie-star driven – Bruce Willis headlined *The Sixth Sense* and Will Smith starred in *Wild Wild West* (a poor film, but one that did okay courtesy of Smith's star leverage) – it's telling that the bigger films were less reliant on them. Even *The Sixth Sense* arguably sold more strongly on the back of word of mouth than through good, old-fashioned star wattage. What's more, 1999's biggest hit, *Star Wars: Episode I – The Phantom Menace*, probably could have had Daffy Duck in the lead and still have topped the charts.

Go down the US top 20 for the year, and surprise hits such as *The Blair Witch Project*, *American Pie* and *Stuart Little* proved that a star wasn't vital (each would get at least two sequels). Furthermore, a fresh wave of independent talent was bubbling up and coming to prominence, and many of these new names would go on to become notable, high-profile voices in Hollywood cinema.

Sam Mendes, for instance, made his movie directorial debut with the Oscar winner

American Beauty. It'd be a huge hit in 1999 and indirectly lead to Mendes helming two hugely successful James Bond ventures, *Skyfall* and *Spectre*. David Fincher, meanwhile, bounced back from his horrid studio experience on *Alien 3* by following up *Seven* with 1999's *Fight Club*. This film is notable for being one of the edgiest features of the era to be actively backed by a studio, much to the unhappiness of 20th Century Fox's ultimate owner, Rupert Murdoch (who declared that he wanted more films like *Titanic* instead).

Elsewhere, David O Russell (*Joy*, *American Hustle*) broke through with *Three Kings*; Doug Liman (*Edge of Tomorrow*) released his second feature, *Go*; while Brad Bird (*The Incredibles*) would realize his stunning animation, *The Iron Giant*. Not all of the films were hits, but they got enough prominence to ignite the careers of their directors, each of whom would go on to steer major studio blockbuster movies.

Two particular turning points in the decade are worth citing, because they both managed to show movie studios there was a path that didn't involve paying $20m to a star attraction (as Columbia did in 1996 to lure Jim Carrey to play the lead in the surprisingly dark film *The Cable Guy*). The first of these turning points is 1993's *Jurassic Park*.

If *Terminator 2* had demonstrated at the start of the decade the new power that special effects held in helping to realize a

American Beauty (above and top) was a modest production but turned into an Oscar-snaffling, $356m-grossing smash hit.

character, it was Steven Spielberg's film-take on Michael Crichton's dino-book that utterly turned heads. Given how effects-dominated modern blockbuster cinema is, it's easy to overlook just how much of an impression *Jurassic Park*'s dinosaurs first made. Yet the other blockbusters of 1993 were primarily star-driven – Harrison Ford in *The Fugitive*, Clint Eastwood headlining *In the Line of Fire*, Sylvester Stallone in *Cliffhanger*, Arnold Schwarzenegger in *Last Action Hero* – and the audacity of hinging the spectacle of a film around computer-generated characters was new to the movies. The resultant box office – over $300m alone for a film that cost just north of $60m – was a real eye-opener. Universal's expert marketing campaign taught the industry a few tricks, too, holding back key reveals until they were really needed, though such spoiler protection has long since been abandoned at the altar of the marketing department.

> **Fast-forward to 1999...a proverbial grenade was being lobbed into the action by The Matrix**

It didn't take Hollywood long to heed other lessons *Jurassic Park* was teaching. Studios latched on to the idea that a movie star was an expensive risk compared with cheaper effects work. Furthermore, while a computer might crash and struggle to send an email, it didn't need coaxing from its trailer and it didn't demand a slice of the gross takings. Special effects, too, had universal appeal. Hire Jim Carrey for a movie and he'd play in some countries better than others. Get in a load of effects, and they'd become the universal language of generally pretty dumb blockbusters.

Fast-forward three summers to Fox's *Independence Day*. Headlined by Will Smith – who wasn't at that stage the star draw he became – it was sold off the back of an effect of the White House being blown up. (Ironically, this was a practical effect rather than a computerized one, thanks to the use of a particularly intricate scale model.) It held off

The infamous *Independence Day* trailer shot, that sold hundreds of thousands of tickets at least.

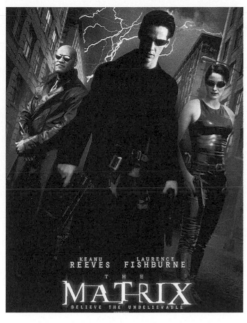

Warner Bros. top brass infamously didn't quite get *The Matrix*, but took a gamble on it nonetheless. It released *Wild Wild West* the same year.

(although their work continues to warrant more interest than it gets), but the host of imitators that followed wouldn't either. *The Matrix* was led by Keanu Reeves, of course, but he wasn't the centre of the film's marketing. Instead, the stunning effects work was the focus – along the "bullet time" technique of slowing the action right down. *The Matrix* was a warning for the more traditional blend of star-led action cinema that the 1980s and 1990s had thrived on.

The decade that followed would see the explosion of the comic-book movie (with 2000's *X-Men* the next catalyst) and the gradual eroding of the number of movie stars who could be banked on to attract an audience with their name alone. Franchises, sequels and computers all became safer bets than a star's paycheck. As a consequence, the 1990s proved to be a dramatic turning in blockbuster cinema – though not necessarily one for the better.

another relatively starless effects-fest, *Twister*, from the top of the US box office. Meanwhile, a more traditional Arnold Schwarzenegger vehicle, *Eraser*, found itself in 14th place when 1996's US box office takings were totted up. Computers were out-powering stars.

Fast-forward again to 1999, and while *Star Wars* was using increasingly digital sets rather than heavily relying on extensive location work, a proverbial grenade was being lobbed into action blockbusters by *The Matrix*, the second turning point in the decade. Hugely influenced by Hong Kong action cinema, the film had done much of the running beforehand, but what directors Lana and Lilly Wachowski managed to do was wrestle those influences, visual effects and a cyberpunk narrative into the must-see summer blockbuster of the season.

The Wachowskis would never quite capture lightning in a bottle in the same way again

WARNER BROS. AND *THE MATRIX*

Warner Bros. in the 1990s traditionally worked on talent relationships, which saw it fund film after film from the likes of Kevin Costner, Clint Eastwood and Mel Gibson

●●●

When the Wachowskis pitched *The Matrix*, the studio's long-established top brass – Terry Semel and Robert Daly – struggled to get their heads around it. The Wachowskis went away to prove they could direct (with 1996's *Bound* being one of their best films), but it ultimately took a 600-page storyboard pitch to the studio's bosses before the $60m budget was approved. Things were never quite the same again.

THE MAN WHO'S MADE THE WORLD'S MOST EXPENSIVE FILM: FOUR TIMES

The most expensive film ever made is said to be *Pirates of the Caribbean: On Stranger Tides*. The 2007 sequel is thought to have cost some $375m just to make. The second-most expensive film is its follow-up, *At World's End*, which looks a bargain in comparison at $300m.

Four times in his career, however, writer/editor/director James Cameron has seized the crown for having made the most expensive film of all time. And while his most expensive production – *Avatar* (2009) – today wouldn't even crack the top ten with its $237m budget, four of his productions did hit the top spot at different times in the past

TERMINATOR 2: JUDGMENT DAY (1991)

The first of Cameron's films to break the record, this sequel to his ironically low-budget indie *The Terminator* (1984) was the first to leave its financiers with a $100m bill for the negative alone (before marketing and distribution costs). It arrived the year after *Die Hard 2: Die Harder* had cost some $75m to make and had led to questions as to how such an expensive film could ever make money. Today, $75m is classed as mid-budget for a Hollywood movie.

The money, as with all of Cameron's films, is clearly on the screen in *Terminator 2: Judgment Day*, with the technical advances in the creation of Robert Patrick's villainous T-1000 the key example. As a bit of added movie trivia, Adobe's first Photoshop software was used to

help with some of the visual work. The film was a massive hit, bringing in over $500m in box office takings, and leaving Cameron inking a production deal with 20th Century Fox.

TRUE LIES (1994)

The first fruits of that deal would not be cheap – as Cameron opted to team up with Arnold Schwarzenegger for a third time, on a remake of the French comedy *La Totale!*. In Cameron's hands, it became the 1994 action comedy *True Lies*, the second instance for which his film was the most expensive ever. Ironically, given the $120m or so it cost to make the film, Cameron had declared, "I was looking for a small drama after 'the most expensive movie in history'". He did not find one.

To give an example of how the costs ramped up, one sequence in the screenplay was a shootout in a washroom. In the original draft, this was half a page, after which things moved on. Cameron, though, expanded it to a washroom three times as big, with real tiles, a genuine mosaic on the floor, strobing lights and water everywhere. What became a major action scene in the film took five

True Lies: James Cameron films come with a bill, but few quibble he leaves every dollar on the screen.

days to shoot. It was as straightforward as the making of *True Lies* got. Production was delayed so much owing to the expanding ambition of the film that Bill Paxton shot some scenes, went off and made another film, and then came back to complete his work. Yet Cameron, again, delivered – and the well-received film took $370m worldwide.

TERMINATOR 2: 3-D RIDE (1996)
The third time Cameron broke the most expensive production barrier was with the creation of this ride for Universal Studios in Florida. This 12-minute feature cost $60m to put together (over half of this being spent on the movie part of the ride), it cost more per minute to make than any film in history. At $5m per minute, the ride outspent even the notoriously expensive film *Waterworld*. Yet something water-based saw Cameron smash his spending record one last time...

TITANIC (1997)
Books have been written about Cameron's 1997 epic, *Titanic*. The combination of Cameron's perfectionism and a shoot that was incredibly difficult technically saw the movie go way past its intended finish date. "It was difficult, difficult. Because if you were there

you would know why," noted one of its cast, David Warner. "Having to put the ship at a certain angle at a certain time of the day, and then when flooded and you wanted to do two takes, you had to clean the place up and that would take four or five hours to get it back."

It was expensive, too. The bill for *Titanic* began to soar, to the point where 20th Century Fox sold the US distribution rights to Paramount Pictures, to help shoulder the financial burden. Originally budgeted at $80m, *Titanic* would be the first film ever to cost $200m to make. It would be nearly a decade before one did again, with 2004's *Spider-Man 2* and 2005's *King Kong* both reported to have cost around that sum.

Cameron, once again, had the last laugh. *Titanic* would go on to become the first film to break the $600m mark at the US box office, the first to break $1bn at the global box office on its initial release, and the winner of 11 Oscars, 3 of which went home with Cameron. In fact, *Titanic* would have stood as the biggest film of all time, were it not for the only film to topple its numbers to date: *Avatar*, written and directed by... James Cameron.

CLEOPATRA

Stories of heavy spending on movies aren't an exclusively modern phenomenon, of course. Adjusting for inflation, the $31m budget for 1963's *Cleopatra* comes out at around $240m in today's funds, putting it at about the price level of *The Dark Knight Rises* or *The Avengers*. Through its production, the historical epic – *Cleopatra*, not *The Dark Knight Rises* – changed director, cast, shooting location and script. It proved so expensive that it very nearly took down 20th Century Fox.

POST-
PRODUCTION

IS MOVIE MARKETING SPOILING FILMS?

•••

How many times have you sat in a cinema and thought you'd already seen the key parts of the film? Chances are you may well have done.

There were lots of things wrong with *Terminator Genisys* (2015), the fifth entry in the *Terminator* movie franchise, and one that was all set to launch a new trilogy of films (even including a sting during the end credits, to set up the next movie). But one thing that certainly didn't help was a major spoiler for the film being released as part of the movie's marketing campaign. Without going into specific detail, an important plot twist was revealed in one of the trailers for the movie – which meant that when a dramatic turn took place in the narrative of the movie, a lot of the audience already knew it was coming.

Its inclusion in the film's marketing was certainly a moment of regret for director Alan Taylor, who mourned to the website of media company Uproxx, "I certainly directed those scenes with the intention that no one would know", before adding, "I think they [the film's marketing team] felt they had to do something game-changing in how the film was being perceived".

Those efforts didn't really work, but they were built on a growing trend for giving more and more of the game away as a trade-off for luring people into buying a ticket for a film – not always with the blessing of the filmmakers behind the project. Animators at DreamWorks, for instance, were widely reported to be aghast at one of the trailers for 2014's *How to Train your Dragon 2*, which gave away a major moment in the movie. Granted, there was a lot more in the movie to enjoy,

but it still seemed odd, not least because there was plenty of other material to work with. But then, as those who cut trailers point out, they're there to do a job.

The whole point of a trailer is to entice people into buying tickets, and it is regarded as the single most effective promotional tool for a film. Obviously, nobody wants to spoil a movie, yet put yourself in the shoes of a movie executive for a minute. If you believe that including a moment in a trailer will bring in extra millions at the box office, what would you do? Multiplexes are littered with the answers to that question.

Not that this is a new complaint. Notoriously, the trailer for the Charlton Heston-headlined sci-fi flick *Soylent Green* (1973) is one of the worst of all time in this respect. "What is the secret of Soylent Green?" it asks, time and time again, teasing the audience and luring them toward investing in a ticket to find out – until the point in the trailer when it gives away the answer, the film's ending and the big twist, all in one go. Modern trailers rarely go that far, however. Even posters used to give away more than they should. Some of the promo artwork for 1983's *Superman III*, for example, opted to depict the big battle in the final act of the movie, leaving audiences who traipsed past the poster on the way into the cinema in little doubt where it was headed.

Still, movie marketing is pretty much omnipresent in the current climate, be it on the side of a bus, targeted ads on social

Are spoilers increasingly prevalent in movie marketing? Perhaps a little. There does seem to be more of it, and it's in more places. And with big corporations sinking nine figures of investment into a blockbuster movie now, it's a problem that's not going to get better.

As 1973's *Soylent Green* demonstrates, spoiler-filled trailers are not a new invention.

media and across the internet, expensive Super Bowl commercials or ads on your chat show of choice. Spoilers have become a potent currency, with studios knowing full well that if a star drops a solid spoiler about a film in an interview, it'll be a news story on at least 100 websites around the world in a day or so.

That's the key difference. For anyone remotely interested in movies now, spoilers are tricky to avoid. Most big films have three trailers at least, several promotional clips and umpteen images, which in turn are spidered across the web. Thus, for 2012's *The Amazing Spider-Man*, Sony released at least ten video promos (including trailers), and when totted up they gave away just shy of ten minutes of footage from the final film (about seven per cent of the final feature). It doesn't sound much but those minutes had to include the big, popular action moments and some significant story beats, just to get people interested.

THE EXCEPTION

Every now and then, there's a piece of movie marketing that potentially spoils the film before it is released, but does it in such a way that you can't help but grin. Entirely in keeping with the style of the movies, then, how about this tagline on the poster for *Crank: High Voltage*?

'HE WAS DEAD...BUT HE GOT BETTER'

INCREDIBLY LATE CHANGES TO MOVIES

•••

Following the huge global success of the first *Despicable Me* film, production firm Illumination Entertainment quickly got cracking on a sequel. *Despicable Me 2* was confirmed and scheduled for the summer of 2013, just three years after the release of the original (a speedy turnaround in the world of animated movies). The original creative team was due to return, and Illumination landed a real coup when it lured Al Pacino to voice El Macho, the villain of the follow-up. Nothing could go wrong.

However, if you're one of the many who sat through the film, you might struggle to recall his contribution – and with good reason. Just six weeks before the release of the film, over two and a half years into production, Al Pacino abruptly quit, for reasons that weren't given (but were bountifully rumoured). Illumination Entertainment had a massive problem, speedily bringing in Benjamin Bratt to re-record the entire part from scratch. As producer Chris Meledandri told *Variety* at the time, "I'm not aware of any of the major animated films of the last 15 years that…has brought an actor in at such a late stage." He was right, too.

However, 2016's *Kung Fu Panda 3* had a go. Rebel Wilson had been lined up for a role but couldn't complete the role. That wasn't down to her, though. When DreamWorks Animation extended the production schedule on the movie, Wilson found herself unable to commit to the extra work, because of other projects she was already working on. She thus bowed out with around six months left until the movie's release, and Kate Hudson was drafted in. However, it wasn't a simple change. Not only did Hudson have to go back and re-record

the lines that Wilson had already laid down, but director Jennifer Yuh Nelson and her team had to make subtle changes to the animation work they'd completed thus far, to ensure that the character on screen – Mei Mei – matched Hudson's voice and inflections.

People quitting isn't the only reason for late changes to films. In the aftermath of the release of James Cameron's *Avatar* in 2009, Hollywood studios were greedily eyeing the extra premium that the film brought in from 3D screenings. With its added ticket-price premium, this was significant in *Avatar*'s record-breaking takings, and as a result, a rush of "bolt-on" 3D retrofits were ordered.

Most notably, Warner Bros. had its 2010 remake of *Clash of the Titans* nearly ready to go but ordered a 3D version to be turned around in post-production. *Clash of the Titans* was neither shot in 3D nor designed for it, and Warner Bros. allowed just three weeks for the stereoscopic work to be completed. Commercially, it was a solid decision. Artistically, it was a disaster. The Den of Geek review at the time read, "I cannot emphasize this enough, do not pay out for the 3D, as it simply isn't there. The director didn't even

Clash of the Titans boasted 3D so poor, its director would describe it as "famously horrible". He was right.

want it apparently, but lo and behold *Clash of the Titans* was retrofitted to turn a fast buck and the result is shocking."

In hindsight, the film's director, Louis Leterrier, agreed. He told *The Huffington Post* a few years later that he'd all but disowned the film. Of the 3D, he said, "It was famously rushed and famously horrible. It was absolutely horrible, the 3D. Nothing was working, it was just a gimmick to steal money from the audience." No shortage of money, either – over half of the film's $163m US box office takings came from 3D screenings (and even more 3D money came in from around the world). Warner Bros. won its gamble, although audiences would subsequently decline to turn out in the same numbers for *Wrath of the Titans* – a sequel that Leterrier declined to direct.

That said, more and more movies are editing right to the proverbial wire, especially in the age of digital filmmaking, editing and distribution. That means that the changes we've discussed are the ones we know about. There's a whole treasure chest of alterations, made very late in the day, that never become known outside of the production team.

ATROCITIES

It would be remiss not to mention the very late changes that come about as a result of real-life atrocities.

For example, the Idris Elba-headlined thriller *Bastille Day* had already begun its worldwide cinema roll-out in 2016, but after the horrific terrorist attack in Nice, France, in July of that year, when 86 people died after a truck was deliberately driven into a crowd of people on Bastille Day itself, changes were made. The film was promptly pulled from French cinemas, and for its subsequent North American cinema release, and worldwide DVD roll-out, the film became known as *The Take* instead.

• • •

Following the atrocities of 11 September 2001, several productions quickly introduced changes. Edits were made to films as varied as *Serendipity*, *Zoolander*, *Kissing Jessica Stein* and the trailer for the first *Spider-Man* movie, to remove the World Trade Center. *The Bourne Identity*, which was then filming, also underwent significant reshoot work, to take away the original impression that the CIA weren't on the side of good. Over time, several more films – including *Home Alone 2: Lost in New York* and *Armageddon* – have had edits made for television screenings, out of respect for those killed.

FILMS THAT REMAINED UNRELEASED FOR YEARS & WHY

Hundreds of movies are completed each year in the US and UK; Britain, for instance, sees around 15 new releases each week and over 60 new films a month coming from Hollywood (not all of which get to see the inside of a cinema). That said, there are some films that are completed and yet remain on the shelf for years. Often, it's nothing to do with the quality of the film.

A prime example is Drew Goddard's terrific horror movie *The Cabin in the Woods*. The widely acclaimed film, which Goddard penned with Joss Whedon, was shot in the first half of 2009, but it would languish in the vaults of parent company MGM until its eventual release in April 2012. This wasn't because of a lengthy, troubled post-production – the film came together in time for the planned February 2010 release, though it was then rescheduled for early 2011 to allow a post-production 3D conversion to be explored.

Yet when MGM hit sizable financial troubles, *The Cabin in the Woods* found itself mired in with a bunch of films. The studio quickly had to find a new distributor for it and for the not very good remake of *Red Dawn* (which likewise suffered a long delay as a consequence), such was the need to rapidly bring in funds. While staving off creditors, MGM was also desperately trying to get *Skyfall* and *The Hobbit* trilogy off the ground. Lionsgate snapped up *The Cabin in the Woods* and was rewarded with a small but enduring hit. Other affected films, such as the aforementioned *Red Dawn* and the

Kevin James vehicle *The Zookeeper*, also found new homes, and eventual releases.

———

Money is one reason that films tend to remain unreleased; lawsuits are another. Emma Thompson penned the screenplay for *Effie Gray*, about the real-life relationship between Victorian art critic John Ruskin and his teenage bride, the Effie of the film's title. The film was written, Thompson took on a supporting role and director Richard Laxton wrapped filming in November 2011. It would

The remake of *Red Dawn*: some movies are worth waiting for. This one, less so.

be three years before it got a release, thanks to a series of lawsuits that alleged plagiarism. Things got very mucky before they were resolved in Thompson's favour, although she was still stung by a ruling over costs. She notably didn't promote the film when it was eventually released in October 2014.

Sometimes, a film simply remains in limbo. The film **10 Things I Hate About Life** isn't a direct sequel to 1999's terrific *10 Things I Hate About You*, though the key creative team from the 1999 film was shepherding it. The film shot for four weeks at the end of 2012, before a dispute arose with its lead, Evan Rachel Wood. A legal battle broke out, which left the second half of the film unfinished, and likely to remain that way.

A political comedy by the name of **Nailed**, from acclaimed director David O Russell (*Three Kings*, *Black Swan*), took seven years to escape the vaults following assorted battles. It was shot in 2008, although production was shut down on four separate occasions, amid reports of the cast not being paid for their work. Furthermore, James Caan, one of the key parts of the ensemble, quit halfway through. The story follows a waitress, played by Jessica Biel, who is accidentally shot through the head with a nail gun. Without the required medical insurance, she can't afford to have an operation to remove it. So commences a screwball comedy as she heads to the heart of American government to campaign for better healthcare. Jake Gyllenhaal co-stars.

Although the film was effectively shot, financial woes stopped it from being completed. Russell would finally quit the picture – which he'd also co-written – in 2010, and the producers upped sticks as

By the time *Nailed* was released, seven years after it was filmed, its marketing campaign looked nothing like this.

well, leaving it in the hands of its unnamed money people. They scrambled a cut together and staged a test screening, but it was not a very successful one, and not one that David O Russell or any of the cast and crew were informed of.

Yet the film wouldn't die. It first changed name to *Politics of Love*, and then to *Accidental Love*, and under that last moniker was finally released. Although it was credited to director Stephen Greene, Stephen Greene doesn't actually exist – it's a pseudonym for Russell, who had stuck to his word of having nothing to do with it. Come the start of 2015, the film finally got a low-key release, was promptly savaged by critics and was forgotten about again. Which seems to be fine with the people who got the project going in the first place, seven years previously.

SECRETS FROM THE BBFC & MPAA EXAMINERS' ARCHIVES

•••

Why was *Alien* given an 18 rating? How much screaming is too much in a *Doctor Who* movie? We take a look back through the archives of the British Board of Film Classification (BBFC) and the Motion Picture Association of America (MPAA).

ALIEN (1979)

Ridley Scott's space horror *Alien* was rated X on release – not because of its gore and violence, but because of its sexual imagery. The BBFC examiners' notes praise the film's technical achievements in florid style but also wrestle with the rating it should be given. Like *Jaws*, the examiner argues, *Alien* is "far more frightening to adults than to children" – and could therefore qualify for an AA rating (allowing teenagers aged 14 or over to see it) rather than an X, which would restrict it to the over-18 crowd.

The examiner continues, "At first, the British distributors were also in two minds, urging us to consider an AA in order to widen the audience. We replied that if we were to grant an AA to *Alien*, it would be hard ever again to give an X to similar entertainments."

A later document explains why the BBFC plumped for an X: too many pulsating orifices. "I feel uneasy at passing for 14-year-olds a film which uses sexual imagery in a horror context […] Occasionally the image is explicit as when the leathery egg opens up to reveal a glistening pulsating membrane which erupts into the squid-like creature. It was more or less on the strength of a shot like this that *Invasion of the Body Snatchers* was made X, and

I object to this on the same grounds – ie, that it presents a perverse view of the reproductive function. I don't want to flash ideas like this to teenagers who might not have come to terms with the normal sexual functions."

BRAINDEAD (1992)

The very words "classification board" may conjure up images of dusty old people sitting in the dark with clipboards, tutting at the sight of a bullet wound or the occasional nipple. Yet the notes from Peter Jackson's violent comedy horror *Braindead* hint at a more enthusiastic relationship with horror than the BBFC's outward appearance might suggest.

"I don't much care for horror spoofs," the examiner wrote, "but this is wonderfully funny – a genuinely entertaining grand guignol farce in which the comic invention never flags […] I was on this basis sorely tempted to go for '15' despite the endless succession of amputated limbs, torn-off head-skins, beheadings, buckets of blood, dismemberments, pustules bursting, arms being devoured […]"

A document from a second examiner concurs, and notes that someone else at the same screening "boldly floated a 15, on the grounds that there's nothing here

POST-PRODUCTION

Peter Jackson's *Braindead*: the BBFC feared the film may upset "girls especially".

to harm or disturb a 15-year-old, and that most teenagers would love it".

Ultimately, the decision was made to give *Braindead* an 18 certificate, partly because the examiner thought that some more sensitive teenagers – "girls especially", the writer adds – "are disturbed and upset by blood and visceral detail, even in a comic context".

"They would not thank us for lowering the rating (which they use as a guideline)," the document continues. "Obviously more research is needed into teenagers' attitudes to splatter; don't let's push the boat out before we've consulted them properly!"

CARRY ON FILMS

In its heyday, the *Carry On* franchise was a great British institution, offering a string of saucy innuendo and cheeky slapstick. The movies' suggestive dialogue often gave the BBFC a headache, however, as a document about 1969's *Carry On Camping* proves. It provides a faintly comical list of the lines that would have to be excised to meet the requirements of an A certificate:

Reel 1 *Remove the line "She's been showing me how to stick my pole up."*

Reel 3 *Remove the line "There's quite a lot of difference between our legs." Remove all the dialogue relating to phallic symbols.*

Reel 7 *Delete the line "Erection is fairly simple; it's getting it to stay up." Re-edit the scene when the two men and two girls are in the tent in such a way as to remove, or greatly reduce, the innuendo in the lines "How about those two things sticking out in front." "Get hold of them with both hands."*

Even in 1987, the *Carry On* team's antics were still being scrutinized by the BBFC. For a video re-release of 1968's *Carry On Up the Khyber*, the board's examiner had to decide whether the film's jokes were appropriate for a PG rating; although one line, "He's just a travelling fakir," once cut for an A certificate, was back in, two similar jokes ("Fakir off") were still cut out.

Carry On films infamously caused headaches for the British Board of Film Classification.

"I must admit that I would be prepared to pass this U," the examiner wrote, "but there is an endless stream of smutty jokes, and a scene at 41 minutes where the adventurous four fondle the busty 'ladies of the night' that have been provided for them. I'll take the easy way out and pass it PG."

DR. WHO AND THE DALEKS (1965)

Swearing, nudity and violence are a common bones of contention among BBFC examiners, but what about screaming? When it came to the script for *Dr. Who and the Daleks*, the Doctor's first feature film outing, the amount of screaming made the examiner uneasy. "My main objection to what I read," said the examiner, "was the number of screams, quite excessive and unnecessary and not always redeemed by the fact that what has been screamed at turns out not to be frightening after all."

Simply put, it was the jump-scares that were the problem. To underline the point, the examiner listed all the places in the script where someone shrieks or screams in terror. "Barbara wakes Ian – he wakes in a scream," one entry reads. "I know he is meant to be a

figure of fun, and Roy Castle has a reassuring personality, but still there is too much yelling in this script."

In a letter summarizing the examiner's points, the BBFC's director John Trevelyan explained, "In U films, we are always anxious not to have shots of people who are terrified, particularly close shots."

GREMLINS (1984)

The year 1984 proved to be something of a flashpoint when it came to film classification. In the US, the complaints about the levels of violence in such films as *Poltergeist* and *Indiana Jones and the Temple of Doom*, both released with PG ratings, led to the creation of the PG-13 certificate. The UK wouldn't get a similar rating until the 12 certificate emerged in 1989, which left the BBFC in something of a quandary when it came to a film like *Gremlins*.

The BBFC's examiner's notes reveal an appreciation for the movie and its adept fusion of cosy suburban life and anarchic horror, and there's a clear reluctance to cut the movie for a PG rating – even though a list of potential cuts is provided.

One of *Gremlins*'s most infamous scenes would have had to go to get a family-friendly rating.

"[If] we are forced to cut for 'PG', I would consider cutting: the death of the teacher; the terror of the Futtermans as they are attacked; the 'comic' death of the nasty old lady, which may not be so funny for kids (I am unsure about this one); the attack on the man dressed as Santa; Kate's story of the death of Santa [...]"

Yes, one of the greatest monologues in 1980s cinema would have had to go if the film was to get a family-friendly rating. In fact, a document from a second examiner took a dimmer view of the film's black comedy:

"I was appalled at Katie's description of her father dressed as Santa Claus dying in the chimney [...] Are we supposed to laugh at this? Are we supposed to condone children laughing at this?"

Gremlins was ultimately released uncut with a 15 rating, though a later release saw it reduced to a 12A.

TERMINATOR 2: JUDGMENT DAY (1991)
Unlike the original *Terminator* – an 18-rated, grungy action thriller brimming with violence and a hint of soft-focus sex – *Terminator 2* dialled back the bloodshed for a story that says (as the BBFC put it) that "delinquent young boys just need a machine to protect them and a mother to love them".

THE MPAA

In the US, the MPAA, the country's own ratings board, is more secretive about its process than the BBFC. Yet the descriptions that follow the MPAA's ratings provide at least a vague insight into their decision-making. Some of those descriptions are unintentionally hilarious:

WAR OF THE BUTTONS (1994):
"Rated PG for mischievous conflict, some mild language and bare bottoms"

JEFFERSON IN PARIS (1995): "Rated
PG-13 for mature theme, some images of violence, and a bawdy puppet show"

FOR THE MOMENT (1993): "Rated
PG-13 for sexual situations, language and a poignant death"

BATS (1999): "Rated PG-13 for intense
sequences of bat attacks"

ALIEN TRESPASS (2009): "Rated PG for
sci-fi action and brief historical smoking"

War of the Buttons: a little-seen gem, albeit with BBFC-alerting backsides.

WHY TERRIFIC MOMENTS END UP ON THE CUTTING ROOM FLOOR

From scenes chopped in the editing suite, to the moments that turned up in the trailer and then disappeared, the movies are full of stories of scenes that never made the final cut. Join us as we dig into some of the stories.

Stephen King has passed on no shortage of terrific advice about writing, not least in his unmissable tome *On Writing*. But one tip that resonates with screenwriters around the globe is "kill your darlings". King isn't the first to say this, but in the aforementioned book he implores wannabe writers to "kill your darlings, kill your darlings, even when it breaks your egocentric little scribbler's heart, kill your darlings". In other words, sometimes you have to cut some of your favourite parts, simply because they're not serving the story.

It's advice, too, that resonates with filmmakers. DVD releases are often blessed with a menu option for deleted scenes, letting you browse the moments that people believed in enough to shoot and put together, but had to cull when deep into the editing process. Sometimes there are some corkers. The DVD of *The Wizard of Oz*, for instance, restored a dance sequence to the song "If I Only Had a Brain", which quadrupled the running time of the scene. The original *Anchorman: The Legend of Ron Burgundy*, meanwhile, ended up with so much chopped footage that a second movie was cut together – *Wake Up, Ron Burgundy: The Lost Movie* – and distributed in a special package with the original film on DVD.

INFAMY, INFAMY

Sometimes, deleted moments become so infamous that they finally get an airing. Back in 1992, James Cameron got to present an extended version of his 1986 sci-fi sequel *Aliens*. This version added some 17 minutes, making it a good hour before Sigourney Weaver's Ripley and her colleagues finally encounter an alien in earnest. The reinstated footage brought back the heartbreaking moment when Ripley discovers that her daughter has died at the age of 66. She sees a picture of said

The extended version of *Aliens* adds crucial narrative moments.

Blade Runner: it's taken a few attempts to get to "The Final Cut".

daughter and is left mourning that she was originally aiming to get back in time for her 11th birthday. Cameron, incidentally, would also, in time, present longer versions of his 1989 film *The Abyss* and his 1991 film *Terminator 2: Judgment Day* and, in the case of the former, significantly deepen the film as a consequence.

Even more infamous was Ridley Scott's cut of his 1982 film *Blade Runner*. Studio interference is a common story when it comes to editing rooms, although the modern-day contracts that movie directors sign tend to prohibit them from talking about it. It was little secret, though, that Scott hated parts of the original cinematic cut of *Blade Runner*, including the forced-upon-him voice-over narration (see page 144, How Films Were Affected by their Test Screenings), and material – including a paper unicorn – that broadly hinted that Harrison Ford's Deckard was a replicant. Scott finally got to present his Director's Cut, released in cinemas ten years after the film's original release. He wasn't done tinkering, though, as his Final Cut was released 15 years after that, in 2007.

THE TV CUT

Sometimes previously deleted scenes appear where you don't necessarily expect them. For a period, movie studios would provide different cuts of their films for television stations, for instance. The demands of television scheduling meant that sometimes films needed to be extended or shrunk to accommodate them. Where the productions were stretched, that's where extended edits of films appeared, often introducing scenes that weren't shown in the theatrical cut. Not surprisingly, directors have in the past asked for their names to be taken off the TV versions of their work.

Assorted broadcast versions of *Airplane!* (1980), for instance, throw in little extra jokes that otherwise don't appear (example: a moment near the start where someone shouts "Hi, Jack!" in the airport terminal, with predictable results). A US television version of *The Bodyguard* (1992) inserted a chattering beaver figurine in a suspicious package, while 1988's classic Yuletide feast *Die Hard* earned another cut scene when premiering on the US television channel FX, as an initial attempt to shut down a block of city power doesn't quite go to plan.

The opposite sometimes applies, though. Michael Mann's crime thriller *Heat*, from 1995, was set to debut in the US on NBC on 3 January 1999. The problem? It only had a three-hour slot, including adverts, and so the 170-minute film wouldn't fit. Mann offered to cut another 17 minutes of material from the movie – NBC opted to chop 40 minutes out instead.

―――――

FANTASTIC SCENES AND WHERE TO FIND THEM

Fortunately, the digital era has rescued a lot of footage that would otherwise have been lost, and has made it available. From discs with deleted scenes, through to clips that pop up online, a lot of the time it's easy to see why the scene in question has been chopped. But every now and then, you can't help but think that a movie would have been better if a chopped moment had stayed in place.

―――――

SCENES THAT WERE IN THE TRAILER, NOT IN THE FILM

A film's trailer is often cut before the final version of a movie is locked down, and a consequence is that you sometimes see in a trailer a bunch of little moments that don't make it to the final feature. Here are ten quick examples.

The Truman Show: We get a brief moment where we see the "cast" of Truman's life behind the scenes, reading their lines.

Star Trek: J J Abrams's 2009 big-screen *Star Trek* reboot includes a flashback scene in its trailer in which Winona Ryder is seen cradling the newborn Spock. In the final cut, we just got Ryder in aging make-up.

The Empire Strikes Back: The moment in the first trailer for this 1980 film in which Luke and Leia lean in for a kiss was excised when the film followed a year after it.

L.A. Story: The Steve Martin-penned comedy's trailer includes a line where John Lithgow tells Martin that skipping to a meeting is a bad idea. And one where Martin skips. Neither made the final cut.

Who Framed Roger Rabbit: The ground-breaking hybrid of live action and animation included a moment in its promo where Bob Hoskins's Eddie Valiant had an animated pig head. The full deleted scene it was from finally made it to DVD decades later.

The Transporter: The trailer showed Jason Statham fighting off a grenade with a tea tray, but the scene is missing from the film. Thankfully, there's enough joy from The Stath elsewhere in the film to compensate.

Paranormal Activity 3: This is an infamous example, and one that suggests major recuts. In essence, about four-fifths of the first trailer for the film isn't seen or hinted at in the final version of the film that was released.

Spider-Man: The original trailer for Sam Raimi's 2002 *Spider-Man* movie included shots of New York's World Trade Center's Twin Towers. These were digitally removed from future promos, following the terrorist atrocities of 11 September 2001.

Harry Potter and the Order of the Phoenix: The trailer for this one had Michael Gambon's Dumbledore saying, "Don't fight him, Harry, you can't win". But what this relates to is unclear, with no mention in either J K Rowling's source novel or the final cut of the film.

Shaun the Sheep Movie: Here we have not so much a scene, as a background detail. The initial promos for the Aardman Animations film had a shop in the background called Costly Coffee. By the time the film came around, it was Gulpa Coffee. Aardman had apparently decided to stay on the safe side of the Costa Coffee chain.

THE SPECIALLY SHOT TRAILER

Sometimes, we get trailers that have been specifically shot for promotional purposes, and thus the footage was never intended for the final movie. The *Alien* prequel *Prometheus*, for instance, was built up to via a series of promos featuring Guy Pearce as billionaire CEO Peter Weyland. He was set to have a more prominent role in the final film than he got, but also, some of his material was specially filmed for promos.

Furthermore, the 1990s saw a rise in specially shot teasers for big films, often playing a year before the movie itself was released (back when this was a novelty). Thus, *Terminator 2: Judgment Day* had a promo where we see a Terminator being put together. Arnold Schwarzenegger teased his return to action cinema in 1993's *Last Action Hero* by telling the audience to "come back later". Meanwhile, Roland Emmerich's 1998 *Godzilla* film was teased a year in advance with footage of the titular creature's foot crushing a skeleton of a Tyrannosaurus Rex – an obvious dig at 1997's *The Lost World: Jurassic Park*. The latter, somewhat inevitably, made a lot more cash.

The teaser for *Godzilla* (1998) attempted to get audiences excited for the movie a year in advance.

THE MUPPET CHRISTMAS CAROL

Each year, Google services thousands of searches from people wanting to know about the mysterious story of *The Muppet Christmas Carol*'s missing song. A song by the name of "When Love Is Gone" is sung by the character Belle to Michael Caine's younger Scrooge. But the then Disney chief, Jeffrey Katzenberg, insisted it be cut, over the protests of director Brian Henson.

The scene did reappear on the subsequent VHS and LaserDisc releases of the movie, and the initial DVD release in the US. But not all DVDs include it in the feature, although it's an easy scene to find online. It tends to be chopped out of television screenings of the movie, too, which reflect the original cinematic cut of the film.

THE CHANGING FACE OF MOVIE MARKETING

•••

Before the internet, selling a movie generally involved a trailer, a poster and the purchase of advertising space on billboards, in newspapers and on the side of buses. Oh, and a movie star helped. It'd be fair to say that a lot has changed.

When the first movie in the *Fast & Furious* series, the cunningly entitled *The Fast and the Furious*, sped into cinemas back in 2001, its promotional campaign followed a familiar pattern. At that time its cast – led by the then up-and-coming pairing of Vin Diesel and the late Paul Walker – weren't deemed sufficiently famous to have their names prominent on the poster. Universal pursued a conventional promotional campaign, issuing posters and a trailer or two. It's likely that the studio, as

well as box office pundits, were taken aback by the size of the success the film enjoyed.

The franchise would go through a few bumps by the time it became the global juggernaut we know today, the one that's seeing Universal greenlight films right through to *Fast & Furious 10* in 2021. But what's also interesting is how, in a space of around 15 years, the series has given

Vin Diesel's social media channels are far more popular than any individual movie studio's own.

a stark demonstration of the power shift in movie marketing.

Fast-forward, then, to the announcement of the trailer for *Fast & Furious 8*, which was made toward the back end of 2016. Ahead of the movie's release in 2017, Diesel had already been using his sizable presence on Facebook in particular to alert followers to the progress of the film (and his assorted other projects, including 2017's *xXx: Return of Xander Cage*). When it comes to social media, too, the studios are allowing their stars to take the lead, for Diesel is, along with Dwayne Johnson, the kind of movie star whose social media reach far outweighs that of the studio he makes films for. Universal is thus happy for Diesel to make key announcements, understanding that his 100 million fans, and counting, dwarf the few million that the studio's official page can muster.

Dwayne Johnson tends to break news of his films via Instagram and Facebook, ahead of studio announcements.

The number of movie stars in the traditional sense may be dwindling (just putting Tom Hanks on a poster is no path to riches any more, as *Inferno* and *A Hologram for the King* proved in 2016) but the social media impact of many actors is changing the marketing strategies behind blockbuster cinema – so much so, in fact, that it's now sometimes written into actors' contracts. That applied, for instance, for some of the cast of 2016's *Teenage Mutant Ninja Turtles: Out of the Shadows*, who were teasing the reveal of footage from the film – a trailer for a trailer, if you will – in the days before said promo material was released.

The practice is increasingly common. Star contracts for a film already tend to lock in, say, ten days of promotional work, but now a line is being added to the deals to ensure they give projects support via their personal Twitter, Facebook and Instagram accounts.

This is new territory for studios, as it's a prominent promotional tactic over which they don't have direct control. They can retweet a new post from Dwayne Johnson to their heart's content, but they can't control the fact that the majority of people will see the original source, rather than their reposting.

But such is the impact of social media – it's almost *de rigueur* now to announce when your trailer has been viewed more than 100 million times on YouTube – that studios have little choice but to embrace it. Some of the tactics are interesting, too. As one insider explained, a particularly effective approach is the "social roadblock". We saw this with 2016's *Suicide Squad*, whose marketing campaign took advantage of its sizable ensemble's individual social media presences. Each member of the cast posted their own character poster on their social media accounts at a given time, all using the given hashtag #WorstHeroesEver.

Suicide Squad leveraged the social media power of its ensemble cast.

Several online tactics are now used to raise awareness of movie trailers. The most unfortunately effective is the trailer for a trailer, a 10–15-second preview of the fuller preview that's to follow. In the case of 2013's *The Wolverine*, 20th Century Fox even went so far as to release a trailer for the trailer for the trailer. But returning to the *Fast & Furious* movies, Universal actually held a premiere at which it revealed the first *Fast & Furious 7* trailer, toward the end of 2014. Streamed online, it featured interviews with the cast, a red carpet (genuinely) and the subsequent release of what was, at heart, an advert. But it certainly worked. Not for nothing do major movies now tend to have at least three trailers a piece.

Such was the presence of the likes of Will Smith, Margot Robbie and Jared Leto that the term was trending in double-quick time. It's also interesting that *Suicide Squad* was a critically mauled film, yet awareness of it was through the roof.

But this is the new status quo, and social media presence is a cornerstone of film marketing. The wise stars, therefore, are the ones who work their backsides off to generate the kind of social media presence that a film production company can only dream of.

The Wolverine's marketing campaign was not unusual in trying to trail the trailer itself.

WHEN A FILM STAR TURNS ON THEIR OWN MOVIE

A film's promotional tour is supposed to be full of positive messages. But sometimes, things don't go to plan.

PROMO PROBLEMS

The modern-day film star, as part of their contract for making a movie, invariably has a few days, sometimes weeks, of promotional duties built into their deal. You probably know how this works: the star in question gets shepherded between comfy hotel suites around the world, and answers similar-sounding questions from journalists of assorted nationalities. Bonus points are awarded for managing to look interested for the duration of this exercise.

The party line, it'd be fair to say, is almost always exclusively toed, not least because said movie stars tend to be media-trained in a no doubt luxurious special underground bunker. Yet sometimes, things go awry.

Bruce Willis, for instance, notoriously conducted video interviews for the fairly forgettable *Red 2* in a dressing gown live on British television. In a further discussion with London reporter Jamie Edwards, we got the odd moment where the journalist appeared to be defending the film, while the star was, let's charitably say, "a bit dismissive of it".

Daniel Craig, meanwhile, didn't attack *Spectre* outright, but he certainly earned a fair amount of ink for saying in the midst of its press tour that he'd rather "slash his wrists" than play James Bond again. A comment from which he has since backtracked.

STARS PUTTING THE BOOT IN

Most of the time, if a filmmaker or star expresses regret about a project, it's long after a movie has left cinemas. (Shia LaBeouf has arguably turned this into an art form, earning headlines for his unenthusiastic views on the likes of *Transformers: Revenge of the Fallen* and *Indiana Jones and the Kingdom of the Crystal Skull*.) But there are instances, of course, when the stars have been negative about their movies very early on.

Burt Reynolds's career revival in Paul Thomas Anderson's 1997 ensemble drama *Boogie Nights* impressed many worldwide, earning Reynolds his only Academy Award nomination. It's a terrific performance, with Reynolds playing adult-film director

Burt Reynolds and Mark Wahlberg in *Boogie Nights*. Reynolds has always stood by the problems he had when working on the movie.

Jack Horner, against Mark Wahlberg's Eddie Adams/Dirk Diggler. Critics were quick to pour praise on Reynolds's work, and the man who was once the biggest movie star in the world was on the verge of a major comeback. (Reynolds, it should be recognized, had lost two years of his working life to the aftermath of an accident on the set of 1984's *City Heat*, with Clint Eastwood, when Reynolds was just at the height of his box office powers.)

Reynolds would win a Golden Globe as Best Supporting Actor for *Boogie Nights*, noting in his acceptance speech, "I'm flabbergasted". Few doubted it. It was little secret that he wasn't keen on the role, having gone as far as firing his agent when he caught a rough cut of the movie in advance. It was suggested that this ultimately cost Reynolds his chance of converting his subsequent Oscar nomination into a win. (Robin Williams took home the statue that year, for *Good Will Hunting*.)

Not that Reynolds had regrets. In his entertaining 2015 memoir, *But Enough About Me*, Reynolds noted, "Though I've seen parts of *Boogie Nights* I've never sat down and watched the whole thing," adding, "I asked family members not to see it, and they don't."

He recalled that "I was less and less thrilled about going to work every day" and, while he expressed his gratitude to the director, Paul Thomas Anderson, and his appreciation of his work, he also noted that "he just isn't my kind of director".

What made the story so big was that Reynolds's dislike of *Boogie Nights* was revealed at the time the movie was playing. Such instances are notable by their rarity, especially when the movie and work concerned were so acclaimed. In contrast, few batted an eyelid at David Cross's comment about *Alvin and the Chipmunks: Chipwrecked* (a film in which he had just played a ship's safety monitor dressed as a penguin) – at around the time of its release, he described the movie as "a big commercial for Carnival Cruise Lines", heavily implying that audiences should give it a miss. Which they didn't.

Still, perhaps the late Marlon Brando takes the crown here. Even before it was released, he'd passed judgement on 1990's *The Freshman*, in which he co-starred with Matthew Broderick. Chatting to the Canadian newspaper *The Globe and Mail* ahead of the film's release, he predicted that the pretty

Marlon Brando (*left*) has a reputation for having been quite hard work on movie productions.

Babylon A.D. was written off by its director even before it arrived in cinemas.

decent comedy was "going to be a flop", declaring it "a stinker". It was nearly the former, but certainly not the latter.

DIRECT DIRECTORS

Finally, it's not just talent in front of the camera that sometimes defies the script. The 2008 Vin Diesel-headlined sci-fi clunker *Babylon A.D.* was directed by Mathieu Kassovitz. In the run-up to its release, in protest at interference from 20th Century Fox during the making of the movie, Kassovitz declared that the final cut of his film was like "a bad episode of 24 [the TV series]". Many agreed: the film bombed.

Even more notoriously, the director of 2015's critically slaughtered *Fantastic Four* movie, Josh Trank, announced on social media – and then promptly deleted (but not before half the internet seemed to get a screengrab of it) – that "a year ago I had a fantastic vision of this. And it would've received great reviews. You'll probably never see it. That's reality though". That single post was estimated by 20th Century Fox to have cost the film at least $10m of business on its opening weekend.

HINDSIGHT CORNER

Here's what five movie stars have said of their own films, long after their release:

George Clooney on *Batman & Robin*: "I always apologize for *Batman & Robin*."

•••

Sam Worthington on *Clash of the Titans*: "I think…we kind of let down some people."

•••

Arnold Schwarzenegger on *Red Sonja*: "It's the worst film I ever made."

•••

Brad Pitt on *The Devil's Own*: "It's the most irresponsible bit of filmmaking – if you can even call it that – that I've ever seen."

•••

Sylvester Stallone on *Stop! Or My Mom Will Shoot*: "I made some truly awful movies. *Stop! Or My Mom Will Shoot* was the worst."

POST-PRODUCTION

HOW FILMS WERE AFFECTED BY THEIR TEST SCREENINGS

•••

The process of test screening a movie before its release dates back even as far as the 1930s. Back then, a preview audience for The *Wizard Of Oz* reported back to the powers that be that Judy Garland belting out "Somewhere Over The Rainbow" was slowing the film down, the suggestion being that it should be cut. The studio, in that case, resisted, but as these stories of test screenings testify, that's not always the case.

BABE: PIG IN THE CITY (1998)

The original *Babe* was and is a family treat, a hit out of nowhere for Universal Studios, and a Best Picture Oscar nominee, too. Whereas the original was produced by *Mad Max* helmer George Miller but directed by Chris Noonan, Miller took the director's chair for what would become *Babe: Pig in the City*, and the studio left him to it. Come the first test screening, though, it wished it hadn't. This took place at Anaheim Hills in California, and parents quickly complained that the film – which features scenes of animals basically being dragged to within an inch of their death – was too scary. However, Universal was nearly out of time, and so only some minor amendments were made (including deleting good chunks of Mickey Rooney's clown character). Upon the film's release, stories soon emerged of children leaving the cinema in tears. *Babe 3* was quickly abandoned.

CLIFFHANGER (1993)

There's a moment in the Sylvester Stallone vehicle *Cliffhanger* – the film that arguably reignited Sly's career in the 1990s – where he has to leap from one cliff to another. It involved a 40-foot jump (aided by ropes), but when a test audience was presented with the scene, they guffawed. They just didn't accept that it could be done. Some computer work was done to make the jump appear shorter. The irony? The jump was pretty much done for real but people didn't believe that was the case.

THE EMPEROR'S NEW GROOVE (2000)

This hugely underrated Disney animated feature is all but unrecognizable from its original form. At first, the film was to be a musical by the name of *Kingdom of the Sun*, boasting songs by Sting, and with an environmental slant. Test screenings didn't

Universal realized it had a big problem when it eventually screened *Babe 2*. *Babe 3* would not happen.

go well, though, so virtually all the songs were stripped away, the original director quit, Sting was unhappy and the final cut would be very funny, but very different. Sting's wife, Trudie Styler, would make a documentary blocked from release by Disney (aside from a brief leak onto YouTube) called *The Sweatbox*, that told the behind-the-scenes story of the film's major changes.

WHAT IS A TEST SCREENING?

When a studio has a film in a near-finished form, it'll recruit a third-party company to select an appropriate audience to see the rough-cut of the movie concerned. These screenings try to find a relevant demographic: one test audience for 2010's *Kick-Ass*, for instance, was put together by asking customers of a comic-book store if they fancied seeing an early version of the film.

More often, though, it's select cities, shopping malls and venues across the US where the blockbusters with the broadest market are tested. Filmmakers tend to sneak in the back at the last minute to see what's happening, and audiences after the film have to fill in a questionnaire. Based on that, the studio has a gauge of how well its film has played, and whether to make changes or order more screenings.

In extreme cases, sizable reshoots may end up being ordered. The 1993 notorious box office disappointment *Last Action Hero*, for instance, ended up with new action sequences being shot off the back of test-screening reports. It wouldn't, ultimately, save the film from being trampled at the box office by *Jurassic Park*.

FOR LOVE OF THE GAME (1999)

Kevin Costner's third and least successful baseball movie became notable for an incident involving his penis. The original cut of the film earned an R rating in the US, restricting access to over-17s unless accompanied by an adult. The point of contention, so to speak, was a shower scene where Costner's dancing wolf was in full view. According to *New York* magazine, a test audience "giggled at Kevin's penis". It was duly cut.

LICENCE TO KILL (1989)

It wasn't the actual content of Timothy Dalton's James Bond swansong that was altered as a result of a test audience – it was its name. The movie was originally set to be called *Licence Revoked*, before test audiences reportedly fed back that they figured 007 had

The Shawshank Redemption is one of the world's most loved films. Its biggest flaw, though, was the result of a test screening.

lost his driving licence. *Revoked* was revoked. *To Kill* was recruited.

Oddly, this worked the other way around for *Erin Brockovich*, the 2000 film that won Julia Roberts her Oscar. The studio weren't keen on using the name as the title, but test audiences were behind it. It stayed, and the film hit big.

THE SHAWSHANK REDEMPTION (1994)

Adapted from a Stephen King novella, Frank Darabont's film *The Shawshank Redemption* is regarded as a near-faultless modern classic. But the prison drama has one very obvious fault: an ending that over-explained, leaving not one sniff of ambiguity. Whereas King's text ended on the words "I hope", uttered in voice-over by Morgan Freeman in the movie, the film then fails to stop until we've seen a tacked-on reunion between Freeman's character Red and Tim Robbins's Andy. Over two decades later, it still sticks out.

SEVEN (1995)

"I'm standing in the back of the theatre," director David Fincher once said of a test screening for his astounding thriller *Seven*, "and these three women come by and one of them says to the other two, 'the people who made that movie should be killed'." Thankfully, they weren't, but test audience scores for the film still came in low, with the pitch-black ending high on the list of complaints. Fincher, along with Morgan Freeman, who starred in the film with Brad Pitt, would only budge an inch, adding some narration at the very end. Even then, they weren't keen, but in this instance, by pretty much ignoring a test audience, they produced a modern classic.

SUICIDE SQUAD (2016)

The muddled final cut of David Ayer's *Suicide Squad* was reportedly caused by the company

Bram Stoker's Dracula marked a sea-change in how Columbia Pictures approached movies of its ilk.

well go as big as possible straight away, with as broad and wide a release as possible. It's a conventional tactic now but was quite radical then, particularly given the horror leanings of the film. The tactic worked: over $200m at the global box office was duly banked.

FIRST BLOOD (1982)

A movie series – and quite possibly Sylvester Stallone's career – could have been very different had test audiences not had their say. The original cut of the 1982 feature debut of the *Rambo* series came with a much darker ending, where the character of John Rambo dies of his self-inflicted gunshot wound. (Fact: Rambo doesn't actually kill anyone in the first movie. By *Rambo III*, he seems to kill everyone.) But the test audience revolted. They wanted Rambo to live, and they got their wish.

that cut the trailer being brought in late to have a stab at editing the main feature, too. Three months before the movie's release, two versions of the film were tested in California. One was the director's gloomier, darker cut, whereas the other was a lighter version. Because the test audiences veered toward the latter, some late and expensive reshoots were ordered, resulting in the compromise version that played in cinemas.

BRAM STOKER'S DRACULA (1991)

A test screening doesn't determine just the film itself, but also how it's marketed. With *Bram Stoker's Dracula*, director Francis Ford Coppola tried different cuts of the movie, but none found favour with test audiences. Columbia Pictures, which was backing the movie, changed its plan. It had set out a release strategy that would see the film open in a few cinemas first, and then gradually expand. Instead, they figured they might as

THE INFAMOUS EXAMPLES

In the last 30 years or so, the most famous examples of test-screening tinkering have been 1987's thriller *Fatal Attraction* and the 1982 sci-fi classic *Blade Runner*. In the case of the former, a virtually nonsensical softer ending was used following test-audience objections, only for the excellent original finale intended by director Adrian Lyne to be included in a VHS release, in an alternate cut.

With *Blade Runner*, a lengthy and pretty hated narration was added at the behest of test audiences, as well as a happy ending. These were removed for the 1992 Director's Cut – which was followed in 2007 by the Final Cut, over which Ridley Scott finally had complete control.

FILMS THAT CHANGED DRAMATICALLY IN POST-PRODUCTION

From edit room scuffles to extensive new sequences being shot, films are often substantially retooled once they're in the edit suite. Sometimes it's for the best, but other times it's not...

A big-screen take on television series *The Avengers*, the 1998 film of the same name, starring Ralph Fiennes, Uma Thurman and Sean Connery, is by now a fairly infamous flop. Released off the back of reports of poor test screenings, the movie arrived with a running time of 89 minutes and reviews that highlighted the incoherence of what was on the screen. The critical reception and box office returns were weak. For director Jeremiah Chechik, it was particularly frustrating. "That failure of that movie changed my life," he admitted. Not that it was

The promos for *Rogue One: A Star Wars Story* feature material that was cut out late in the day.

fully in his control. Originally, the film boasted a darker music score, by the late Michael Kamen, and Chechik's cut "was 20 minutes longer. All of the absurdity of it was connected in its own logic. You could understand it", he said. But a new regime at Warner Bros. ordered a different cut. "By the time the studio was done [...] they had cut out all the internal logic," Chechik mourned. "It was chaotic and absurd [...] the movie that was finally released was not the movie that I made."

▬▬▬▬

His is not an unfamiliar tale. 2010's **Jonah Hex** was expected to be a solid comic-book movie hit for Warner Bros., but when word came in that the final cut was just 81 minutes long, alarm bells started ringing. Short films aren't bad, but short comic-book movies are rare.

When director Jimmy Hayward, who would go on to direct the animated movie *Free Birds*, delivered his first cut of *Jonah Hex*, Warner Bros. wasn't impressed. It was so unimpressed, in fact, that it ordered big changes, bringing in Francis Lawrence – who would later direct all but the first *The Hunger Games* movies – to oversee them. The resultant final cut showed the signs of having had too many cooks. While its star, Josh Brolin, initially defended the movie, telling MTV he was "extremely" happy with the final cut prior to release, he would subsequently say that he "hated it" and the process of "reshooting 66 pages in 12 days".

That said, not all stories of post-production tussles end up badly. In 2016, the build-up to the release of **Rogue One: A Star Wars Story** was troubled by sizable reshoots, with talk of as much as 40 per cent of the movie being reconfigured. Screenwriter Tony Gilroy was brought in to write fresh screenplay material, and director Gareth Edwards confirmed that a thousand extra visual effects were ordered in. "There were a ton of reshoots," actor Riz Ahmed confirmed to the *Los Angeles Times*.

Successful reshoots in particular were credited with overhauling the hugely successful final third of the movie. Edwards had wanted a documentary war-movie style approach to *Rogue One*'s denouement, and he duly got it. The back end of the movie was the most widely praised part of it.

World War Z's final act was successfully overhauled following major changes in the edit suite, while Pixar stuck a delay on

The Good Dinosaur and stripped it right back in spite of its nearly being finished in 2014. The (middling) resultant movie would finally land at the end of 2015.

It's only recently that reshoots have become headline news. For decades, they were part and parcel of Hollywood production, without the accompanying brouhaha that they seem to attract today. After all, sometimes it takes the perspective of being in an edit suite with a working cut of a feature to see just what's wrong with it. But with online outlets needing daily copy, a reshoot tale is often made out to be far more dramatic than it actually is.

THE BATTLE OF *BRAZIL*

Perhaps the most infamous tale of a director who went into battle with a studio over the final cut of a movie was that of Terry Gilliam, his film *Brazil* and Universal Pictures. Now regarded as a sci-fi classic, the 1985 movie was significantly recut in the US at the behest of the studio, with Universal's then chief Sid Sheinberg demanding a happier ending. Gilliam hated the new cut, known as the "Love Conquers All" version, and his version of the film was released outside of the US.

In America, the film remained unreleased while the battle of *Brazil* raged. Gilliam was holding private screenings, without the studio's permission, in the US, to the point where the unreleased movie was awarded Best Picture by the Los Angeles Film Critics Association. Gilliam would duly take out a full page advert in entertainment trade magazine *Variety* urging Universal to release the movie, which it eventually did. The excellent book *The Battle of Brazil*, by Jack Mathews, tells the story in absorbing detail.

THE LITTLE MOMENTS THAT CHANGED A FILM'S FORTUNES

•••

Sometimes, it turns out that even wildly popular films have had a surprising burst of luck that helped transform them. They range from Oscar winners to the movie that turned Hugh Grant into a major film star.

FOUR WEDDINGS AND A FUNERAL

Production resources were not plentiful when it came to making this huge British surprise hit of 1994. The film earned a Best Picture Oscar nomination, swept up nearly a quarter of a billion dollars at the box office alone, and made Hugh Grant a movie star. Yet the budget for the film had already been cut down from the planned $8m to $6m by the time filming started, and production had been delayed by over a year. Inevitably, things were stretched, to the point where producer Duncan Kenworthy had to stand in as one of the faces in the photo montage at the end of the movie. But fate was on the film's side.

It followed the modestly successful Anglo-German movie *Backbeat* into UK cinemas by a few weeks. *Backbeat* had been heralded by *Empire* magazine, but when the same publication sent a reviewer to watch *Four Weddings and a Funeral*, they came back unimpressed, wanting to score the film two out of a possible five. The magazine's editor wanted a second opinion, got one and went with it. The movie was upgraded to four stars, was given a splash in the magazine and as a result got a useful boost for its British release.

Yet an even bigger slice of fortune was on its side when it came to cracking the American market. No British film had topped the US box office since *A Fish Called Wanda* in 1988, and *Four Weddings and a Funeral* would achieve this in early 1994. It relied, though, on one cinema in New York City to spark its American momentum.

At the time, Michael Kuhn was heading up PolyGram, the company that funded the film. He recalled in his memoir, *One Hundred Films and a Funeral*, that the US distributor of the film, Gramercy, could barely afford to release it. It ordered five prints, two of which were set to play in New York and the other three in Los Angeles, with the aim being to build up word of mouth, and justify paying for more prints.

The problem, though, was that early projections for the film's opening were still very "soft", and by Saturday lunchtime of the movie's opening weekend, the movie looked doomed. If it couldn't post a good revenue per screen average by the end of the weekend, then other screens wouldn't take up the film and its release would splutter.

Gramercy identified the New York multiplex that was causing the shortfall, and duly investigated. It turned out that the multiplex concerned was playing it on a smaller screen, which was selling out, while

A cinema in New York helped make Hugh Grant (*right*) a movie star and Andie MacDowell (*left*) very rich.

its larger screen was promised to a big studio release. The manager of said cinema, though, agreed to break the rules. Wagering that the studio behind the other film wouldn't find out – and it apparently didn't – he swapped the screen bookings. *Four Weddings and a Funeral* thus played in the bigger studio, which meant it could accommodate the many more people who wanted to see it, and its box office was transformed. Had that one manager not made his fateful decision, the film was set to gross just shy of $19,000 on five screens. Instead, it took $176,000. As Gramercy hoped, other cinemas took note, and the film's fortunes and profile were transformed.

LOCK, STOCK AND TWO SMOKING BARRELS

Another British movie, *Lock, Stock and Two Smoking Barrels*, also needed someone to make a stand for it, to help transform it into a hit. In this case, though, that person was Tom Cruise.

This small British independent movie would eventually kick-start the careers of Jason Statham, Vinnie Jones, director Guy Ritchie and producer Matthew Vaughn (who went on to build a very successful directing career of his own). But in spite of encouraging business in Britain, it couldn't get a distributor willing to take a chance on it in the US – until Matthew Vaughn played his trump card. He dropped a call to Trudie Styler, one of the investors in the film, and asked her to invite Tom Cruise – at that time the world's biggest movie star – to a preview screening of the movie. Crucially, this was to be a screening for potential buyers of the film.

It took place in a small screening room on the lot of Sony Pictures. Just before the film was set to roll, Cruise duly walked in, to the astonishment of those around. As Vaughn recalled in BBC Radio 4's *The Business of Film with Mark Kermode* programme, "It was hysterical. You had all these mid-level executives sitting there, and Cruise walked in. He saw them all sit up and pay attention, all getting on their phones, and suddenly all these senior executives joined the screening."

The moment that iced that particular cake? Cruise standing up at the end of the film, turning to everyone, and saying, "This is the best movie I've seen in years, you guys would be fools not to buy it." A bidding war commenced, and *Lock, Stock and Two Smoking Barrels* became an international hit.

> **"This is the best movie I've seen in years, you guys would be fools not to buy it"**

Vinnie Jones probably owes Tom Cruise a couple of drinks…

DRIVING MISS DAISY

Winning four Academy Awards, including Best Picture, at the 1990 Oscars, *Driving Miss Daisy* earned over $140m at the global box office, off a production budget of just $7m. It inspired a cracking, and best left unprinted, line in the 2008 comedy *Role Models*, but it owes a chunk of its success to the failure of a Bruce Willis movie.

For the winter of 1989, Warner Bros. reckoned it had a critical hit on its hands. The film concerned was *In Country*, directed by Norman Jewison and starring Bruce Willis and Emily Lloyd. This being an era before studios channelled pretty much all of their promotional work into one opening weekend, the plan with *In Country* was to open it at the end of September 1989, and rely on slow word of mouth to build over the following months. Yet it soon became clear that it was no Oscar contender. Although Bruce Willis would earn a Golden Globe nomination for Best Supporting Actor, the $18m movie was soon dribbling out of cinemas. Warner Bros. suddenly had a gap in its schedules and did a quick recce of its slate. *Driving Miss Daisy* caught its attention.

The film's director, Bruce Beresford, recounts the story in his book *Josh Hartnett Definitely Wants to Do This: True Stories from a Life in the Screen Trade*. He noted that Warner Bros. had invested a modest $2.5m of the film's budget, but at the point at which it realized the movie was "promotable", it "turned the publicity machine on full blast, transforming an art-house film into a major hit".

Among the beneficiaries of its success was the late Jessica Tandy, who became the oldest person ever to win an Oscar for their acting. *Driving Miss Daisy* would subsequently also become a Broadway show and a good seller on home formats. As regards *In Country*, it has enjoyed a small DVD release.

CINEMA GOLD

Films are full of little coincidences and quirks, and small moments that help define them. Take the 1988 movie *Die Hard,* for instance. One of the scene-stealers in that film is the character of Ellis, played by Hart Bochner. Even though he was going toe-to-toe with the late, great Alan Rickman (who plays the criminal Hans Gruber), Bochner's sneery embodiment of the late-1980s coke-head yuppie is cinema gold. Yet the film's director, John McTiernan, hated his interpretation of the character. "My take on Ellis," said Bochner, "was that I always feel that when you're playing a bad guy, you look for their insecurity, which drives their behaviour. While the character was a bad guy, he was certainly ridiculously obnoxious, and a fly in everyone's ointment. So I came at it from it's coke behaviour, and the coke masks his insecurity."

But John McTiernan was not impressed. He told Bochner, "I don't know what you're doing. I hate it. It's not what I envisaged for this character. I want smooth. I want Cary Grant."

Bochner, though, stuck to his guns, and on his second day of shooting, when he was about to be admonished again by McTiernan, the director heard laughter and saw producers Joel Silver and Larry Gordon in hysterics by a monitor. He walked over to them, consulted, and returned, telling Bochner, "You know what, man, you do whatever you want to do". Bochner duly did, and a classic supporting character of modern cinema made it to the screen intact.

FILMS THAT ARE HARSHER THAN THEY SEEM

Most of us, by now, pretty much know what we're going to get when we pop in a DVD of *Watership Down*. Cuddly animals, sure, with lifelong trauma as a side dish. Likewise, even the DVD cover suggests that something like *Panic Room* is hardly going to be a barrel of laughs. But what about those films that look light and fluffy, but turn out to be anything but?

MURIEL'S WEDDING (1994)

A huge hit in its native Australia, this 1994 film brought the talents of Toni Collette to a global audience. As the film travelled around the world, it was sold as a comedy centred around the songs of Abba, and, to a degree, that's what you got. This is, after all, the story of a woman who dreams of her wedding day, of getting married and of greater things. And there are, indeed, Abba songs.

Yet it's got a hell of a sucker punch, too. Muriel's story is not that of a traditional romcom, and by the end, there's more of a sombre, downbeat feel than any sign of a happy-ever-after. In among the many human tragedies as the film progresses, Muriel's garden burns down, too.

It is a terrific film – both quirky and brave. But it's not top choice for an uplifting night in. *Mamma Mia* is a far safer way to scratch the upbeat-movie Abba itch.

THE FOX AND THE HOUND (1981)

The Disney marketing department in the early-1980s must have thought they'd hit pay dirt when they first started getting the drawings across for *The Fox and the Hound*. Disney's 1981 tale of two friends who traditionally should have been enemies boasted a cute fox and an even cuter dog, and the pair's friendship would no doubt survive the pressures that nature and expectations throw at it. Cute animals! Lots of merchandise! What could go wrong?

Er, let's just say that the film would struggle to get through the Disney system. *The Fox and the Hound* is barely two notches down from *Watership Down*, and one above *Babe: Pig in the City*, in its ability to distress small children. To give you a flavour of what's in store, the IMDb categorizes the film under the following keywords, among others: tragedy, gun, yelling, hit by a train, porcupine. You have been warned.

An Officer and a Gentleman: a dark choice for a date movie.

AN OFFICER AND A GENTLEMAN (1982)

The final scene of this 1982 film, in which a uniformed Richard Gere scoops up Debra Winger in his arms, is a pretty iconic piece of cinema now. Lampooned and referenced widely – and with the classic movie ballad "Up Where We Belong" playing behind it – it's the main reason the film is renowned primarily as a romance.

Without that single scene, though, the reputation of *An Officer and a Gentleman* would surely be very different. Far from being a love story between a navy cadet and a local woman, the film leans more toward dark, often bleak drama. Louis Gossett Jr won an Oscar for his portrayal of drill sergeant Emil Foley, and the brutal training he puts his cadets through wouldn't be trumped until *Full Metal Jacket* arrived – with R Lee Ermey in tow – five years later.

But the darkest core is found when one cadet – David Keith's Sid Worley – gets into a relationship with Lynette Pomeroy, played by Lisa Blount (who tragically died in 2010 at the age of just 53). Lynette desperately wants to

escape her life, and get married to an officer, enjoying being stationed around the world. Sid is less keen, until he learns that Lynette is pregnant. It turns out that she isn't, setting off a trail that leads to Sid's suicide, not that many minutes of screen time before Joe Cocker and Jennifer Warnes's singing starts up again.

It'd be remiss to call the ending tacked on, because even though it was conceived quite late in the day, there is a logic to it. But far from a date-night treat, *An Officer and a Gentleman* is one of the darkest mainstream movies of its era.

THE FULL MONTY (1997)

The most successful British comedy of the 1990s, Oscar-nominated for Best Picture. A very, very funny ensemble movie. A Broadway show. The catalyst for Hot Chocolate's lead singer, the late Errol Brown, going back on tour. Yep, *The Full Monty* went, in quick time, from being a small blip on the cinema-release radar to a genuine phenomenon.

Wisely sold as the very funny film about everyday men who turn to removing their assorted knitwear and baggy smalls for money when things get tough, there's a core of steel – in more than one sense – at the heart of *The Full Monty*. The actual guts of the film are dark. This is a story about what happens to a community when the industry on which it relies shuts up shop. Where do you find hope? How do families stay close-knit? How do you keep your self-respect and determination when it looks like there's no way forward? How do you pull yourself back from suicidal thoughts?

The Full Monty delves deep into such tricky human material, as *Brassed Off* had done in the previous year and as *Pride* would go on to do in 2014. It knows, too, to give its audience no shortage of things to laugh at, and bottoms to admire. It also appears to end with a light shining out of Tom Wilkinson's

The Full Monty earned a Best Picture Oscar nomination, with a deep political core beneath its surface story of male strippers.

The underrated *This Year's Love*.

backside (genuinely: dig out your copy and see). But it also makes sure it lands its hefty, darker punches.

PAY IT FORWARD (2000)

This 2000 film is a bit of a bumpy road, positioned as a heart-warming drama in advance of an ill-fated Oscar run. It has a great cast, it's based on a popular book, and the central theme – to pay kindness forward, and make the world a better place – is complete Oscar bait.

But the rosy, warm-blush DVD cover disguises a film with devastating turns, often brought to the screen with the subtlety of Godzilla in a game of hopscotch. Even as Sunday afternoon viewing, *Pay It Forward* – in spite of a genuinely positive idea at its core – is more likely to leave you feel bludgeoned than inspired. The book handles its ideas a good deal better.

THIS YEAR'S LOVE (1999)

A dark British ensemble drama from director David Kane, *This Year's Love* has a quality cast led by the likes of the brilliant Kathy Burke, alongside Jennifer Ehle and Ian Hart. But for all its qualities – and it has many – it certainly leaves you a little bruised come the end credits.

Unhelpfully, the 1999 film was sold in the UK as a love story and as a suitable film for a Valentine's treat, thereby demonstrating either extreme gallows humour or sheer chutzpah. It was thus released for the weekend at the end of Valentine's week, and many date nights across the UK were ended prematurely as the story of relationships going very wrong played out on the screen. The romcom of the film's very funny trailer was, let's charitably say, "notable by its absence".

BATTERIES NOT INCLUDED

The intriguing-looking box cover for Matthew Robbins's 1987 movie *Batteries Not Included* – co-written by Brad Bird, no less – suggests another Spielberg-produced mid-1980s funfest. The marketing was certainly not shy about using Spielberg's name.

There are lots of fun things about *Batteries Not Included*: the little alien spaceships for a start, along with the terrific cast, the practical effects and a promise of some more family-friendly Amblin Entertainment.

Originally planned as part of the 1980s *Amazing Stories* television series on NBC, and conceived by Mick Garris (there's a clue for a start, given the number of Stephen King stories Garris subsequently adapted for the screen), *Batteries Not Included* isn't the family-friendly film it's often regarded as.

Early on in the film, for instance, we see how a building development is advancing, and how the people behind it want the last apartment building and café standing in their way pulled down. (A not dissimilar theme would pop up in another Spielberg-overseen production, *Gremlins 2: The New Batch*, in 1990.) The residents all get sizable monetary offers but don't want to move, and so the heavies are sent in.

This alone is put across in a fairly brutal way. But re-watching *Batteries Not Included*

Batteries Not Included had its roots in US TV show *Amazing Stories*.

today, two things really come across: first, that the film stands up really very well; and second, that the late Jessica Tandy's performance is both haunting and wonderful.

In the midst of the story, there's a heartbreaking relationship between Tandy and her screen husband, Hume Cronyn (they were real-life husband and wife, too). While Tandy's character at first comes across as a dotty old lady, the reasons gradually present themselves, and the heart of the film's story is revealed: the loss of her son. That's a big thing to explore in such a movie. But then, it's a far more interesting, deeper film than it may at first appear. It's all the better for it and, as a consequence, resonates deeper than all the *Ice Age* films you can find in the family corner of the DVD shop.

WATCHING FILMS

SPOILER ALERT!

INSIDE OUT, TRANSFORMERS: THE MOVIE, THE NEVERENDING STORY, THE IRON GIANT, WATERSHIP DOWN

FAMILY MOVIES THAT TRAUMATIZE SMALL CHILDREN

Best Picture Oscar nominee *Babe* is regarded as something of a family treat, yet it begins with a truck backing up to take pigs off to the abattoir. There's a subset of family movies that go still further and find ways to traumatize the younger audience they're trying to entertain. You probably already know about some – hello, *Bambi* and *Chitty Chitty Bang Bang* – but here's a list of some films to watch with ankle-biters only at your peril.

INSIDE OUT (2015)

A moment that seemed to break slightly more grown-ups than children, but is nonetheless a real gut-wrencher, is the point in Pixar's outstanding *Inside Out* where the character of Bing Bong sacrifices himself. This is so that the protagonist of the story, 11-year-old Riley, can have Joy (metaphorically and literally) in her life. "Take her to the moon for me," Bing Bong says, as half the audience breaks on the spot.

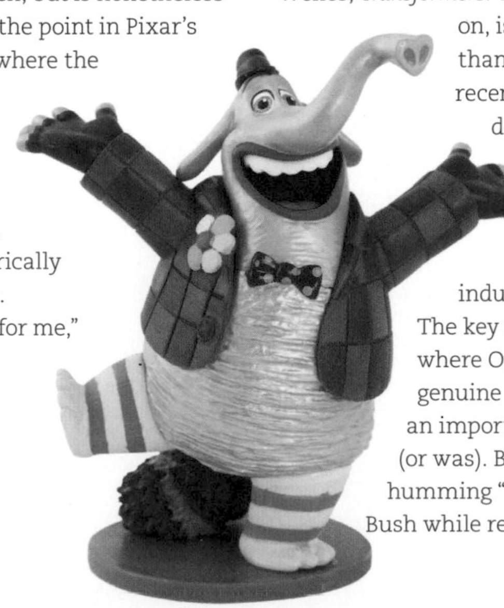

Inside Out's Bing Bong.

TRANSFORMERS: THE MOVIE (1986)

Infamously the final screen work of Orson Welles, *Transformers: The Movie*, decades on, is a whole lot better than Michael Bay's more recent series of live-action destructathons. But to a generation of *Transformers* fans, the 1986 animated feature induces tears at 20 paces. The key moment? The part where Optimus Prime falls, a genuine surprise given just what an important character he is (or was). Bonus points to anyone humming "The Touch" by Stan Bush while reading this bit.

The NeverEnding Story ended soon enough for Artax.

THE NEVERENDING STORY (1984)
Notwithstanding the inevitability of a film called *The NeverEnding Story* getting sequels, this is a movie that also proves something else: if you want to upset small (and big) children, take out an animal. In this case, Artax the horse. He doesn't even get a quick demise, slowly sinking into the Swamp of Sadness. The more he moves, the more he sinks. Deeper, and deeper, and deeper. Until…sob.

THE IRON GIANT (1999)
One of the most criminally underseen family movies of recent times, Brad Bird's exquisite adaptation of Ted Hughes's *The Iron Man* does more in under 90 minutes than the majority of multiplex fillers can do in twice the time. It ends on a majestic moment, as our hero flies toward the sky, uttering the word "Superman". It proves to be more upsetting than the entirety of *Superman IV: The Quest for Peace*.

THE HUNCHBACK OF NOTRE DAME (1996)
A hugely underrated Disney venture, this film stumbled at the box office a little. Granted, adapting Victor Hugo's source book and making it family-friendly was always going to be a challenge. What's surprising is just how dark the film got. There's a mob berating the central character, sexual undertones and, most surprisingly, the main antagonist, Judge Frollo, singing a song – the terrific "Hellfire" – about his lust for the character of Esmeralda. You might be surprised to hear that Disney got a few complaints…

WILLY WONKA & THE CHOCOLATE FACTORY (1971)
Not the tame and neutered 2005 take on the Roald Dahl classic *Charlie and the Chocolate Factory*, which starred Johnny Depp. No, for an unnerving family movie, the 1971 version of the story is your go-to. The late Gene Wilder is particularly wonderful and

unsettling, not least when his Willy Wonka takes a bunch of children on a sinister, psychedelic boat trip on a chocolate river. His "you lose" rant at the end is a bit of a shake-up, too. Dahl never liked the 1971 film take on his story, but it would be fair to say that most people disagree with him about it.

INDIANA JONES AND THE TEMPLE OF DOOM (1984)

A film that was given a PG certificate both in the UK and the US, *Indiana Jones and the Temple of Doom* barely warrants such a soft rating. (The uncut version was since classified a 12 in the UK, but even that's pushing it.) George Lucas, who was the executive producer and who came up with the story, would admit in a subsequent documentary about the making of the film that he was "not in a good mood" when making it, in part because of the divorce he was going through. Director Steven Spielberg, too, had concerns over just how dark the film is. And with good reason. For all its merits (and there really are many), this is the *Indiana Jones* movie with the chilled monkey brains, with people being lowered onto flames, and a human sacrifice being burned to death. Cheery stuff.

WATERSHIP DOWN (1978)

Most parents and guardians by now are oh-so-familiar with the golden rule of not showing their children the film of *Watership Down* unless they're willing to deal with the consequent emotional meltdowns. Based on the book by Richard Adams, director Martin Rosen's film is pretty much a full-on traumatization assault. Take the slow death of Hazel the rabbit as one example.

"You've been feeling tired, haven't you?" goes the voice, as Hazel is gently encouraged to die. He duly lies down, his soul leaves his body and children around the world wonder why they weren't allowed to watch *The Jungle Book* instead. It's a strong film, this, but not an obvious choice for a kids' party.

WHO FRAMED ROGER RABBIT (1988)

A film whose title is written without punctuation, given that Hollywood has decreed that films with a question mark in the title tend to fail, *Who Framed Roger Rabbit* was a ground-breaking piece of work in 1988. It still stands up today, and it still manages to scare the life out of viewers of a certain age. The reason? Christopher Lloyd, oh-so-friendly and warm in the *Back to the Future* films, as the genuinely terrifying Judge Doom. The toxic-chemical dip early on in the film instantly marks him as a character to genuinely fear. And then there are those eyes.

Christopher Lloyd (*right*) in *Who Framed Roger Rabbit*: a performance terrifyingly against type.

Perhaps the most infamous animated movie that Disney has ever made, *The Black Cauldron* came together when the studio was on the verge of abandoning animation altogether. An adaptation, although not a particularly close one, of Lloyd Alexander's *The Chronicles of Prydain* books, it was in development for over a decade, finally arriving in cinemas long after the deadline and over budget in 1985.

The film had been all set to be unleashed in 1984, but a private test screening horrified Disney's top brass. Children in attendance, traumatized and upset by what they'd seen, were reported to be leaving before the end. Jeffrey Katzenberg had just been appointed as chairman of the Disney studio, and he had no intention of letting the film out in the state it was in. He

ordered cuts and changes, to which producer Joe Hale objected. Katzenberg duly went to the editing room and started cutting the film himself, and it took Disney's CEO, Michael Eisner, to persuade him to stop. Katzenberg then insisted the release be delayed to the summer of 1985, to allow modifications to be made.

Even with the modifications – which removed further scenes of violence, and one of partial nudity – the final version remains brutal. Once the cheery Disney logo has gone, the film opens, for example, with dark clouds and a sinister voice-over about a cruel king being thrown into molten iron. At least they don't show it, right? Well, hold tight, because by the end there has been death, peril, pretty relentless threat and the small matter of the Horned King. Unusually for Disney, there's

little levity, either. There aren't the moments to punctuate the doom and gloom, and you're left with a relentlessly dark and downright scary movie, with a nice cuddly Disney logo at the start.

The film marked a turning point for animation at the studio, with Katzenberg becoming more hands-on, and projects no longer allowed to drift through development. Within four years, *The Little Mermaid* would be released, starting a second golden wave of animation at the studio.

As for *The Black Cauldron*, Disney has never quite known what to do with it since. It has had the odd quiet DVD and video release, but there's little chance, it seems, of a detailed special edition. You can probably guess what chance it has of getting a proper cinema re-release, too, or finding a ride based on it in a Disney theme park. The studio has not deleted *The Black Cauldron* or entirely hidden it away (and there's an awful lot to like in it). But it is unlikely ever again to have its name up in lights.

The Black Cauldron: one Disney animation you won't find in any of its theme parks.

HOW HOME MOVIE FORMATS HAVE EVOLVED

Since the mid 1970s, technology has been in place to let us watch movies at home. It explains why so many of us have multiple copies of *Die Hard* that work on different machines. Here are the key home movie-watching formats.

VHS

LAUNCHED: 1976
DEVELOPER: JVC

It may have been technically inferior to Betamax, but the Video Home System (VHS to its mates) was marketed better, was more inclusive and cost less. JVC made the VHS standard an open one, meaning other manufacturers could easily support it. They did, and VHS was the dominant home entertainment format for the best part of two decades as a result.

BETAMAX

LAUNCHED: 1975
DEVELOPER: SONY

The first, and technically superior, videotape format, this was ultimately hamstrung by its higher cost, among other factors. Betamax quickly gained market share on launch, but was ultimately defeated by VHS. Sony would switch to making VHS decks in 1988. Betamax, though, still found use as a professional format and wasn't retired until 2016.

LASERDISC

LAUNCHED: 1978
DEVELOPER: MCA

The first movie disc format (albeit one grounded in analogue technology), LaserDiscs offered a notably better level of quality than VHS tapes. The inconvenience of often having to flip a disc over mid-movie won it fewer friends, but, even today, LaserDiscs are regarded warmly by film collectors, not least for some of the extra feature content, some of which never made it to DVD.

The humble video cassette (above). Now piling up in second-hand shops near you.
The laserdisc format (right) enjoyed some niche success, particularly in the later 1980s and early 1990s.

DVD

LAUNCHED: 1995
DEVELOPERS: SONY, PHILIPS, TOSHIBA, PANASONIC

A natural successor to VHS and LaserDisc, DVDs – or Digital Versatile Discs – became the fastest-selling format of its ilk at launch. Affordable, good-quality and introducing special features on discs to a broader audience, DVD established itself as the most popular physical format on which to watch a film.

HD DVD

LAUNCHED: 2006
DEVELOPERS: DVD FORUM, TOSHIBA

With the introduction of high-definition televisions came the disc formats to take advantage of the better resolution such sets offered. HD DVD was first, but it would lose a bitter and expensive format war with Blu-ray – though not before a few hundred titles had been released. Toshiba pulled the plug in 2008, after Warner Bros. opted to release high-definition films exclusively on Blu-ray instead.

BLU-RAY

LAUNCHED: 2006
DEVELOPERS: BLU-RAY DISC ASSOCIATION, SONY

Sony had to spend big to ensure Blu-ray prevailed over HD DVD, but it got its victory: the format became the second-biggest seller, behind Blu-ray, and, until the launch of Ultra HD Blu-ray in 2016, was the format of choice for home cinema enthusiasts.

ULTRA HD 4K BLU-RAY

LAUNCHED: 2016
DEVELOPERS: BLU-RAY DISC ASSOCIATION, SONY

Quite possibly the last disc-based movie format, as more and more people switch to streaming services such as Netflix and iTunes, Ultra HD Blu-ray has a far greater capacity than standard Blu-ray and is designed to support the new generation of 4K televisions. Take up at the launch was a little sluggish.

AND DON'T FORGET...

VCD

As the name suggests, video CD – or VCD – was simply packing films onto a compact disc. Unfortunately, the data demands of a film meant that the resolution/quality of movies on VCD was notably on the poor side, even with later, evolved versions of the format, such as SVCD. VCD, however, continues to enjoy success in parts of Asia.

UMD

When Sony launched its PSP hand-held games console, it introduced the UMD, or Universal Media Disc. It released movies on the format, but take-up was poor. UMD movies swiftly became settled in their new home: the bargain bin.

MYSTERIES LEFT BEHIND BY THE *BACK TO THE FUTURE* TRILOGY

When you've watched a film series that you love time and again, you can't help but come up with a few questions, and notice things you might not have seen before. Anything to do with time travel – from the joyous *Time After Time* through to half of *Doctor Who* – opens up further paradoxes and questions. To give a flavour of just how this can go, here are a few questions left over from the *Back to the Future* trilogy. They don't make us love the films any less, mind.

WOULDN'T GEORGE AND LORRAINE RECOGNIZE MARTY?

Most long-standing couples will remember the moment they first got together, and the people around them. In the first *Back to the Future* film, George and Lorraine are brought together by their son, Marty. He, of course, has zoomed back to 1955, and needs to make sure his parents fall in love, lest he won't exist in 1985.

Surely, at some point, as George and Lorraine grow older, they would look at their offspring and begin to think that he might look awfully familiar. Or maybe, after having three kids, anything that happened pre-parenting was wiped from their memory.

1885, AND ITS MULTIPLE DELOREANS

Stay with us. At the end of *Back to the Future Part II*, Doc Brown is flying the DeLorean and gets zapped by lightning, heading back to 1885. At the start of *Back to the Future Part III*, Marty goes back from 1955 to 1885 to rescue Doc, and hides the time machine in a cave. But what happened to the version of the DeLorean that Doc got zapped in? Sure, he left it for Marty to find in 1955, but at some point wouldn't two versions of it have been in 1885 at the same time? Your head has permission to hurt at this point.

WHY NOT PAY BUFORD TANNEN THE $80?

In *Back to the Future Part III*, we learn that Doc's demise in 1885 is because he was shot by Buford Tannen over the matter of $80. But – hold on again – Doc in 1885 is the older, 1985 version. The 1955 Doc discovers the reason for his death, and thus – following this still? – the 1985 Doc would have this information, too. He arrives back in 1885 with plenty of

In 30 years' time, this moment should kick-start a conversation or two...

time to settle the debt or take preventive action. He's had 30 years of his own life to come up with a plan, after all.

DOC'S NOTE

At the end of *Back to the Future Part II*, Western Union delivers a note to Marty, immediately after the lightning bolt has hit the time machine. Why, then, didn't Doc leave a longer note? Again, he knows what's coming, so why not ask Marty to just pop back with some fuel, or some parts from the future that might be useful? Maybe some nice snacks?

SURELY THERE'S A BETTER TIME TO STEAL BACK THE ALMANAC?

In *Back to the Future Part II*, Biff Tannen is given a copy of *Grays Sports Almanac* in 1955 for his future self, which in turn transforms his life, and 1985. Doc and Marty thus go back to 1955 to take the book off him pretty much straight away. But wouldn't it be easier to wait until, say, 1956? We learn that Biff doesn't place bets for a year or two, so isn't there a more secure time when Marty could pinch it back?

THE ANSWER

Of course, the answer to all these conundrums – some of which have inspired much internet debate – is that you wouldn't have half as much fun with the movies without these paradoxes. They service the story that the filmmakers wanted to tell and, had rules been stringently obeyed, it's a fair bet that *Back to the Future Part III* would barely exist. And that just wouldn't do.

ALSO...

- If Doc can make a time machine and a freezer in 1885, what's stopping him tracking down some kerosene and getting hold of some gasoline from it?
- There's no way that the bear would have been able to appear suddenly out of that cave in *Back to the Future Part III*.
- If Doc is committed in 1955, when does he get to invent the time machine in the first place?
- Our heads now hurt even more...

STAR WARS: WHY DOES THE EMPIRE KEEP BUILDING DEATH STARS?

•••

Given that they want to win, why does the Empire and its offshoots keep on building Death Stars when they consistently fail? There are two explanations for this.

In 1977's *Star Wars* (aka *A New Hope*), the first Death Star is destroyed at the end, as a result of the Rebel Alliance capitalizing on a structural weakness. It was replaced by a second Death Star, which was destroyed at the end of 1983's *Return of the Jedi* after the Rebel Alliance capitalized on a structural weakness. In 2015's *Star Wars: The Force Awakens*, the First Order's base of operations is a mobile ice planet. Whereas the Death Stars could wipe out whole planets, this Starkiller Base could destroy whole systems. It was destroyed at the end of the film because the Resistance capitalized on a structural weakness. One of the explanations is based in the real world and one in the Star Wars universe.

THE IN-REAL-LIFE EXPLANATION

The Death Star is iconic. It blows up a whole planet. It went straight into our collective imaginations as shorthand for evil, epic, destructive capabilities. Likewise in *Star Wars: The Force Awakens* as soon as we realize that the planet is a Death Star, we know the score. That's why it keeps coming back, because it's cool and scary.

THE IN-STORY EXPLANATION

According to the legends, a long time ago, the Sith used huge Kyber crystals to build superlasers capable of obliterating entire planets, which – to cut a long story short – led to the evil Emperor pressing ahead with his Death Star battle station project.

Princess Leia came into possession of technical readouts for the station after the Rebel Alliance noted that anything called a Death Star can't be good, and sent in troops to recover the plans. It's worth noting that Grand Moff Tarkin really wanted the Death Star to succeed. He'd dedicated nearly 20 years of his life to a project that had some resistance within the Empire, as well as the sheer administrative nightmare of building a space station the size of a small moon in secret using the famously placid Wookiee race as slave labour. When you've spent a long time on a passion project, you do sometimes allow your heart to rule your head.

When it failed, the Emperor was miffed. He had the designer of the Death Star killed for allowing it one weakness, and then cloned him so he could begin work on the second

Make sure to fix that exhaust port next time, eh?

The second Death Star was constructed on the edge of the galaxy above Endor. The most rebellious planets would be hemmed in by the Imperial fleet until the new Death Star could arrive, with the logic being that destroying the planets with the bulk of the enemy on them would be a decisive blow against the rebellion. Fortunately, the Empire would never put up to two million military personnel in one location, so the same thing couldn't possibly happen to them. Twice.

Next, in *Star Wars: The Force Awakens*, the First Order was clearly inspired by the history of the Death Stars, which was in turn inspired by legends of the ancient Sith. And yet its destruction may have been averted if the First Order had watched *Jurassic World*. The underlying theme of that film was "bigger equals better", whereby the dinosaurs in the park were not deemed sufficiently awesome for tourists, and so a new, made-up creature had to happen.

The First Order regarded a planet-sized, galaxy-destroying battle station as the next step up from the Death Stars. However, to destroy a star system required a different and greater power source that was large enough to be dangerous to the planet itself. It needed to be regulated, thus providing a weakness for the base. The shield for the planet also had a weakness because of its size, and its controls were located in one place. In an attempt to prove themselves mightier than their predecessors, the First Order ended up failing in much the same way.

Conclusions? Building a moon-sized gun is somewhat overambitious. Trying to use said gun once the blueprints for it have been stolen is optimistic at best. And yet in both cases the possibility of success, with one decisive move, kept inspiring them to repeat their mistakes. As a wise man once said, "Don't get cocky, kid."

one. This just goes to show that a high-profile failure is not necessarily the end of your career, so much as an opportunity to get your name out there. It also shows the Emperor is perhaps blinkered in his vision, dedicated to destroying the rebellion and returning to the legendary days of Sith power. Hence, a second Death Star.

It was overseen by Tiaan Jerjerrod, who was afforded less time and money to build a superior battle station. While he ensured that the exhaust shafts were secured on this model, he was being asked to achieve the impossible by the Emperor in terms of rapid construction and deployment. When the Emperor arrived on the Death Star II, it was still unfinished. Nonetheless, he felt safe because of the security measures in place guarding the shield generators on Endor. There's almost certainly an excellent reason why the shield generators could not be kept behind the shield.

DO BOX OFFICE FLOPS ACTUALLY FLOP?

Once you make a film, in theory, it's out in the marketplace for ever. After all, we still buy and rent movies that are decades old. Why, then, is the world so quick to declare a film a "box office bomb"?

Even before its opening weekend was over, Disney's ever-efficient marketing department had fired out a press release championing the admittedly impressive box office numbers of 2016's *Doctor Strange*. The film, the press release told us, "has outperformed the opening weekends of *Captain America: The Winter Soldier*, *Guardians of the Galaxy* and fellow Marvel origin film *Ant-Man*". This news was duly parroted around the world, and with some reason: box office stories make popular new stories.

What they don't often make, however, is accurate ones. The film press – and film business as a whole – moves so quickly in the modern era that whether a film is a hit or a flop is defined both quickly and savagely. Granted, a home-formats release can turn a relatively modest box office performer – the original Austin Powers and Bourne movies, for instance, or the more recent *John Wick* (2014) – into a hit. But few seem to come back and write that story.

Most notably in box office reporting, there's the story of the "box office bomb" or "box office turkey". These are films that have seemingly done very badly, and no doubt lost the companies behind them lots of money. However, in the modern era, it's rare for a big film to lose an inordinate amount of money. Disney's ***Tomorrowland: A World Beyond* (2015)**, for instance, cost around $190m to make, and took $209.2m at the global box office. Bear in mind that Disney does well to get close to half of that box office revenue once cinemas and local distributors have taken their slice, and that's red ink aplenty. Headlines were formed, stories were written.

Because movie studios tend to be shareholder-owned, they need to provide regular financial reports, several times a year. Thus, when *Tomorrowland: A World Beyond* – and other financial disappointments for the studio, such as *John Carter* (2012) and *The Lone Ranger* (2013) – fell short, Disney announced to its investors a "write-down" on its expected earnings. "Disney could lose $140m on *Tomorrowland* flop," roared the headline in the *Hollywood Reporter*.

But could it? Box office returns are a significant, but far from exclusive, part of a film's takings. In days of old, the cliché was that a film's (expensive) cinema release was effectively a trailer for its home-video debut (which tended to be a lot more lucrative). DVD sales have long since peaked for studios, who enjoyed the significant riches they brought in the early to mid-2000s, in particular, before piracy and streaming really took hold. But even now, they bring in notable revenue.

Tomorrowland led to headlines of a Disney financial write-down.

As do on-demand streaming services. As do soundtrack albums. As do toys and merchandise, in-flight screenings, television premieres and suchlike.

Revenues for films may depreciate over time, but a movie can and often does keep earning for many decades after its original release. Whether that proves to be enough to plug the gap in *Tomorrowland*'s finances remains to be seen. But it's a fair bet that the reported $140m loss will turn out to be anything but.

<hr>

The 1995 movie **Waterworld**, starring Kevin Costner, tends to be routinely dismissed as a box office flop. *TIME* magazine, for instance, listed it in its "top 10 blockbuster bombs". CNBC described the film, wrongly, as "a commercial and critical disaster that almost destroyed his career". Yet the irony is that *Waterworld* turned a profit for Universal Studios.

The reason it attracted such notoriety is that, for a while, it was the most expensive movie ever made (until, two years' later, James Cameron sailed off with the crown with his Oscar-winning *Titanic*). Through 1994 and early 1995, stories of money being splashed away filled industry trade papers. *Waterworld* had the juicy ingredients: a big movie star deemed ripe for a fall, a production that seemed out of control, and a price tag of a then unheard-of $175m just for the negative. Throw in marketing and distribution costs, went the theory, and Universal would need to see around $500m in cinema takings to clear a profit.

In the end, it actually grossed $264m in cinemas, but turned out to be a strong hit on video. Between those two factors, the red ink would have been just about scrubbed out. In the meantime, Universal introduced Waterworld theme-park attractions and a range of merchandise. DVD and Blu-ray releases have also followed (including an

Waterworld: one of the most lucrative box office flops in history!

extended cut). It's a regular on TV stations around the world, and those, too, are a continual source of income.

There's a further factor that – thanks to some accountancy work that must have earned someone a tasty pizza – ensured *Waterworld* actually made a generous profit. At the time the film was being made, Universal's then-parent company, MCA, was in the process of selling the studio to new owners, Seagram. As part of the deal, Seagram ensured that the production costs for *Waterworld* didn't come with the package, and thus it took on post-production expenses, but not much more than that.

With the bulk of the expenditure lost in the midst of a multi-billion dollar company takeover, the bill to Universal, under its new owners, was estimated to be closer to just $12m in the end, plus distribution costs. Without that world class Microsoft Excel work, the film would have turned a modest profit. With it, the movie proved to be a very profitable project – but that makes a much less exciting headline.

Ironically, Kevin Costner's next-but-one film, 1997's *The Postman*, would prove to be a far costlier box office disappointment. It was made for $80m and took just $17.6m at the box office. With poorer home-video prospects, too, it's probably safer to call that one a box office failure.

There's a world of difference between a flop and a film that has killed off a franchise. On paper, the following three films all did good business. But they either didn't do enough of it, or they left audiences cold.

PLANET OF THE APES

2017's *War for the Planet of the Apes* brought to a conclusion of sorts a reboot for one of 20th Century Fox's most famous franchises. This particular strand started with 2011's *Rise of the Planet of the Apes*, but Fox had tried before, back in 2001, to get *Planet of the Apes* moving again. That time, it recruited Tim Burton, who would bemoan working on a studio movie in the aftermath of its release. The film did good business ($362m in cinemas), but you'd struggle to find someone to take a bullet for it, Burton included. (Even its star, Mark Wahlberg, would belatedly admit that "they didn't have the script right".) Fox agreed, and came to the conclusion that a sequel to a not-popular film would be a riskier venture than it had envisaged. It would take a decade for the reboot button to be pressed.

SUPERMAN

Bryan Singer's 2006 continuation of the Superman movie franchise (right down to the swoosh of the opening titles), with Brandon Routh in the blue tights, was intended to springboard a new series of films, as *Batman Begins* had done for *The Dark Knight* the year before. It struggled to do so, though the movie's reputation as a financial failure is unfair. It grossed $391m worldwide, against a $200m production budget. Warner Bros. abandoned its plan for an outright sequel, choosing to reboot again, with Henry Cavill in the lead role, for 2013's *Man of Steel*. A lack of audience enthusiasm for *Superman Returns* was reckoned to be the key reason.

SPIDER-MAN

Sony had great plans for a standalone Spider-Man movie universe, with films based around villains and supporting characters. The box office take of 2014's *The Amazing Spider-Man 2* ended those plans. Incredibly, the movie still took $708m at the box office, tripling its reported budget. The reason it is regarded as a flop is that the figure was down on the previous film, at a point when Sony was looking for growth. It thus called in Marvel, and Spider-Man – in the guise of Tom Holland – duly joined the Marvel cinematic universe in 2016's *Captain America: Civil War*, and 2017's *Spider-Man: Homecoming*.

Superman Returns did solid box office, but failed to win over its audience.

REMAKES THAT WORKED

With scores of films getting the remake treatment at any given moment, Hollywood won't stop poring over its back catalogue any time soon. But what's the obsession?

When director Steven Soderbergh embarked upon 2001's *Ocean's Eleven*, a remake of the 1960 film, he addressed the San Francisco Film Festival and had a strong point to make on movie remakes. "Why are you always remaking the famous movies? Why aren't you looking back into your catalogue and finding some sort of programme that was made 50 years ago that has a really good idea in it, that if you put some fresh talent on it, it could be really great?" he queried. He subsequently ripped up a few pages of his rulebook by remaking the Russian epic *Solaris*, but in fairness to him, he did get it down from 2¾ hours to just over 1½ hours. In contrast, the Brad Pitt vehicle *Meet Joe Black* was a three-hour glossy version of a film less than half its length. (Incredibly, the original movie – *Death Takes a Holiday* – was released as a DVD extra on a subsequent release of *Meet Joe Black*!)

Internet comment boards, with good reason, are quickly filled with groans and despair when it's revealed that the Hollywood system has another remake in mind, and it's not hard to see their point. In an era when getting people to go to big, expensive movies that aren't based on a pre-existing property is increasingly tricky, hearing that a new version of *The Naked Gun*, *Flatliners* or *Splash* is on the way rarely incites much joy.

That said, when a Martin Scorsese movie finally won Best Picture at the Oscars, it was for a remake (*The Departed*, a remake of the excellent Hong Kong thriller *Infernal Affairs*). Few, too, would quarrel with the different take he brought to his remake of *Cape Fear* in 1991.

That's the key thing, too. Although there is a large swathe of remakes that ultimately earn the "lazy" badge, there are also filmmakers who have seen something in previous material and tried to bring something different to it.

The 1986 version of **Little Shop of Horrors**, for instance, was a significant upgrade on the Roger Corman-directed 1960 original (a film

Robert De Niro in 1991's *Cape Fear*.

A solemn warning to clean your teeth courtesy of *Little Shop of Horrors*.

Even a heavily criticized remake, such as the 2012 retooling of *Total Recall*, brought some degree of interest and an in-built audience. The movie overcame scathing reviews and fan resistance, grossing nearly $200m at the box office. Granted, it was hardly a cheap venture – the budget was reported to be around the $120m mark – but without the *Total Recall* name, would its takings have climbed that high? Unlikely.

At any given time, there are a hundred or so remakes of some form or another in the works, even to the point of American hits being remade elsewhere in the world (a Japanese remake of *Ghost*, for instance, landed in 2010). Until audiences start giving them the short shrift that internet commenters tend to call for, they're going to keep on coming.

itself not without charm, nor Jack Nicholson), with an increased budget allowing a richer seam of comedy talent to be mined. The 1986 film was actually based on a 1982 musical, which in turn was based on the original movie. Furthermore, the musical's songs by Alan Menken and the late Howard Ashman injected something utterly fresh into the material. (The pair would pen the music and songs for Disney revival hits *The Little Mermaid* and *Beauty and the Beast*.) Plus the 1960 original didn't have Steve Martin's iconic dentist in it.

——————

Elsewhere, John Carpenter's 1982 take on **The Thing** is regarded as a modern(ish)-day horror masterpiece, but it too was a remake of sorts of 1951's *The Thing from Another World* (and it would be remade again, less successfully, in 2011, although that film is technically classed as a prequel). But more off-radar, director Breck Eisner took George A Romero's 1973 sci-fi horror *The Crazies* and found modern things to add in 2010, while not losing the thread of the original. Horror, in particular, has an up-and-down relationship with remakes (mainly down, in truth), but it's also the genre that plays host to a large share of them.

The reason remakes are so prevalent, as you'd expect, is that they're an easier sell.

ACCLAIMED FILMS THAT ARE ACTUALLY REMAKES

THE MAN WHO KNEW TOO MUCH (1956)

THE MAGNIFICENT SEVEN (1960)

INVASION OF THE BODY SNATCHERS (1978)

HEAVEN CAN WAIT (1978)

SCARFACE (1983)

THE FLY (1986)

DIRTY ROTTEN SCOUNDRELS (1988)

TRUE LIES (1994)

TWELVE MONKEYS (1995)

THE PARENT TRAP (1998)

THE THOMAS CROWN AFFAIR (1999)

INSOMNIA (2002)

TRUE GRIT (2010)

WHAT MAKES A GREAT SCREEN VILLAIN?

•••

The late film critic Roger Ebert once wrote, "Each film is only as good as its villain." There's a good reason for this: although the protagonist appears to do all the hard work in any given movie, it's the antagonist who gives them the work to do in the first place.

Although settings and genres are subject to constant change as tastes and fashions shift, it's the archetypal movie villain, perhaps, who has changed the least. Whatever genre you choose – western, fantasy, sci-fi, horror, realist drama – in the best of them you'll always find a compelling antagonist. Their goals and methods may vary, but ultimately their function is always the same: to make life hell for the other characters in the story.

This is probably why the typical villain changes relatively little from story to story; they can be convincing or cartoonlike, human or alien, male or female, but they're essentially performing the same task every time – they test the mettle of the protagonist or create a situation that the hero (or heroine) must somehow resolve.

Louise Fletcher in *One Flew Over the Cuckoo's Nest*.

Without Darth Vader, Luke Skywalker would still be a miserable farmhand on the lonely planet Tatooine. Had *Die Hard*'s Hans Gruber stayed at home instead of taking over the Nakatomi Plaza, cynical cop John McClane would never have rebuilt his relationship with his estranged wife, Holly. James Bond would probably have a desk job, and possibly even be married to Miss Moneypenny.

The evil exploits of villains are the hidden engines of any great movie, testing the resolve of the rest of the cast and altering the course of their lives, whether it's for the better (as in *Die Hard*) or for the infinitely worse (see *Seven*, in which the central character is left in psychological tatters by his nemesis, John Doe). Villains are the hero's worst enemy and the screenwriter's best friend.

None of this is to say that movie villains have to flaunt their wickedness as boldly or cartoonishly as Darth Vader, or as Loki from the *Thor* movies; some of the most disturbing big-screen antagonists are often the most mundane. As an example, take the flat-out terrifying Nurse Ratched from Milos Forman's classic 1975 drama *One Flew Over the Cuckoo's Nest*. As played by Louise Fletcher, Nurse Ratched rules over the inmates of an Oregon psychiatric hospital with a rod of iron. Jack Nicholson's spirited criminal Randle McMurphy soon winds up as Ratched's nemesis and gamely tries to overturn her strict regime; but as he ultimately learns, it's a battle of wits he simply can't win. Fletcher won an Oscar for her role, and it's strange to think that Nurse Ratched could have been played by any one of a number of other major actresses in contention, including Angela Lansbury.

These days, it's hard to imagine anyone else playing such a chilly character so effectively. Fletcher speaks in a calm, soothing tone, yet her eyes portray a steeliness and resolve that are impossible to argue with. In one quietly effective scene, Ratched gently overrules McMurphy's demands to have the music turned down in the rec room, proving herself to be a master of subtle manipulation. "If Mr McMurphy doesn't want to take his medication orally, I'm sure we can arrange for him to take it some other way."

Then there's Bill Lumbergh from Mike Judge's cult 1999 comedy *Office Space*. Lumbergh is the kind of mundane villain most of us will have encountered at some point in our lives. Thanks in no small part to a wonderfully beige performance from Gary Cole, Lumbergh is the ultimate horrible boss: with his precise hair and carefully pressed shirt and tie, he prides himself on being a casual, laid-back employer, yet spends his waking hours filling his workers' lives with psychological torment. Usually prefacing his sentences with the words, "Mmm. Yeah," Lumbergh's cool-guy self-image masks a heart of ice. Just look at the way he relentlessly pursues burnt-out programmer Peter Gibbons (Ron Livingstone) for "TPS reports". Or the callous way he orders permanently bewildered office drone Milton Waddams (Stephen Root) to move his desk down to the basement.

If the devil exists at all, he probably walks around offices with a mug in his hand saying things like, "Hello Peter, what's happening? Um, I'm gonna need you to go ahead and come in tomorrow. So if you could be here around nine that would be great. Oh, and I almost forgot – I'm also gonna need you to go ahead and come in on Sunday too, mmm, okay?"

Of course, movies offer a distorted reflection of the real world. In reality, people go about their daily lives and rarely come into conflict with each other. The heroes and villains of movies are our myths, as detached from our complicated yet mundane existence as the characters in ancient folklore.

It's often said that the good-versus-evil battle commonly depicted in movies is a comfort, because it simplifies the more nuanced and complex struggles of reality. This is why, perhaps, superhero films have soared in popularity in recent years; as warnings of terrorism and financial collapse have filled contemporary headlines, we've taken refuge in movies, where the boundaries of what is right and wrong are more clearly defined. Just as stories need villains to create compelling action, so audiences have needed entertainment to make sense of the real world, and also divert their attention from it.

There is, however, a more fundamental reason why we need good-versus-evil stories, and plots with compelling villains in particular. Where dramas and more realistic thrillers such as *The Godfather* or *Heat* attempt to offer a limited reflection of the real world – featuring complex, conflicted characters with their own agendas, as opposed to clearly defined heroes or villains – movies such as *The Avengers* or *The Dark Knight* trilogy are a reflection of a very different struggle: the one going on inside our heads.

In every person, there's a desire to fit in with the structure of society: to go to work, go to school, make friends, be successful and generally do one's bit as a good citizen. But then, there's also that part of the brain that is full of childlike mischief, that wants to kick over sandcastles, drive a bit faster than the speed limit or maybe run through a crowded shopping centre in a bear suit.

Freudian psychologists might refer to this internal conflict as the struggle between the superego, the ego and the id. But this is Den of Geek, so we'll illustrate the point with a film quote from *Apocalypse Now* instead: "there's a conflict in every human heart, between the rational and the irrational, between good

> **Sure, he's the bad guy, but wouldn't it be fun to be him, just for a while, to zap a few people?**

Loki (*left*): the Marvel cinematic universe's finest foe.

and evil. And good does not always triumph. Sometimes the dark side overcomes what Lincoln called the better angels of our nature."

This is why we quietly enjoy watching Tom Hiddleston's Loki swagger around and grin with his cape and horns in *The Avengers*; sure, he's the bad guy, but wouldn't it be fun to be him, just for a little while, to zap a few people with a magic spear and sneer at Robert Downey Jr? We might cower at the Joker's capacity for evil in *The Dark Knight*, but don't we also wonder what it would be like to be as joyfully, insanely uninhibited as he is? Doesn't he treat Gotham City in precisely the same way that players of, say, Grand Theft Auto IV do? Just as the heroes embody all the traits we might like for ourselves (bravery, strength, courage under fire, good hair), so the villains get to revel in the negative traits we all carry, but are required to suppress.

Movies like *The Avengers* allow both parts of our nature to play out – the bit of us that wants to see chaos and destruction, and the other part, the sensible piece that holds the darker side of our being in check. This is why, eventually, the bad guy usually has to lose. We've been entertained by their evil antics, but we also know that society couldn't function if everyone ran around behaving like a maniac. We've had a little look in Pandora's box, and we've been engrossed and perhaps a little disturbed by how much we've enjoyed what we've seen, but ultimately the lid has to close. The irrational part of our brain enjoyed the chaos, but the rational part understands that logic and order must be restored.

This is why the world needs movie villains. We may want to see light triumph over dark, but not before we've enjoyed the thrill of seeing evil throw off its shackles, run riot and maybe smash up a few cars for an hour or two. In a strictly ordered world, villains are everyone's favourite guilty pleasure.

FIVE UNDERRATED VILLAIN PERFORMANCES WORTH CHECKING OUT

SAMANTHA EGGAR: *THE BROOD*
Wild-eyed and unforgettably intimidating, Samantha Eggar is a mother of monsters in David Cronenberg's horror.

BRIAN COX: *MANHUNTER*
Casually psychotic, Brian Cox's turn as Dr Hannibal Lecter is a masterclass in understatement.

JOSEPH COTTON: *SHADOW OF A DOUBT*
Cotton hints at a murderous appetite beneath a respectable exterior in one of Alfred Hitchcock's best thrillers.

ANDY ROBINSON: *DIRTY HARRY*
Playing crazed killer Scorpio, Robinson equals Clint Eastwood's surly charisma. One of the best villains of all time.

RAY LIOTTA: UNLAWFUL ENTRY
Liotta's unhinged performance as a maniacal cop enlivens this by-the-numbers 1990s shocker.

Unlawful Entry: a middling thriller with a great villain.

SMALLER FILMS THAT HIT BIG

Writer and director Kevin Smith was pleased with the box office returns for 2006's *Clerks II*. The follow-up to his 1994 breakout hit had cost just $5m to make and had grossed $27m in cinemas. In the context of modern cinema, some saw $27m as a flop, but Smith was quick to counter that, actually, his nimbly budgeted film would see a profit – which hardly made it a flop.

That said, there are films with relatively tiny budgets that have gone on to make huge returns. Without needing to pay percentages to movie stars or to incur huge upfront costs, these are the movies that studios really crave. Here are ten of the biggest surprise breakout hits. (Note that marketing and distribution costs aren't accounted for in the budget figures – but even so…)

MAD MAX

COST: $200,000
BOX OFFICE: $100M

ROCKY

COST: $995,000
BOX OFFICE: $225M

THE BLAIR WITCH PROJECT

COST: $60,000
BOX OFFICE: $248.6M

MY BIG FAT GREEK WEDDING

COST: $5M
BOX OFFICE: $369M

GERARD DAMIANO'S
DEEP THROAT

HOW FAR DOES A GIRL HAVE TO GO TO UNTANGLE HER TINGLE?

The $100m takings from *Deep Throat* (above) are the ones that are (roughly) known about. Plenty of pirate copies did the rounds. The success of *Open Water* (below left) led to an unrelated film being badged *Open Water 2*.

DEEP THROAT

COST: $47,500
BOX OFFICE: $100M*

MAGIC MIKE

COST: $7M
BOX OFFICE: $167M

OPEN WATER

COST: $500,000
BOX OFFICE: $52M

THE FULL MONTY

COST: $3.5M
BOX OFFICE: $257.9M

PARANORMAL ACTIVITY

COST: $15,000
BOX OFFICE: $193.4M

GREASE

COST: $6M
BOX OFFICE: $394.9M

* There's no definite number here, with some claims putting the infamous adult film's takings closer to $600m. The $100m total is, of all things, an FBI estimate!

Grease (below) hit big. *Grease 2* did not.

HOW DOCTOR STRANGE AND PINK FLOYD ARE CONNECTED

•••

Doctor Strange and the rock band Pink Floyd both got their start during the 1960s, a decade of mind-expansion, psychedelic experimentation and the pushing of cultural and artistic boundaries. Yet neither was exactly in step with the rest of the genre.

Unlike his Spandex-clad and heavily muscled contemporaries, who employ brute force, the eponymous hero of the 2016 film *Doctor Strange* uses occult practices like black magic and astral projection to defeat his foes. He was based on Marvel's superhero Doctor Strange, who first appeared in 1963 in the comic entitled *Strange Tales*. Unsurprisingly, the *Doctor Strange* comics were popular on college campuses as the counterculture revolution of the 1960s began to take hold.

Nods to Pink Floyd are present and correct in Marvel's 2016 *Doctor Strange* blockbuster.

Founded in the mid-1960s, the band Pink Floyd was never really the kind of post-Beatles psychedelic pop group that was becoming more common by then, nor was it one of the blues-based hard rock or technically oriented progressive rock bands that dominated the 1970s. It's easy to imagine stoners disappearing into the surreal artwork of the *Doctor Strange* comics while early Pink Floyd records play, and to understand why psychedelic rockers were more drawn to these comics than to traditional superhero fare.

Scott Derrickson, director of the *Doctor Strange* film, dropped a number of Pink Floyd references on Twitter during production of his 2016 movie (as well as mentions of Bob Dylan, The Talking Heads, and other bands) and duly dropped a Pink Floyd song into a Marvel film for the first time. It highlights an interesting intertwine between movies and music.

The song, "Interstellar Overdrive", comes from the first Pink Floyd album, *The Piper at the Gates of Dawn*, released in 1967. The album abandoned the melodic but skewed psychedelic pop of their early singles "Arnold Layne" and "See Emily Play", for a collection of songs that were more metaphysical, sinister, and occasionally (as in the case of "Interstellar Overdrive") free-form explorations of sound

The original TV movie of *Doctor Strange*.

and feedback. The album version of this song clocks in at nearly ten minutes, but live versions could run longer – as long as the band wanted, really – and were accompanied by a psychedelic light show and oil projections that added to the whole mind-expanding mood and wouldn't have looked out of place in a *Doctor Strange* comic.

Pink Floyd's guitar player, singer and driving creative force in the early years was Syd Barrett, who left the group in 1968 because of his worsening mental illness, which was probably accelerated by his voracious appetite for mind-altering drugs like LSD. Marvel's *Doctor Strange* movie certainly leans heavily on imagery consistent with the visuals associated with LSD, psilocybin and mescaline trips (Strange even accuses the Ancient One of spiking his tea with psilocybin), which is fitting even if it isn't a direct connection to Pink Floyd.

Barrett was still present on a few tracks of the band's second album, 1968's *A Saucerful of Secrets*, which has a semi-hidden image of Doctor Strange on the cover. Not only is the collage effect reminiscent of the band's light shows and a representation of the psychedelic experience, but also the placement of Strange himself makes it look as if the whole album cover is a spell being cast by the Master of the Mystic Arts. The Strange elements come from

a story in 1967's *Strange Tales* comic, issue 158, with art by Marie Severin. (*Doctor Strange* co-creator Steve Ditko had left Marvel almost a year earlier.)

The album's title track, "A Saucerful of Secrets", could be seen as a sequel to "Interstellar Overdrive", as it's another extended instrumental that places more emphasis on experimental sound than it does on anything resembling a traditional rock song structure. In other words, it's the perfect accompaniment to your reading of weird *Doctor Strange* comics from the era. As an aside, you can also spot the Marvel cosmic entity the Living Tribunal in the upper left-hand corner of the album cover.

Doctor Strange was still on the band's radar enough that they included him in the lyrics of "Cymbaline" from their third album, 1969's soundtrack to the Barbet Schroeder film *More*.

The debut of *Doctor Strange*.

Benedict Cumberbatch, in 2016's *Doctor Strange* movie. A film rightly not shy of its Pink Floyd connections.

"Suddenly it strikes you/That they're moving into range/And Doctor Strange is always changing size," Syd Barrett's replacement, David Gilmour, intones solemnly. Funnily enough, "Cymbaline" was known as "Nightmare" when it was performed as part of the suite of songs *The Man and the Journey*, meaning it shared a name with the first villain that Strange ever fought in the comics.

Soon the band's lyrical focus drifted away from metaphysical concerns and into more earthly ones. While they continued to produce extended musical compositions, the atonal sounds of "Interstellar Overdrive" and "A Saucerful of Secrets" gave way to the more melodic "Echoes" and "Shine On You Crazy Diamond".

Returning the favour, if *Doctor Strange* was an influence on the band in their early days, you can perhaps see hints of Pink Floyd in the 1978 *Doctor Strange* TV movie. That one has a synth-heavy, at times funky, electronic soundtrack and an astral-trip visual sequence

that looks like some of the light-show projections for which they were known. "The Master of the Mystic Arts", the final song on Michael Giacchino's score to the 2016 *Doctor Strange* movie, subtly evokes some of the band's 1970s work, too.

One final piece of Doctor Strange/Pink Floyd synchronicity popped up in the month before the Marvel feature was released. *Doctor Strange* star Benedict Cumberbatch joined former Pink Floyd guitarist David Gilmour on stage to sing "Comfortably Numb", a song that started life as a demo called, funnily enough, "The Doctor". Whether this is coincidence, or simply the universe bringing the Pink Floyd/Doctor Strange connections full circle, is up to you to decide.

SPOILER ALERT!

BIG, TURNER & HOOCH, SLEEPLESS IN SEATTLE, YOU'VE GOT MAIL,
THE TERMINAL, CAST AWAY, FORREST GUMP

THE COLLATERAL DAMAGE OF TOM HANKS MOVIES

•••

With the best part of $10bn banked for his movies across his career, Tom Hanks remains one of the biggest and most interesting movie stars on the planet. He's got Oscars, he continues to pick interesting roles and he's someone who's stayed at the top of their particular game for the best part of three decades.

When you consider that Tom Hanks has achieved his successes without public meltdowns, without signs of turning into a diva and without putting us through many poor films the man is frankly a hero. But it comes at a cost – for, pouring through the Hanks back catalogue, it becomes clear that for him to enjoy a heroic ending, others must suffer. Here's the case for the prosecution.

BIG (1988)

This film earned Hanks his first Oscar nomination and was his breakthrough as a movie star. What's more, *Big* also still stands up as an endearing and much-loved comedy drama.

But spare a thought for Elizabeth Perkins's character, Susan. Hanks's Josh starts the film as a young boy, he spends most of the film as a grown-up and Susan falls in love with him. She leaves her (horrible) boyfriend and lets a man-child squeeze her bits and pieces, they sleep together, they bounce on a trampoline, and then they're callously parted by a Zoltar machine. It makes the ending far more haunting than you may remember.

We hear, but don't see, Josh's reunion with his mother (a pre-Oscar Mercedes Ruehl), with director Penny Marshall instead focusing on Susan's car driving up the street, as she comes to terms with the fact that she's just

Best not to think about the ending of *Big* too much…

Turner & Hooch. You're on emotionally safer ground with the James Belushi-headline *K-9*, released at around the same time.

dropped off a kid who's been missing for six weeks. Who she just happens to have slept with.

The least she could expect? A broken heart. The worst? Prison time, and lots of it.

TURNER & HOOCH (1989)

This is the one where Tom Hanks plays a police investigator by the name of Scott Turner, who has his working life perfectly in order. But what's this? He's paired with a big, slobbering dog, who turns his life upside down! It's like that James Belushi film, just without the German Shepherd and the car wash.

Turner, then, begs for and is given a murder case that has come in, and the key witness is indeed Hooch. Hooch is a talented beast, too: not only does he wreck Turner's house and car, but he also proves the catalyst for a romance with a vet. He is rewarded for this by

the screenwriters killing him off, a decision that Hanks has since admitted cost an awful lot of money at the box office. Hanks would bound up to the Oscar stage within five years. Hooch, er, wouldn't.

SLEEPLESS IN SEATTLE (1993)

The second pairing of Tom Hanks and Meg Ryan remains a well-loved romantic comedy, which takes inspiration from (the far superior) *An Affair to Remember*. Here, Hanks plays Sam, a man who has lost his wife to cancer, and lives with his young son. When he, for important plot reasons, goes on the radio on Christmas Eve to talk about his loss, his story bewitches a reporter on the other side of the country, Annie (which is where Meg Ryan comes in). The scene is set for a heart-warming mix of comedy, romance and drama.

But what's this? Annie Reed already has a boyfriend?! In fact, she's engaged to Walter – Bill Pullman, no less, future president of the United States (in *Independence Day*, that is) – and was presumably planning her happy life with him. At least until Tom turned up. Walter is summarily dismissed with a bit of dialogue, his life presumably wrecked off-screen. Cue the swirling music, as Hanks and Ryan unite, and get about plotting to upset someone else's life with yet another relationship broken-up in 1998's *You've Got Mail*.

THE TERMINAL (2004)

In Hanks's (limited) defence, this film is based on a true story, that of Viktor Navorski, who finds himself stranded at New York's JFK airport. The reason? Thanks to the outbreak of civil war in his homeland of Krakozhia, said country loses its recognition as a sovereign nation. Navorski thus can't enter America and can't go home. He has no choice but to begin living at the airport, as he does for the best part of a year.

The Terminal had the largest single set ever built for a Steven Spielberg movie. Not that it helped the janitor...

At the end of the film, the aforementioned civil war comes to an end. Viktor finally gets his chance to leave the airport and step outside into America, using an emergency one-day visa. However, when this becomes problematic, all looks doomed – until in comes janitor Gupta Rajan! He, too, has been stuck in America, in his case to avoid returning to India where he'll be arrested. But on learning that Viktor was about to give up and go home, Gupta runs in front of a plane, setting in train the events that lead to his own deportation. Viktor gets to go to America, Gupta gets to go to prison. Smashing.

CAST AWAY (2000)

Those who doubted the acting talents of Tom Hanks were served with a wonderful riposte in the form of his second collaboration with director Robert Zemeckis. In *Cast Away*, Hanks puts in a remarkable piece of work, holding the screen almost single-handedly for the film's running time.

He plays a FedEx systems analyst, who finds himself marooned on an island in the middle of nowhere. Time passes, Hanks gets hairy and thin, and friends are few and far between. With good reason, as it turns out. If he is to survive, the most brutal sacrifice of Hanks's career must take place: Wilson must float away, so that Hanks may live.

FORREST GUMP

Perhaps still Hanks's iconic role, *Forrest Gump* saw him win his second Oscar, just a year after he'd snared the first. But heck, across his near 2½ hours on screen, Forrest left his fair share of damage in his wake.

These are the characters who had to suffer so that Hanks could win his Oscar:

Lieutenant Dan Taylor, who just wanted to die like the rest of his platoon, but Forrest rescued him.

●●●

President Richard Nixon, as Forrest proves instrumental in exposing the Watergate scandal, which brings Nixon down.

●●●

Every shrimp boat but Forrest's. The only way he can build his successful Bubba Gump Shrimp Company is for a hurricane to wreck every other fishing boat in the vicinity, presumably destroying the livelihoods of a whole bunch of families in the process.

●●●

Jenny, who gives Forrest a son, who turns out to be that kid from *The Sixth Sense*. Jenny and Forrest don't get a happy ending, of course, as Jenny dies, leaving Forrest and Forrest Jr to have the uplifting ending together.

●●●

His mum. But that was down to old age, so we'll let Forrest off the hook on that one.

THE UNEROTIC EROTICA OF RELATIVELY MODERN MOVIES

Universal Pictures knew what it was doing when it scheduled the film adaptation of the non-porn-really-honest *Fifty Shades of Grey* for a Valentine's Day release in 2015. And after the studio watched over half a billion dollars in takings roll into its coffers, *Fifty Shades Darker* and *Fifty Shades Freed's* film versions were also given romantic February release dates. But the movies, we've learned over time, are as good at discouraging bedroom activities as they are at inciting them.

VICIOUS COMEDY

In fact, Hollywood is well aware of the cinematic value of a great big row, which must make a terrific night out for a couple trying to leave domestic disputes behind them. The delightfully vicious 1989 comedy *The War of the Roses*, with Danny DeVito in the director's chair, saw Michael Douglas and Kathleen Turner taking verbal chunks out of one another, with DeVito sort of acting as referee.

Jennifer Aniston and Vince Vaughn struck box office gold with a good barney, too: *The Break-Up*, from eventual *Ant-Man* director Peyton Reed, wasn't at the same level, but it was a summer success. However, it did lean heavily on romantic comedy trappings – and marketing – to help sell the picture in the first place.

The War of the Roses: a perfect (last) date movie.

INHUMAN RELATIONSHIPS

Often, it's the films not billed in the first place as romantic comedies that tend to go a little off-piste with their more tender moments. It's hard to think of too many examples as offbeat as the already completely bonkers *Howard the Duck* movie of 1986, which was regarded by some as an infamous box office turkey, but by others as an underrated treat. Yet all would surely agree that they have not seen a film quite like it.

Yeah. A caption can't really explain this. Um, can we move on?

The most bizarre moment? Surely, *surely*, it's the bedroom scene. Just the year before, Lea Thompson had been seen on the big screen in the first *Back to the Future* film, a huge box office success and one that, decades later, is still at least as popular as it was then. But the year after its release, she would be lying in bed in luxurious undergarments, alongside a man dressed as a giant duck. There have been films in the past that have tried to make an affection for animals into a central plot device, yet *Howard the Duck* plays it in a matter-of-fact way. It's a case of blinking twice to see if your eyes are deceiving you. Incredibly, the film got a "PG" rating on its US release.

A few more recommendations if you're looking to be put off sex entirely. Brett Leonard's 1992 virtual-reality sci-fi movie, originally entitled *Stephen King's The Lawnmower Man* became infamous when Stephen King demanded his name be taken out of the title. It had been sold as being based on a King short story, but the author objected, claiming in court that the finished film bore no resemblance to his original story, and the court agreed. Nowhere in his writing will you find a scene where two metallic gloops embrace on screen. For a more modern

equivalent, try digging out the extended version of James Cameron's *Avatar*, in which two blue and hairy creatures indulge in a little plug and play.

If these examples don't put you off, then spare a thought for Jeff Goldblum and Geena Davis, who manage to break through an assortment of mental firewalls and begin a relationship in David Cronenberg's 1986 classic sci-fi horror film *The Fly*. When Goldblum's Seth Brundle starts sprouting bristly hairs on his back, Davis's character becomes justifiably alarmed, and matters go from bad to worse. As Renée Zellweger put it in *Jerry Maguire*, it would run "a distant second to a good book and a warm bath".

The Fly's love scene. One of those moments where it might have been best to pretend to have a headache.

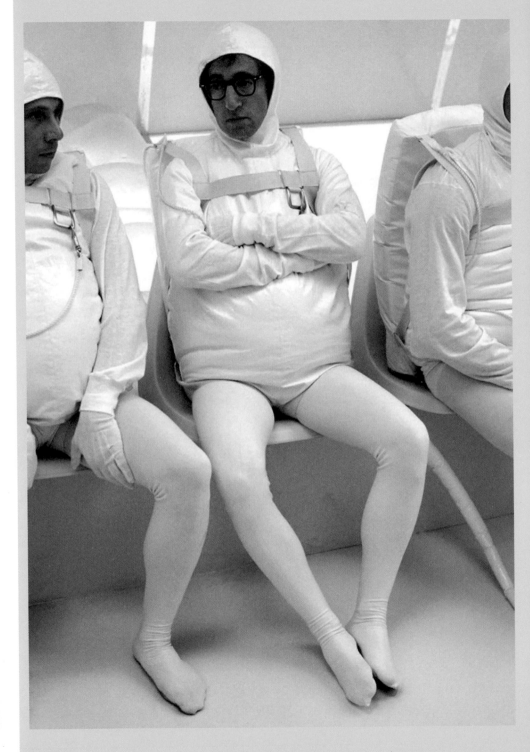

SAFE SEX

The mid- to late-1980s were notable for a public health crusade to educate people in the need for safe sex, and in particular the use of condoms. Trust, then, the team of 1989's *The Naked Gun: From the Files of Police Squad!* to take this to its logical extreme. Anyone settling down with their date would have been confronted with Leslie Nielsen and Priscilla Presley wrapped in full body condoms, with barely the risk of touching each other, yet alone infecting one another.

The towering comedy moment to put any couple off coupling, though, is surely the final sequence in Woody Allen's majestic 1972 film *Everything You Always Wanted to Know About Sex* (But Were Afraid to Ask)*. This movie would be a curious choice for a first date at the best of times, but the final segment of the film sees Allen playing a sperm – still in his glasses – about to make his exit.

DISPASSIONATE KISSES

Animators will tell you that in the days of hand-drawn animation, a kiss was the hardest thing to realize. In truth, some humans also really struggle with it. Take the 1994 apparent rom-com *I Love Trouble*. It was no secret that co-stars Julia Roberts and Nick Nolte really couldn't stand each other, and the moments where they're supposed to be drawn together in a romantic coupling have all the chemistry of rusty fridge-freezers. The year before, the off-screen coldness between Sharon Stone and Alec Baldwin was entirely reflected in cinemas worldwide, where *Sliver* was projected many feet high.

Mind you, a good old-fashioned smooch has been used for horror purposes to top effect a few times. In 1991's *Bill & Ted's Bogus Journey*,

Granny's kiss is treated as a nightmare (rightly in this instance – no disrespect to your own granny). Three years later, Donald Sutherland's open mouth heading for the camera lens jolted audiences back in their seats in a dream sequence for *Disclosure*.

FURTHER VIEWING

If you're a sucker for the anti-erotic erotic movie, then Paul Verhoeven's 1995 *Showgirls* is better as an advertisement for swimming pools than as any kind of aphrodisiac.

Without going down Spoiler Avenue, it'd also be fair to point out that a scene near the end of Neil Jordan's superb 1992 thriller *The Crying Game* may not hold universal erotic appeal.

That same year, Peter Jackson's *Braindead* answered the rarely asked question, "What do zombies look like when they're limb mingling?"

Jason Statham's approach to public interaction sees him in the middle of a muddy racing track, generating necessary sparks with Amy Smart in the utterly bananas *Crank: High Voltage*. There are many times in which a *Crank* film is appropriate viewing, but date night might just be pushing it.

The latest "imminent" Woody Allen release.

A FEW REMARKABLE THINGS ABOUT REMARKABLY BAD MOVIES

Even the worst movies have their highlights. If you're stuck indoors on a wet day with one of the following to watch, keep an eye out for some of the surprising highlights to be found in, um, "less impressive films".

SPECIES MAY HAVE A CONNECTION TO A BLOODSUCKING MONSTER IN PUERTO RICO

Reviews for the 1995 horror-thriller *Species* weren't particularly favourable, but its box office was strong enough to hasten the making of one theatrical sequel (*Species II*, 1998) and the direct-to-video outings *Species III* (2004) and *Species: The Awakening* (2007).

Weirdly, *Species* lives on in modern culture in a way that its makers couldn't have possibly foreseen. In the mid-1990s, reports began to surface that livestock in Latin American countries had been found dead and apparently drained of their blood. Puerto Rico resident Madelyne Tolentino claimed to have seen the culprit: a short, athletic humanoid creature with dark reptilian skin and spines running up and down its back.

Species: the original film is okay, the sequels less so.

Writer and crypto-zoologist Benjamin Radford spent several years investigating the legend of the chupacabra (literally, "goat-sucker") and published the book *Tracking the Chupacabra: The Vampire Beast in Fact, Fiction and Folklore*. Radford concluded that Tolentino's description of the creature was almost certainly influenced by the appearance of the H R Giger-designed monster in *Species* – the witness even admitted she'd seen the film, which came out just one month before she reported her sighting.

Since 1995, reports of chupacabras and animal slayings have proliferated all over the Americas. In most instances, experts have concluded that the sightings were probably of mange-ridden coyotes rather than something unexplainable.

IN 1986'S *KING KONG LIVES*, MRS KONG FALLS THROUGH A BARN

Given the reduced budget that *King Kong Lives* was faced with, it's little surprise that the sequel can't afford to restage the 1976 remake's climax atop the World Trade Center. Instead, writers Ronald Shusett and Steven Pressfield stage a similar confrontation at a barn dance.

King Kong has rescued Lady Kong from an army "Primate Holding Division" – which suggests the army makes a habit of capturing apes, for some reason – and is on the run from a horde of soldiers. But with Mrs Kong heavily pregnant and about to go into labour, she falls through the roof of a barn, sending locals scattering and leaving King Kong to face the assembled army by himself. Kong fights valiantly, smashing tanks and stomping soldiers, even as his body is riddled with stinging bullets. Although mortally wounded, Kong manages to crush the villain with a clenched fist, before collapsing next to the barn where Lady Kong is in the throes of childbirth. King Kong's final scene is unique, in that it's both absolutely ridiculous and moving. The sight of Mrs Kong, in bed in a barn and holding her oddly proportioned baby while King looks on with tears in his fading eyes is strangely affecting – mostly because, despite all the variable special effects and silly storytelling, King Kong remains a noble, likable movie creation.

Although the film's lower budget is obvious in almost every effects shot, it's the flirting and eye-batting apes that make this maligned sequel so entertaining. Even the filmmakers realize that the Kongs are the true stars of the piece, with the actors who play them listed first in the end credits. So despite – or perhaps because of – some iffy men-in-hairy-suits effects, some notably flat cinematography and rushed sound design, *King Kong Lives* remains a curiously charming relic in King Kong's film history, even though it sits firmly in the camp of, say, Ishiro Honda's *King Kong Escapes* rather than the majestic 1933 original. But then again, making daft sequels to King Kong

King Kong Lives: a film hampered by its obviously limited budget.

films is as old as the series itself, with the largely forgotten *Son of Kong* rushed out within months of the first film's huge success. What *Son Of Kong*'s screenwriter, Ruth Rose, said of that film also applies perfectly to *King Kong Lives*: "If you can't make it bigger, make it funnier…"

out of the water and, with surgical precision, chomps off the poor chap's arm. Sean's screams for help are drowned out by the warbles of carol singers, and he, along with a fair percentage of his boat, is hungrily devoured. Ho, ho, ho!

IN *SUPERMAN IV: THE QUEST FOR PEACE,* A FEW FIRE HYDRANTS TURN A UK TOWN INTO MANHATTAN

Where the directors of previous Superman movies had the budget to film in downtown Manhattan, Sidney J Furie had to make do with various hurriedly dressed locations in the UK for 1987's *Superman IV.* An early scene, in which Lois Lane (Margot Kidder) is trapped on an out-of-control Metropolis subway train, is clearly shot in the London Underground – all the "This is America, honest" posters dotted around can't disguise the distinctive shape of Britain's Tube trains.

The film's most infamous money-saving location, though, is its use of a bus station in Milton Keynes, UK, as a stand-in for New York's United Nations Headquarters on 42nd Street. As Christopher Reeve gloomily put it in his autobiography *Still Me,* "we had to shoot at an industrial park in England in the rain with about a hundred extras, not a car in sight, and a dozen pigeons thrown in for atmosphere".

It's impossible to imagine just how depressing it must have been to set up this particular shot. You're in Milton Keynes, you have a

JAWS: THE REVENGE IS A CHRISTMAS MOVIE

This is a fact easily missed, mostly because you'll be alternately yawning and laughing, but tawdry sequel *Jaws: The Revenge* can be counted alongside *Die Hard, Gremlins, It's a Wonderful Life* and *Jingle All The Way* as a Christmas movie.

It's a few days before Christmas when *Jaws: The Revenge* begins, and all around Amity Island snow has fallen. Sean Brody (Mitchell Anderson), son of Martin and Ellen, is now a police deputy and will soon become the first victim of yet another killer shark. As Sean is removing a log from a buoy floating in Amityville harbour, the Great White lunges

Oddly, since *Superman IV*, no filmmakers have tried to get Milton Keynes to double for New York City again.

Halle Berry went from Oscar-winning glory in *Monster's Ball* to, er, this…

few dozen extras, and Christopher Reeve walking around in his cape, yet the location still doesn't look like New York; it looks like a lonely part of a modern British city. Fortunately, one of *Superman IV*'s production designers decided that the use of a few props – a hotdog seller, a woman carrying an "I Love NY" bag and a few polystyrene fire hydrants – would help convince audiences that Superman really was on his way to the UN building.

Various other British locations were immortalized in *Superman IV*, too; Clark Kent's Smallville farm was actually shot in Baldock, Hertfordshire, while a disused airfield in St Albans became a US Air Force base.

"Don't worry," a location scout probably said during filming. "We'll stick a couple of fire hydrants around the place, and nobody will suspect a thing."

IN *CATWOMAN*, HALLE BERRY ACTS LIKE AN ACTUAL CAT

The production of 2004's disastrous *Catwoman* took more than a few liberties with the character as depicted by DC comics. As well as being supernaturally strong and agile, Halle Berry's Catwoman can fall from great heights and still land on her feet without harming herself; she gets all excited over little bundles of catnip, hisses at dogs and squeezes through narrow gaps. In one weird scene, she's shown lying on her bed, hungrily devouring cat food. In another bit, she flees in terror from raindrops.

SPOILER ALERT!

BATMAN, FAST FIVE (FAST & FURIOUS 5 IN THE UK), *LETHAL WEAPON 2, DRIVE, ENTER THE DRAGON*

MOVIE VILLAINS WHO KILL THEIR INCOMPETENT HENCHMEN

For the sociopathic action-movie villain, gunning down a slack-jawed henchman is the equivalent of smashing a computer keyboard during a hard day at the office. Usually accompanied by the immortal words, "You've failed me for the last time", the death of said henchman sends a clear message to underlings and viewers alike: this guy means business.

THE JOKER: *BATMAN*

Few scenes sum up the frustration of being a movie villain better than this one from Tim Burton's *Batman*. "He stole my balloons! Why didn't someone tell me he had one of those…things?" Jack Nicholson's Joker wails as Batman foils yet another evil scheme. The Joker politely asks his henchman Bob (Tracey Walter) for his gun – and then shoots him with it. Sometimes, kicking a bin in a fit of pique just isn't enough.

HERNAN REYES: *FAST FIVE*

Drug lord Hernan Reyes (Joaquim de Almeida) doesn't get many scenes in *Fast Five*, but he's at least given his own henchman murder for us to enjoy. Here, Reyes is so frustrated at the loss of a microchip that he beats one of his goons to death with a small bronze

Jack Nicholson as The Joker. If he places a job ad, best not reply.

sculpture sitting on his desk. It's not the most memorable scene on this list, but it does represent one of the few times a bad guy has killed a henchman with an objet d'art. Reyes may be impulsive, but he sure has class.

ARJEN RUDD: *LETHAL WEAPON 2*

In a scene designed to illustrate the vicious streak lurking beneath Rudd's avuncular demeanour, a henchman partly responsible for the loss of a fortune in coins is called into the villain's dimly lit office. "Mind the plastic," Rudd (Joss Ackland) says between mouthfuls of dinner, "I'm having some painting done." Rudd then has his number two, Vorstedt, shoot the henchman in the head while Rudd looks on, chewing. Disgraceful table manners.

AL CAPONE: *THE UNTOUCHABLES*

Having been let down by one of his henchmen, Robert De Niro's Al Capone makes a memorable dinner-table speech before battering a goon to death with a baseball bat. That's more than enough to put the guests off their dinner before the fish course has even arrived.

DARTH VADER: *A NEW HOPE* AND *THE EMPIRE STRIKES BACK*

Darth Vader is famous for venting his anger on British character actors in grey hats.

General Motti is choked but survives *A New Hope*, while the henchmen in *The Empire Strikes Back* are less lucky. Most famously, Vader chokes Admiral Ozzel while uttering the now classic line, "You have failed me for the last time". Later, Captain Needa also feels the wrath of the Sith. The Empire, it seems, had an extremely high turnover of staff while Darth Vader was around.

LARGO/ERNST BLOFELD: VARIOUS BOND MOVIES

The tendency for bad guys such as Ernst Blofeld to send minions to their doom is an oft-parodied element of the 007 movies. In *From Russia with Love*, Kronsteen is killed with a poisoned blade hidden in a shoe. Other memorable henchman deaths can be found in *Thunderball* and *You Only Live Twice*. Blofeld and other Bond villains seem to enjoy spending their money on installing elaborate traps with which to kill their employees. If only they'd invested the cash on a better human resources department, then they might end up with more competent henchpeople and a happier working environment.

BERNIE ROSE: *DRIVE*

Even this classy thriller has a henchman/ villain death scene, this time featuring Albert Brooks's shady crook Bernie Rose. Rose's methods are hideously violent: a fork in the face serves as his starter, followed by a knife to the throat for a main course. All of this occurs in Nino's low-rent Italian restaurant. As the famous song goes, "When a fork hits your eye like a big pizza pie..."

HAN/BOLO: *ENTER THE DRAGON*

In Bruce Lee's hit, the evil Mr Han (Shih Kien) has a Bond villain's tendency to slaughter his less competent staff, with the hulking Bolo (Bolo Yeung) his master executioner. In a stand-out scene, four useless guards are struck, crushed and snapped in two by the brawny right-hand man. In the most eye-watering moment, Bolo essentially hugs a man to death, before throwing his broken body on the floor like so much litter. Ouch.

HORRIFYING INCIDENTAL THINGS FROM THE ORIGINAL STAR WARS TRILOGY

Torture, flesh-eating bears, burnt aunts and uncles – for such a set of family-friendly films, there are some chilling inclusions in the *Star Wars* movies. Here are just a few of the horrifying incidental moments in the original *Star Wars* trilogy.

THE AT-ST IS 28 FEET OFF THE GROUND AND HAS NO OBVIOUS TOILET FACILITIES

We half-wonder whether the Empire lost the Battle of Endor not because of the Rebels' superior fighting skills, but because the pilots in the AT-STs were desperate to go to the toilet.

PRINCESS LEIA WAS BRUTALLY TORTURED

If Skywalker's having a bad day, consider poor Princess Leia. In one scene, we see her trapped in a cell as a hovering droid floats into view, a gleaming syringe jutting forth suggestively. Stoical to the last, Leia never once mentions what hideousness befell her in that cell on the Death Star.

SPACE SLUGS

In *The Empire Strikes Back*, Han Solo parks the *Millennium Falcon* inside an asteroid that is actually an exogorth – a creature capable of

growing to an unfathomably large size. So in the Star Wars universe, there are giant worms hiding inside asteroids, just waiting to snap at passing ships. The more we ponder this, the more terrifying we find it.

THERE ARE BAT-TYPE THINGS INSIDE THE SPACE SLUGS

While Han and Leia are inside the exogorth, they encounter a creature called the mynock. These are bat-like, power-sucking parasites, living inside space slugs. What if one of these asteroids crashed into Earth, killed the massive space slug but let all the bat-type things out in the process? Shudder.

UNCLE OWEN AND AUNT BERU'S TERRIBLE DEATH

Luke Skywalker has what could be described as the worst day of his life in *A New Hope*:

But where are the facilities?!

he returns home to see his aunt and uncle reduced to charred skeletons, then watches as his new-found mentor is struck down before his eyes. Considering everything he's been through, Skywalker is still remarkably chipper by the end of the film.

BEING R2-D2

Here's a scary existential scenario: imagine being R2-D2. You're capable, intelligent, and have a built-in hologram projector. Yet your makers failed to give you the gift of speech – instead, you can only communicate through a series of beeps and warbles. Then fate pairs you with someone like C-3PO, who flatly refuses to shut up.

LUKE SKYWALKER HAD HIS HAND CHOPPED OFF BY HIS OWN DAD

Imagine finding out that a wheezing monstrosity in a black helmet and cape was your father – and when you flatly refuse to join his gang, he tries to kill you. Most of us would probably turn to drink or bicycle theft after an experience like that.

EWOKS ARE FLESH-EATERS

The Ewoks are often condemned for being far too cute, but consider this: were it not for C-3PO, the Ewoks would have eaten Luke, Leia, Han and possibly Chewbacca as well. In a chilling final scene in *Return of the Jedi*, the furry critters use stormtrooper helmets as drums. The stormtroopers' corpses are, presumably, piled up in a corner to be consumed later, along with the cooked remains of Anakin Skywalker.

THE MONSTER IN THE TRASH COMPACTOR

The Death Star is a relatively new battle station, yet it already has some sort of life form living in its trash compactor. This is a Dianoga, a scavenger that feeds on organic waste. If these creatures live in drains and sewers, do the residents of the Star Wars universe live in fear of being pulled into their own toilets by a slippery tentacle?

THE MISERABLE LIFE OF THE PROPRIETOR AT THE CANTINA, MOS EISLEY

Can you imagine owning the bar at Mos Eisley? The blood, the severed arms. Then there's Greedo's corpse, still slumped in the corner. The Mos Eisley Cantina is one of those family pub-restaurants now, with wipe-clean menus and a depressing pit full of plastic balls for the kids.

THE UNREMARKED DEATH OF THOUSANDS

An undisclosed number of cleaners, cooks and engineers were almost certainly killed when the Death Star was destroyed in *A New Hope*. Still, the Star Wars universe at least had one less sewer-dwelling Dianoga to worry about.

THE SUBTEXTS OF FAMILY MOVIES

•••

Some family movies simply play out, entertain the kids and disappear. Others are a little more ambitious and are open to lots of different readings.

It's a frustration to many parents that a family movie can often be little more than a surrogate babysitter. While that has value – who doesn't need 90 minutes' peace and quiet from their offspring now and then? – it does encourage films with precious little to do but dance around on the screen for a bit.

Contrary to that, though, there's a more ambitious subset of family films that are keener to say something to their target audience. Some do it badly: most of us have sat through an animated movie that has smacked us over the head with a less-than-subtle moral to a story. But then you get something like Disney's excellent 2016 feature *Zootopia* (*Zootropolis* in the UK and much of Europe). On the surface is a wildly entertaining detective comedy; bubbling underneath, using a city populated by animals as its setting, is a clever message of tolerance.

Disney has form here. Howard Ashman wrote the lyrics to the fabulous songbook for 1991's *Beauty and the Beast*, a film that is about a misunderstood outsider, about second chances and about looking closer to get to know someone properly. But dig even deeper. The song "Kill the Beast", for instance, contains the haunting lyric "we

don't like what we don't understand, in fact it scares us". As the film's producer, Don Hahn, pointed out, "Howard was struggling with Aids at the same time. The "Kill the Beast" song was almost a metaphor for that. He was really dealing with a debilitating disease, in an era when it was stigmatized. And so, there were so many of those underpinnings to the movie that people may not have seen. And shouldn't have seen. It wasn't about the HIV epidemic at all. But if you study the man, and his struggles, and then look at his lyrics, you understand what he was going through."

Ashman died at the age of just 40 and would never see the success that *Beauty and the Beast* would enjoy (nor the Broadway show, nor the 2017 live-action remake). But the messages in his lyrics still resonate.

Animation is strong for layering in extra meanings to films, many of which, of course, are open to interpretation. Yet live-action family movies also have lessons they sometimes want to get across.

Director Martin Scorsese, for instance, may still be best-known for harder-edged dramas such as *Goodfellas*, *Taxi Driver* and *The Wolf of Wall Street*, but his venture into family filmmaking, 2011's *Hugo*, is certainly worth seeking out. Not least

> *Extra meanings to films, of course, are open to interpretation*

Toy Story: the trilogy that breaks pretty much everyone's heart somewhere along the line.

because Scorsese, a dedicated film archivist, has made a film about the importance of treasuring the past and respecting history. The fact that the film also provides a solid grounding for young movie nerds in training is of real merit, too.

Going a bit further back, *Flight of the Navigator*, the 1986 fantasy adventure (from the director of *Grease*, no less), tells the story of a 12-year-old who finds himself abducted by aliens and sent into the future. Suddenly, even though he's the same person, the problems he ends up dealing with feel a bit more grown-up. Not unlike the Tom Hanks-headlined *Big*, some have posited that the message here is to make the most of your childhood while you still have it.

That said, one film can mean many things to different people, and the examples we've talked about are just a few readings of the movies in question – readings that don't get in the way of the main job, which is to enjoy the film itself. One tip, though, if you're taking children to see a film: 30 minutes after they've finished watching it, ask them

to tell you something about its stories or its characters. Sadly, a surprising number of pretty empty films seem to have leaked out of people's brains even before they've got back home.

THE *TOY STORY* TRILOGY

The films of Pixar – from the *Finding Nemo* movies, through *Monsters, Inc.*, to *Up* – are rich with things going on under the surface. But it's the first three *Toy Story* movies that have invited the most analysis. Certainly one of the most interesting readings of the initial trilogy is that the toys represent parents: they watch their children grow up, with all the anxieties that come with that, and then, eventually, the children need them less and less, eventually moving away and leaving them behind. Cheery, right?

MOVIE URBAN LEGENDS

•••

Perhaps the best-known movie urban legend is the ghost in hit comedy *Three Men and a Baby*. Legend has it that in one scene a figure can be seen behind the curtains of a window: a ghost! The truth? It was a cardboard cutout of co-star Ted Danson, a prop for a storyline that had been chopped from the movie. That didn't stop the urban legend from spreading – which also occurred with the following stories.

THE MANCHURIAN CANDIDATE (1962)

The legend: In the aftermath of the assassination of President John F Kennedy in 1963, Frank Sinatra was said to have personally asked for the withdrawal from

Frank Sinatra in *The Manchurian Candidate*: a film that was absent from cinemas for over 20 years.

circulation of political thriller *The Manchurian Candidate*, in which he starred (and which had a presidential assassination storyline).
The truth: He didn't. The film had just run its course and, in fact, played on US television in the 1960s and 1970s. It was off cinema screens until its 25th anniversary in 1987, but only because nobody had requested it.

THE WIZARD OF OZ (1939)

The legend: Come the end of the sequence with the Tin Man, there's a figure hanging from a tree, which is said to be one of the cast playing a Munchkin in the movie. The legend goes that they committed suicide.
The truth: The high-definition era resolved this once and for all. The Blu-ray, with its sharper resolution, clearly shows that it's a bird, rather than a person hanging. Phew.

DEAD POETS SOCIETY (1989)

The legend: Sets were said to have burned down after the first day of filming, when Robin Williams didn't turn up to filming.
The truth: This one's true. Williams, at that stage, hadn't actually signed a deal to appear in the film, and Disney had gambled that he'd show up anyway. He didn't, the film was

Robin Williams was reluctant to star in *Dead Poets Society*.

which wasn't picked up until the film's eventual VHS release in the 1990s.

The truth: This one's actually true. In 1999, when the breastage was noticed, Disney had to recall over three million copies of the video. Each subsequent release of the film has had the scene corrected.

STAR WARS: ROGUE ONE (2016)

The legend: Ahead of the release of Gareth Edwards's *Star Wars* prequel *Rogue One* in 2016, a story appeared suggesting that the writers had rewritten material and shot fresh scenes with an anti-Donald Trump slant, following Trump's Presidential victory.

The truth: Reshoot work was done on Rogue One ahead of its release, as is the norm, but it had nothing to do with Trump, nor was anti-Trump rhetoric woven into the movie.

put into turnaround and sets were burned. Then the movie's first director, Jeff Kanew, departed the project, new director Peter Weir came in and the film finally got going months later, ultimately earning Williams an Oscar nomination for Best Actor.

THE LAST TEMPTATION OF CHRIST (1988)

The legend: Many have held that the final moment, when the screen goes white as Jesus dies on the cross, was not deliberate.

The truth: It was deliberate in the sense that the scene had been staged that way. But director Martin Scorsese later admitted that a camera fault had leaked light on the film at that precise moment, causing the whiteout.

THE RESCUERS (1977)

The legend: A disgruntled animator was said to have inserted a few frames of a topless woman into the Disney family-friendly animated film, just shy of 40 minutes in,

THESE WERE TRUE!

Jim Caviezel, while portraying Jesus Christ in Mel Gibson's *The Passion of the Christ*, was doing the Sermon on the Mount scene and was struck by lightning.

•••

One story suggested that the word "sex" is formed by clouds in the sky at one stage in Disney's *The Lion King*. This one is two-thirds true. The letters spelled SFX, not SEX, and it was designed as a nod to the special-effects team on the film.

•••

Finally, Harrison Ford did indeed have the runs while filming *Raiders of the Lost Ark*, and, as a result, in what was supposed to be a prolonged 3½-page fight with a sword expert, Indy simply shoots him rather than fighting back. One dose of the squits gave the movie its funniest scene.

MOVIES THAT LED TO A CHANGE IN THE LAW

The impact of cinema can be wide-ranging – and it'd be fair to say that some people are still alive on the planet because of it.

"We realized from the very beginning that the ideas we had were gonna be challenged," director Abel Ferrara mused in 2016, when chatting about his controversial 1979 horror film **Driller Killer**. The aftermath of the movie was still with him, too, as he noted that, even nearly 40 years on, "I'm still being sued". *Driller Killer* had ramifications.

In the UK in particular, it became a member of an elite club – the small bunch of movies that have led to a change in the law. *Driller Killer* ended up being debated in the Houses of Parliament. The flames were stoked by an advertising campaign for the video release, which wasn't shy about highlighting the movie's violence. Complaints rolled in, and a tabloid newspaper campaign took hold. *Driller Killer*, along with movies such as 1980's *Cannibal Holocaust*, would go on to be the catalyst for the Video Recordings Act of 1984, which was enacted into British law in 1985. Under it, films such as *The Exorcist* and *Straw Dogs* would be banned for over a decade from a home-formats release; and, even more than three decades on, uncut versions of some of the affected movies were not available in Britain.

At around the same time, Alan Clarke's terrifying, violent film **Scum** was also impacting British policy decisions. The film was originally conceived for television, as a BBC *Play for Today* in 1977, but the corporation pulled it from its schedules. Clarke, along with writer Roy Minton, remade the project as a film, released in 1979. It offered a glimpse inside a youth detention centre, under the Borstal system (a heavily regimented, ultimately brutal form of corrective custody). *Scum* caused an uproar, with Britain's morality campaigner Mary Whitehouse launching a private prosecution against Channel 4 for screening the film on UK television in 1983 (she won, but Channel 4 won the appeal). It was in the aftermath of the film's original release, however, that the British government abandoned the Borstal system, as part of 1982's Criminal Justice Act (replacing it with Young Offender Institutions). It was never openly acknowledged that *Scum* was the catalyst for this, but, not unreasonably, many assumed that to be so.

Moving across Europe, acclaimed director Krzysztof Kieslowski also expanded a production that was originally for television into a feature. **A Short Film About Killing** (1988) was expanded from his acclaimed Polish television series *Dekalog*. (Consisting of ten episodes, inspired by the biblical Ten Commandments, *Dekalog* is itself worth seeking out on DVD.) *A Short Film About Killing* centres on a young man who kills a taxi driver, and who himself is sent to trial and faces the death penalty. So impactful was the

A Short Film About Killing: within a year, the death penalty in Poland was abandoned.

movie that within a year an 84-minute piece of cinema had been a key factor in Poland's abolition of the death penalty.

Over in New Zealand, Peter Jackson was, in 2010, preparing to embark on filming what would become the three **The Hobbit** movies. However, as a result of a dispute with the International Federation of Actors, Warner Bros. and New Line Cinema threatened to move the productions to another country. Because this would have meant taking the films, budgeted at around $500m in all, out of the New Zealand economy, a change in the law was enacted instead. The Employment Relations (Film Production Work) Amendment Bill was speedily introduced to the New Zealand legislature in October 2010.

Crucially, it made workers in New Zealand's film industry contractors by default, instead of being categorized as employees. Many saw

this as a way of removing the employment rights of those affected, but it ultimately worked: *The Hobbit* production stayed in New Zealand, where *The Lord of the Rings* trilogy had previously been filmed. The amendment was passed less than two weeks after it was originally introduced.

KEEPING UP APPEARANCES

An unlikely film to bring about a major rule change, perhaps, but 1989's *Back to the Future Part II* had a ramification on the acting community. Crispin Glover, who played George McFly in the 1985 original film, didn't return for the sequel, telling SiriusXM Radio in 2013 that he was "asking questions that the producers/director didn't like". There was also an alleged dispute over money, though Glover denied this.

Nonetheless, the decision was made to press ahead with including the character of George McFly in the film. The filmmakers took a mould of his face from the first film and used it to make another actor, Jeffrey Weissman, look like Glover. It's Weissman you see on-screen during George McFly's brief appearances in *Back to the Future Part II*.

Glover wasn't happy and filed a lawsuit in 1990 against Universal Pictures, arguing that the use of his likeness without his authorization, along with footage of him from the first film, was wrong. A ruling was never issued, as the case was settled out of court. However, the Screen Actors Guild subsequently altered its rules, to ban its members from unauthorized mimicking of other members of the Guild. The rule still holds.

BIZARRE MOVIE MERCHANDISE

Many of us have been to see a movie and wanted to buy a T-shirt or soundtrack album, perhaps even an action figure, straight after. But the world of movie and TV merchandise can head off in slightly unexpected directions. Here are a few examples.

TERMINATOR 2: JUDGMENT DAY BOARD GAME

Never mind that the film was restricted to 15-year-olds and above in the UK, the inviting board game of *Terminator 2: Judgment Day* from MB boasted that it was for players aged 7 years and older. The aim of the game? To build up a T-800 Terminator by collecting the required parts, and then to destroy the deadly T-1000 in a vat of molten metal. Fun for all the family.

THE *RAMBO* CHILDREN'S ANNUAL

In the 1980s, Rambo was one of the most famous movie characters on the planet. Following the dark and excellent original, *First Blood*, in 1982, Sylvester Stallone would turn John Rambo into a full-on 1980s action hero in *Rambo: First Blood Part II* (1985) and *Rambo III* (1988). Marvellously, in 1987, and again in 1988, Rambo was turned into a children's book, the *Rambo Annual*, aimed at the Christmas market in the UK. Youngsters could learn about their hero's weapons, see him wrestle a large, fierce dog and enjoy jape-filled comic strips.

THOR DUMBBELL ALARM CLOCK

A real thing. Kenneth Branagh's 2011 *Thor* movie has no dumbbells that we can remember, but that didn't stop one enterprising company from slapping the name of the film on the side of an alarm clock, in the shape of dumbbells. Mind you, they missed a trick not calling it Thor O'Clock.

SEX AND THE CITY THONGS

These came in a four-pack, in case you were wondering – one for each of the four main characters. No idea what you're supposed to wear on a Friday.

TWILIGHT SAGA

The love story between Bella and Edward across the five films of the *Twilight Saga* enraptured a very large core audience, to the point where the merchandising got plentiful and really rather varied. You'd need, for instance, a four-figure sum to have bought the replica of Bella's engagement ring from *The Twilight Saga: Eclipse*. Unofficial fan merchandise inevitably took things further – some of the underwear is best not searched for online.

DANIEL CRAIG ICE LOLLY

For a promotional stunt back in 2009, to celebrate the maiden National Ice Cream Week in the UK, a thousand women were surveyed as to who they wanted on the end of an ice cream stick. Saving you some of the details, a small number of ice creams in the shape of Daniel Craig's torso from 2006's *Casino Royale* were duly produced. "Coldfinger" chirped one of the more printable resultant headlines.

PLAN 9 FROM OUTER SPACE: THE VIDEOGAME

An odd choice for a computer game, this was based on the 1956 film that was unfairly infamous as the worst movie of all time. Ed Wood's *Plan 9 from Outer Space* was a gleefully entertaining bargain-basement piece of B-movie nostalgia. The game, sadly, wasn't much cop – but one edition of it did come with a free VHS copy of the film, opening it up to an audience who, in those pre-internet days, probably hadn't even heard of it.

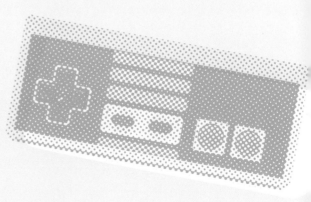

THE DARK ARTS OF THE MOVIE POSTER QUOTE

•••

There has clearly been a bylaw passed somewhere insisting that a modern-day movie poster be packed to the gills with wildly enthusiastic quotes that suggest the film falls just below penicillin, unlimited cinema cards and Jason Statham on the list of humanity's finest creations. But peek behind Oz's curtain and things are slightly muddier. In some instances, dark arts are at work.

A good chunk of review quotes that appear on posters, thankfully, come from the reviews of films themselves. The studio's marketing department will have sifted through reactions to a film and duly picked out some useful terms to help with promotional work. Yet in the days of digital film distribution – where the majority of releases are sent to cinemas on encoded hard disks, rather than in multiple cans of film – movies are being screened for the press closer and closer to release. Other tactics are therefore sometimes used.

On the way out of a press screening of a film, for instance, an email generally lands in the box of the reviewer, asking for a reaction. If said reaction is positive, the follow-up mail asking for a quote for the poster and a star rating is rarely far behind. It's not uncommon for all this to be taking place within an hour of the end credits rolling in the film's first press screening. That's fair enough on a brain-dead comedy, perhaps, but harsher on films that require some thinking and reaction time.

Furthermore, it's been known for marketing departments to send advanced screener discs and (legal) online streaming links for upcoming features, with a specific request to provide a quote that can be used for marketing purposes. In one example, back in 2013, the team selling one major blockbuster went further: they courted websites and magazines for an "anticipation quote", with guidelines provided as to what they were looking for. One of the biggest websites on the planet duly obliged with "the must-see film of summer

One of the films that Dave Manning really liked. Shame he never existed...

2013", notwithstanding the fact that they'd not seen anything close to the finished film.

Still, such tactics are an evolution of different approaches used in the pre-internet days. Perhaps most notoriously, there was the case of David Manning.

THE CRITIC WHO DIDN'T EXIST

Manning was a very enthusiastic reviewer of films from Columbia Pictures in the early 2000s. *Hollow Man* was "one hell of a scary ride", he was reported to have said on its poster. *The Forsaken*, meanwhile, was "a sexy, scary thrill-ride". Manning lauded praise on *The Patriot*, too, and, er, the Rob Schneider comedy vehicle *The Animal*. He also described the late Heath Ledger as "this year's hottest new star" for *A Knight's Tale*.

The problem, though, was that David Manning – or Dave Manning, as he was sometimes credited – didn't exist. He was said to be writing for Ridgefield Press, which at the time was a small weekly publication from Connecticut. But Ridgefield Press didn't know of him and was unaware of – and certainly not complicit in – what was going on.

Mr Manning was a creation of the Columbia Pictures marketing department. Sony Pictures Entertainment, Columbia's parent company, admitted to *Newsweek* magazine in 2001 that Manning wasn't real, with a spokesperson admitting, "It was an incredibly foolish decision, and we're horrified".

The story didn't end there. Although Columbia removed Manning's quotes from its publicity materials, it also faced court action from two Californian movie-goers. In 2005, they brought a case against the studio, accusing it of the "intentional and systematic deception of consumers". Sony didn't admit liability but did cough up $1.5m, and offered a $5 refund for anyone who had bought tickets for the films concerned. Figures aren't available for how many took it up on the offer.

THE KILLER QUOTE

Studios, though, are still willing to push their luck when coming up with a killer critical line, and it's the nature of the beast that they always will. Universal, for one, sold the underrated sci-fi flick *The Adjustment Bureau* as "Bourne meets Inception", citing *Total Film* magazine – correctly – as its source. What the poster *didn't* reveal was that the line came from a preview of the film written months ahead, rather than from the review itself. *Total Film* seemed just as bemused as the rest of us.

Still, sometimes honesty prevails. The poster for *Legend*, the telling of the story of the Kray brothers (featuring Tom Hardy in both lead roles) was awash with four-star reviews. It seemed that everybody loved it. But look carefully, and you'll see that *The Guardian* newspaper's reviewer wasn't as keen.

TOTAL RECOURSE

Sarah Deming, from Michigan, is a woman who seems to take her movie marketing seriously. Enthused by the trailer for 2011's excellent *Drive*, starring Ryan Gosling, she duly stumped up her ticket money. But she was surprised to find that the *Fast & Furious*-style trailer that she'd seen in cinemas weeks before was no reflection of the sombre, dark drama she was presented with. So she decided to do something about it.

Deming sued the film's American distributors, claiming that they were in breach of the Michigan Consumer Protection Act. Her lawsuit noted, "*Drive* bore very little similarity to a chase, or race action film, for reasons including but not limited to *Drive* having very little driving in the motion picture." She lost.

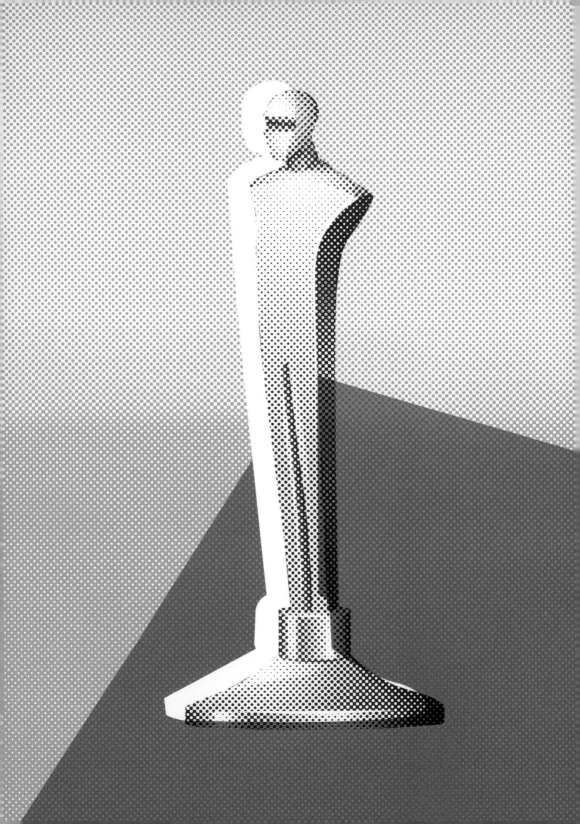

& FINALLY...

BIG BOX OFFICE HITS THAT WERE UTTER SURPRISES

•••

Modern Hollywood seems to have adopted the strict policy that "to hit big, you need to spend big" – that if you want your movie to gross over $100m at the American box office, or edge past $500m worldwide, you need to spend some serious cash in the first place.

The reason this policy has been adopted is that it tends to be true. Every film that's ever crossed the $1bn mark at the worldwide box office has been expensive. *Jurassic Park* is perhaps the most modest, but the $63m it cost to make, back in 1993, was toward the top of the range (although still someway shy of 1991's *Terminator 2: Judgment Day*). The most economical in the list is the 2015 film *Minions*. It cost $74m to make, primarily as a result of its parent company, Illumination Entertainment, tackling the production work in France rather than on the west coast of America, where most blockbuster-movie animation houses are located. However, *Minions* still cost a couple of wheelbarrows of hard cash just to market and distribute.

Every now and then, a film bursts through on a very modest budget that attains a blockbuster level of return. Many studios have a marquee or genre arm to their business – Sony with Screen Gems, and Sony Pictures Classics, for instance – that hunts for such films, given that a small-budget film earning $300m is likely to be far more profitable than an expensive blockbuster taking twice that. It also explains why Sony nailed its mast to Adam Sandler's output for so long.

William Goldman, in his book *Which Lie Did I Tell? More Adventures in the Screen Trade*, argued in the early 2000s that Adam Sandler was effectively the world's biggest movie star. Goldman wrote, "I talked to a top studio guy today and he said this: 'You can absolutely make a case for Adam Sandler being *the* star. His movies cost next to zero and bring in a ton. Huge profits. Isn't that what a star's supposed to do?'" The box office returns for features such as *Big Daddy*, *Anger Management*, *Click* and *You Don't Mess with the Zohan* backed up those words.

Despicable Me made the Minions movie stars.

Teenage Mutant Ninja Turtles (1990) was the most successful independent movie of all time upon its release.

Of course, movie stars are no guarantee of box office gold. Even the world's biggest movie stars – Tom Cruise and Tom Hanks – struggled to rally audiences to the sequels *Jack Reacher: Never Go Back* and *Inferno* respectively in 2016. What's more, the slow decline of the quality and commercial performances of Adam Sandler movies led to his inking a deal to make films for Netflix in 2014. (Sandler, perhaps unwisely, said in the press announcement, "I immediately said yes for one reason and one reason only…Netflix rhymes with Wet Chicks." Ouch.) Sandler is rarely seen on the big screen anymore.

The real prize for a movie studio, though, is the micro-budget film that breaks through. In some ways, the template for this was set by New Line Cinema. Already finding that horror movies were a fine way to bring in big profits, with the *A Nightmare on Elm Street* franchise, the then-independent studio sunk its funds into a screen adaptation of the comic *Teenage Mutant Ninja Turtles*. Its timing couldn't have been better. Turtle-mania was rife when the first film hit in early 1990, and it became the first non-studio film to cross $100m at the American box office. It cost less than $15m to make, and outgrossed in the US the

likes of *Die Hard 2: Die Harder*, *Total Recall*, *Back to the Future Part III* and *Dick Tracy*.

The first two sequels, released in 1991 and 1993, didn't fare as well. But they never cost more than $25m to make, and they comfortably returned that, with change, at the box office. It all started New Line Cinema on a path that would see it gambling on Peter Jackson's *Lord of the Rings* trilogy, before being fully swallowed up by Warner Bros.

Horror is often at the heart of what makes an out-of-nowhere blockbuster. Take 1996's *Scream*, for instance, which built on the postmodern approach that director Wes Craven had employed in 1994 with the *Elm Street* sequel, *New Nightmare*. By knowingly taking affectionate digs at the horror genre, while delivering a quality frightfest in its own right, *Scream* turned its $14m budget into a $173m box office return, three sequels, a TV series and a series of spoof films – the *Scary Movie* franchise – from the same company.

Yet it was 1999's *The Blair Witch Project* that turned the tables. This wasn't the first film to harness the world wide web, then in its mainstream infancy, to bring a film to prominence – notably, the website for Paul Verhoeven's sleazy *Showgirls* earned a million hits, at a time when that used to be a big number – but it did transform film marketing. A guerrilla campaign was used to underpin the mythos of the movie, and a genuine cultural phenomenon was born. *The Blair Witch Project* would cost just $60,000 to make, and earned just shy of a quarter of a billion dollars in cinemas. Its budget-to-takings ratio became a record, blitzing the previous holder, 1979's *Mad Max*.

Surprisingly, the *Blair Witch* franchise didn't build on this return, thanks to a tepid initial sequel and a belated, worthier follow-up in 2016. But others did (see box opposite).

The 2002 film *My Big Fat Greek Wedding*, meanwhile, started life as a one-woman play, written by and starring Nia Vardalos. She was approached by Tom Hanks's production company and agreed to turn it into a movie script. Resisting suggestions for a starrier name, she took the lead in the film herself – it's based on her family – and production began in 2000.

Yet nobody could have predicted what followed. The $5m film got a limited release in April 2002, and gradually, slowly, began to gather positive word of mouth. This accelerated, and *My Big Fat Greek Wedding* stayed resident in the box office charts for months in the US. It never, oddly, hit the number one spot (held off by the likes of *Swimfan*, *Signs* and the first xXx film), but by the time it left cinemas, it had become the highest grossing romantic comedy of all time at the US box office, with $241m banked (and a further near-$130m coming in from overseas). It has kept that position, and the second-placed film, the Mel Gibson vehicle *What Women Want*, is a good $50m+ behind. Vardalos's career stayed grounded afterward, though – a sequel wouldn't follow until 2016 – and nobody has been able to mimic her success in the rom-com genre.

For the granddaddy of the independent

My Big Fat Greek Wedding is America's biggest grossing romantic comedy of all time.

film, though, the box office champion remains Mel Gibson's *The Passion of the Christ*. Granted, you can argue that George Lucas funded his *Star Wars* prequels through his own company rather than a traditional studio, but Gibson himself footed the bill for his 2004 telling of the story of the crucifixion of Christ. It cost around $30m to bring the film to the screen and was picked up by an independent distributor, Newmarket, as opposed to a Hollywood studio.

Newmarket was pleased with its purchase. *The Passion of the Christ* would outgross *Harry Potter and the Prisoner of Azkaban* at the US box office on its way to a $370m take in America. Churches block-booked the film, encouraging people to see it, and the film utterly took off. It found an audience elsewhere in the world, too, ending up with over $610m in the bank by the time it ended its run. Mel Gibson did well enough out of it that he went on to develop a "sequel", telling the story of the resurrection.

Stories such as these are notable by how rare they are. They are the winning-the-lottery moment of the film business: the clichéd case of the right film at the right time. For every independent hit, there are hundreds of indies that can't even get a cinema release, and lean heavily on video-on-demand services. And after all, that is where Adam Sandler spends most of his time.

Few genres offer as much of a path to giant profits as horror, when all goes to plan. Lionsgate, for one, is now effectively a Hollywood major studio in its own right, but it owes much of its success to horror films – in particular, the wildly profitable *Saw* movies. Across the series (for which the seventh film was announced as the final one, but then an eighth was commissioned) Lionsgate was enjoying nine-figure returns in some cases off budgets that never stretched beyond $10m.

It used that money, in turn, to bid successfully for the rights to *The Hunger Games* novels. Even then, the studio had to scrabble around to find the money to make the first *The Hunger Games* film, pinching funds from the budgets of other features it had in the

works. The gamble worked, though, and *The Hunger Games* in turn gave Lionsgate the cash base to acquire the Starz television network.

•••

New Line was built on horror foundations, too, thanks to the *Elm Street* films. And when *Paranormal Activity* and *Insidious* hit, producer Jason Blum put into motion a model for his Blumhouse Productions outfit that became the envy of many.

Blum has acquired a reputation for funding low-budget movies, which allow a director real control over the final cut. But also, he was attracting quality actors and filmmakers. "We shoot all our movies in LA, which means they get to stay at

home. That's a huge bonus, especially if they have kids. That's a big deal – you'd be shocked at what a big deal that is. And now that they know that the movie production's short, and that they can get paid as much if not more than they get at a major studio – it's a good gig for an actor," he explained.

As such, Ethan Hawke signed up for the first *The Purge* movie, which in turn ignited a franchise of films and a spin-off TV show. Further hits in the Blumhouse stable have included *Sinister*, *The Visit*, *Ouija*, and awards-magnet *Whiplash*. The downside of his model is that not all films make it to cinemas, if he can't interest a distributor. Joe Carnahan's sparky *Stretch*, for instance, had to be content with a DVD debut...

3:08:26 AM

Paranormal Activity was reworked for over a year in editing, with Steven Spielberg making suggestions for the final cut.

SPOILER ALERT!

*JURASSIC PARK III, DIE HARD WITH A VENGEANCE, WORLD WAR Z,
TERMINATOR: SALVATION, CASABLANCA, THE LION KING, FIRST BLOOD, ROCKY IV*

THE LOST ENDINGS
OF BIG MOVIES

It's hard to shake the feeling at the end of a movie that there was a better ending than the one we got. In certain cases, that's pretty much on the mark, with some major blockbusters being among the notable examples.

Jurassic Park III is, by distance, the shortest movie of that particular franchise. Measuring a sprightly 92 minutes, including end credits, there's an admirable economy to its production. It throws us back onto an island full of dinosaurs, the dinosaurs attack the latest bunch of human beings, action ensues, box office takings are counted.

Out of the films in the series to date, though, what is notable about *Jurassic Park III* is how abruptly it stops. The latest bunch of dino fodder are on the run, only to get saved pretty much out of the blue by the military, and zip: the film's done. That the ending of the film is weak perhaps shouldn't come as a surprise. When photography on the film wrapped in October 2000, a satisfactory finale hadn't even been written. The cast and crew were duly reassembled in January 2001 – six months ahead of the film's release – to film what we ultimately got in the movie.

A far more cinematic denouement was considered, but never made the cut, which would have seen a battle between the soldiers

Jurassic Park III: the film that stops, rather than ends.

arriving on the beach and the dinosaurs. Also considered was a finale where flying pteranodons would attack rescue-helicopters as they attempted to whisk survivors away. Both of these were ultimately discounted.

It's a little more common than it should be for major movies to start filming without their ending locked down. For both **Pirates of the Caribbean: Dead Man's Chest (2006)** and **Pirates of the Caribbean: At World's End (2007)**, for instance, writers Terry Rossio and Ted Elliott were in each case on location writing the script, with the cast and crew planning ahead off the back of an outline the pair had put together.

The third Die Hard film, **Die Hard with a Vengeance (1995)**, is another example. The ending that ultimately made it to film sees Bruce Willis's detective Lieutenant John McClane looking for something to shoot at to bring down Jeremy Irons's Simon Gruber, before closing on a phone call to his estranged wife. The original, cut ending, though, turned up on a DVD in 2003, and saw Gruber and McClane having a final game of riddles, interspersed with – stay with us here – a game of Russian roulette involving rocket launchers. It was abandoned when studio bosses thought it made John McClane look too cruel. But heck, we'd still be talking about that ending now if it had happened, whereas getting anyone to remember the finale of Die Hard with a Vengeance has now been filed in the medium-difficulty level of pub-quiz questions.

Die Hard with a Vengeance and Jurassic Park III aren't alone in having a potentially more interesting ending lost in the midst of scriptwriting and production battles. More infamously, 2013's **World War Z**, starring Brad Pitt, had effectively the last third of its story rewritten very late in the day (and then the cast and crew had to reassemble

Die Hard with a Vengeance was one of a growing band of blockbusters that started filming without an agreed finale.

for extensive extra shooting). The story goes that Paramount Pictures executives weren't happy with the rough assembly cut they saw, and demanded big changes. In came writers Damon Lindelof (best known for the TV series *Lost*) and Drew Goddard (the director of the film *Cabin in the Woods*), and they wrote the last act we got, as Brad Pitt's Gerry and his team head off to a near-abandoned site in Wales, to sneak around corridors and snicker at Peter Capaldi being cast as a WHO doctor, a good year or so before he landed the *Doctor Who* role.

World War Z is already a film that takes several liberties with Max Brooks's source novel, but the original filmed finale was a little more in keeping with it. The version that Paramount saw and duly rejected was based in Russia, and Brad Pitt's character would grow facial hair, learn to fight zombies and arrive back in America just as the credits rolled. There was no happy family reunion in that version, and there were one or two other darker twists.

Even *Casablanca*'s ending was uncertain for some time.

Terminator: Salvation (2009) also originally had a darker ending than the one we got. In it, our hero – John Connor – would have died, and his exterior would have been placed over that of a machine. Then in would come the assorted heroes, pleased to see who they thought was John Connor, only for him to shoot them all dead. A daring finale, one actually in keeping with the courage of the last ten minutes of the much-maligned *Terminator 3: Rise of the Machines*. The problem in the case of *Terminator: Salvation* – well, one of them, at least – was that news of this ending leaked onto the internet months ahead of the film's release. Director McG was said to have duly amended his film as a consequence of that, although it's also likely that his original finale would have had the associated movie executives reaching for the emergency bottle in their bottom drawer.

Still, some of these stories about endings do have, well, good endings. Few would regard the ending of **Casablanca** as anything but perfect, yet the story of that production suggests that right up to the day of shooting, Humphrey Bogart, Ingrid Bergman and Paul Henreid had no idea how it was all to end. There was no shortage of suggestions. Among the considerations were Bogart's Rick sending Bergman's Ilsa and Henreid's Laszlo off to the airport together (this is the ending of the play on which the film is based). Rick would be arrested in that version.

Furthermore, killing off Laszlo was discussed, as was the death of Rick. The iconic ending we know now was eventually conceived when writers Julius and Philip Epstein were driving down Sunset Boulevard, stopped at a traffic light and instantly said to each other, "Round up the usual suspects". No such moment seemed to happen to the writers of *Jurassic Park III*.

Unusually, an early visual version of an alternate ending to a Disney film, leaked online back in 2008, presented a darker last segment to its huge hit **The Lion King**. The 1994 animated movie originally sees Jeremy Irons's dastardly Scar falling to his death, following a fight with our hero, Simba. But as the original storyboards show, the initial plan was for Scar to lose the fight but endure a more graphic demise. He'd be engulfed in flames.

Several Sylvester Stallone films have undergone revisions, but two changes in particular prolonged his two most famous movie franchises. In the original **First Blood**, for instance, his character, John Rambo, was supposed to die. That was altered following test screenings (see page 147), and assorted sequels followed.

At one stage, the same fate was to befall Rocky Balboa. In **Rocky IV** the Italian Stallion had been battered heavily by, but ultimately emerged triumphant against, Dolph Lundgren's Ivan Drago, so Balboa was supposed to be feeling the after-effects in Rocky V. This is hinted at in the surviving opening of the film, as a weary Balboa is seen after the fight of the previous film. Stallone wrote an ending for Rocky V that would see Balboa die in an ambulance on his way to hospital, with his beloved Adrian by his side. However, he subsequently rewrote the ending, leaving Rocky free to enjoy two of his most popular films, the thoroughly decent Rocky Balboa (2006), and the quite excellent Creed (2015) which earned Sylvester Stallone another Oscar nomination.

ALTERNATE ENDINGS ON DVDS

The advent of the DVD format brought with it mainstream interest in extra features supporting the movie concerned. Studios, therefore, have occasionally been inclined to give us a glimpse at alternate endings, and how things could have been.

Take 2007's I Am Legend, which is regarded as a strong film for the first half, before some shaky special effects elbow pretty much everything out of the way for the rest of the movie. But had the original ending stood, as revealed on the subsequent disc release, the film's reputation might have been a lot better. In the film we got, Will Smith's character makes a self-sacrifice at the end, one that didn't stop chatter about a possible I Am Legend 2 for a few years. But in the original ending, the creatures come for someone Smith's character had rescued earlier in the film, leaving him be. It's a more logical ending, and a strangely moving one – so, naturally, it was rejected in favour of an explosion.

Elsewhere, if you pick up a DVD of 1985's Clue, you can see all four of the endings that were filmed. On the movie's theatrical release, it was pure chance which you'd have got to see, as different prints of the movie had different finales.

Just to keep you on your toes, some DVD releases of the 2004 film DodgeBall also include an alternative finale, with a more downbeat ending. But that was a joke version, included purely for the disc.

ODD REVIEWS OF CLASSIC FILMS

Even the most beloved movies can get bad reviews sometimes, but on rare occasions the criticisms levelled at time-honoured classics can prove to be downright bizarre.

PSYCHO (1960)

Alfred Hitchcock went back to basics and created a masterpiece with his stripped-down, black-and-white adaptation of Robert Bloch's best-selling novel. Along with the likes of *Vertigo* and *Rear Window*, *Psycho* is generally regarded as one of Hitchcock's finest achievements – though that wasn't an opinion shared by the *New York Times* back in 1960. "His denouement falls quite flat for us," wrote the paper's critic Bosley Crowther of the movie's pitch-black ending, before concluding with a curious observation about the film's set dressing, "The one thing we would note with disappointment is that, among the stuffed birds that adorn the motel office of Mr Perkins, there are no significant bats." Whatever you say, Mr Crowther.

Alfred Hitchcock's *Psycho* needed more bats.

THE WIZARD OF OZ (1939)

This movie has become such a cultural staple that it's hard to imagine a time when *The Wizard of Oz* wasn't a cherished moment in 20th-century cinema. But MGM's lavish adaptation of L Frank Baum's book wasn't a huge hit on its release, and while most critics loved the movie, one reviewer in particular wasn't exactly won over. "It has dwarfs, music, Technicolor, freak characters and Judy Garland," the *New Republic* critic Otis Ferguson complained in his oddly hostile write-up. "It can't be expected to have a sense of humour as well, and as for the light touch of fantasy, it weighs like a pound of fruitcake soaking wet." Exactly how much a wet fruitcake weighs – and what Ferguson meant by this analogy – is sadly lost to history.

The Wizard of Oz needed less damp fruitcake.

The Godfather Part II needed less desperation.

THE GODFATHER PART II (1974)

In those conversations we've all had about sequels that are actually better than their predecessors, *The Godfather Part II* is sure to come up sooner or later – just call it Coppola's Law. But while awards piled up at the movie's feet in 1974, one critic in particular failed to see what the fuss was all about. Vincent Canby, the eminent *New York Times* critic, argued that *The Godfather* was better, and that Marlon Brando's star turn in that film was sorely missed. Fair enough, but then Canby went on to compare the sequel to Frankenstein: "It's a Frankenstein monster stitched together from leftover parts. It talks. It moves in fits and starts but it has no mind of its own[...]Looking very expensive but spiritually desperate, Part II has the air of a very long, very elaborate revue sketch."

The Thing is now a highly regarded horror thriller. It was not always so.

THE EMPIRE STRIKES BACK (1980)

You don't need us to tell you that, of all the films in the *Star Wars* franchise, it's *The Empire Strikes Back* that is widely held up as the most intelligent and solidly made. The *New York Times* critic Vincent Canby (yes, him again) thought the sequel was merely "nice and inoffensive" but argued that actually watching it is less edifying than watching a cruise ship coming into dock. "It is amusing in fitful patches but you're likely to find more beauty, suspense, discipline, craft and art when watching a New York harbour pilot bring the *Queen Elizabeth 2* into her Hudson River berth, which is what *The Empire Strikes Back* most reminds me of. It's a big, expensive, time-consuming, essentially mechanical operation. *The Empire Strikes Back* is about as personal as a Christmas card from a bank."

THE THING (1982)

John Carpenter's sci-fi horror is now so widely liked that it's easy to forget how despised it was on its initial release. Mainstream critics were horrified by its gore and violence; Vincent Canby, never one to mince his words, described *The Thing* as "instant junk". What's most surprising is that the seething hatred for the movie extended even to *Starlog*, the kind of sci-fi magazine you might think would defend such a film to the bitter end. Instead, writer Alan Spencer said Carpenter's movie "smells, and smells pretty bad."

STRANGE THINGS IN MOVIE END CREDITS

•••

Never mind the post-credits sting: if you're willing to sit through and read the end credits of movies, you'll find the occasional unexpected treat.

Particularly with modern movies that are effects-dependent, the end credits can be interminable to crawl through. (In some of Peter Jackson's *Hobbit* movies they were pushing 15 minutes.) Good form suggests it's worth doing so, to pay due deference to all the people who worked on a film. But when you've got a child who wants to go home, or a bladder sending out distress flares, sometimes it's best to up and leave. Often, you won't be missing that much. But quite a few features have slipped a few extra bits into the end credits, just to see if you're paying attention.

This is not a new phenomenon. The largely forgettable *Carry On Abroad*, back in 1972, listed its technical advisor as "Sun Tan Lo Tion", while 2016's *Doctor Strange* slips in a warning not to drive while distracted – which, even if you didn't take into account the fate of the title character, is sound advice.

The credits of the world-dominating *Frozen* (2013), meanwhile, seek to assure us that "the views and opinions expressed[…]in the film that all men eat their own boogers are solely his own and do not necessarily reflect the views of The Walt Disney Company or the

The *Hot Shots!* films. Don't leave your seat while the credits roll…

filmmakers". Which is good to know. Also, on Pixar and Walt Disney Animation Studios productions, it has become traditional to list the "production babies", the newborns of the cast and crew who arrived in the world during the three to four years it takes to make a big animated blockbuster.

However, most of the messages you find in the credits tend to lean toward the comedic, with spoof features in particular enjoying themselves. The pair of Hot Shots! movies in the 1990s certainly rewarded anyone who didn't leave their seat when the lights went up. The 1991 original included a recipe for nobby buns, for instance. But for 1993's Hot Shots! Part Deux, you got trivia about co-star Richard Crenna, a baseball joke and a major spoiler for the end of the 1992 film The Crying Game.

Even earlier than those, 1988's The Naked Gun: From the Files of Police Squad! threw in the name of the divorce attorney of producer Robert K Weiss, along with practical advice if a tornado hit ("southwest corner of basement"). For its 1991 sequel, after a listing of the grips who worked on the film, the credits then thoughtfully provided an explanation that a grip was a "person responsible for maintenance and adjustment to equipment on the set". Then, for the trilogy closer, 1994's Naked Gun 33⅓: The Final Insult, there were so many jokes crammed in that at one stage the simple line "don't leave yet" appeared (underneath the credit for, um, "Hairy Butt Boy: Benjamin Cohen").

It's more of an achievement than it probably should be to get such lines into the closing credits. With over 200 names to list, just getting them accurate is a job in itself. (If you're feeling particularly nerdy, there's a very slight typo of the word "assistant" in the end credits of 1996's Mars Attacks!) Furthermore, inclusion in the credits is often contractual on Hollywood films, in conjunction with the key film unions. The main jostling for position

takes place on the opening credits for a film, but it still needs a film's producers to sign off on the lengthy closing crawl.

It tends to be smaller productions that have the most fun, though. The 1981 classic An American Werewolf in London managed to sneak in an ultimately ill-fated congratulations to Prince Charles and Lady Diana Spencer on their wedding (compensation of sort for the remark made about the Prince in the main feature). Plus, if there's a particular favourite, which is entirely in keeping with the tone of the movie concerned, it's perhaps 1987's sci-fi classic RoboCop. Come the end of the credits, on scrolls the standard text urging you not to copy or pirate the film. In the case of RoboCop, though, this warns, "may result in civil liability and criminal prosecution by enforcement droids".

KEEP AN EYE OUT FOR...

A BUG'S LIFE: a spoof list of animals that became extinct during production

SAVING MR BANKS: an audio recording of the real-life P L Travers

HARRY POTTER AND THE PRISONER OF AZKABAN: footprints when the credits turn to those regarding animals and creatures

MONTY PYTHON'S LIFE OF BRIAN: a random film recommendation

GUARDIANS OF THE GALAXY: an assurance that raccoons and tree creatures weren't harmed in the making of the film

& FINALLY...

DEDICATIONS AT THE END OF MOVIES

Occasionally a film is dedicated to someone, or a message may be hidden in the full end-credits crawl. For instance, *Star Trek Beyond* was dedicated to both Leonard Nimoy – the original Spock and a real heartbeat of the franchise – and Anton Yelchin, the young actor who tragically died when the film was in post-production. Here are a few more you may find, and the stories behind them.

BEAUTY AND THE BEAST (1991)

"To our friend Howard, who gave a mermaid her voice and a beast his soul, we will be forever grateful. Howard Ashman 1950–1991". This was a dedication to the lyricist of the 1991 film *Beauty and the Beast*, Howard Ashman, who also served as its executive producer. Ashman was widely credited with being one of the major catalysts behind the Disney animation renaissance, thanks to his incredible work, alongside Alan Menken, bringing the musical side of *The Little Mermaid* and *Beauty and the Beast* to life. Ashman died

in 1991 of complications relating to his HIV-positive diagnosis, and never got to see the absolute final cut of *Beauty and the Beast*, nor the outpouring of positive reviews and the box office success that followed it.

THE EXPENDABLES 2 (2012)

This action sequel is dedicated to the memory of Kun Liu, a 26-year-old stuntman who died in an on-set accident while working on the film.

FROZEN (2013)

Disney's gigantic hit bears a line in its credits to the memory of Poppy, Lola, Caleb and Kayla. Director Jennifer Lee has explained that these were the names of the quadruplets two of the animators were expecting, but sadly lost.

JOHN Q. (2002)

The Denzel Washington-headlined tearjerker is "For Sasha". The daughter of the film's director, Nick Cassavetes, Sasha was born with a heart defect, becoming critically ill at one stage. She's healthy now, thankfully.

Howard Ashman died without seeing the final version of *Beauty and the Beast* (1991).

HELP! (1965)

The Beatles movie has a dedication to Elias Howe, the inventor of the sewing machine. Howe died in 1867 at the age of 48. The Beatles had apparently concluded that without the sewing machine, they wouldn't have anything to wear!

RISE OF THE GUARDIANS (2012)

The underappreciated DreamWorks computer-animated movie is dedicated to Mary Katherine Joyce. She died of a brain tumour at the age of 20, and was the daughter of the source book's author, William Joyce (who was also co-directing the film when she fell ill).

Help! features one of the most left-field dedications in a movie...

THE SHAWSHANK REDEMPTION (1994)

The much-loved 1994 drama is dedicated to Allan Greene, who was the agent of the film's writer and director, Frank Darabont. Greene died just before the film was released.

THE SWARM (1978)

Michael Caine battles bees in 1978's *The Swarm*. The film, though, is dedicated to "the industrious, hard-working American honey bee, to which we are indebted for pollinating vital crops that feed our nation". Not many humans saw the film. Holding out an olive branch to bees seemed a decent idea.

TEENAGE MUTANT NINJA TURTLES II: THE SECRET OF THE OOZE (1991)

A dedication in the credits of this sequel to *Teenage Mutant Ninja Turtles* is to Jim Henson, whose Creature Shop created the turtle suits in both films. Despite this being the last film Jim Henson worked on before his death, his family weren't happy about the dedication, as Henson had not approved of the levels of violence within. *The Muppet Christmas Carol* is also dedicated to Henson.

UNFORGIVEN (1992)

Clint Eastwood, who took home his first Oscar for *Unforgiven*, had dedicated the film to Don and Sergio – namely Don Siegel and Sergio Leone, respectively the director of *Dirty Harry* and the inventor of the "spaghetti western" film genre.

THE WICKER MAN (2006)

Not the original, but the infamously terrible 2006 remake, this movie bears the credit "For Johnny Ramone", after the late guitarist, who died in 2004. It was Ramone who had introduced the film's star and co-producer Nicolas Cage to the original (1973) classic *The Wicker Man*, from director Robin Hardy.

CITATIONS

All box office figures cited from BoxOfficeMojo.com and The-Numbers.com

BRILLIANT OPENING CREDITS SEQUENCES IN MOVIES

15
David Fincher interview, www.denofgeek.com/movies/18487/david-fincher-interview-the-girl-with-the-dragon-tattoo-heavy-metal-and-benjamin-button

THE THINGS THAT INSPIRE MOVIES

16
Jeffrey Katzenberg's memo, www.lettersofnote.com/2011/11/some-thoughts-on-our-business.html

17
Noel Clarke interview, www.denofgeek.com/movies/noel-clarke/21676/noel-clarke-interview-fast-girls-star-trek-mma-and-more

Mark Herman interview, www.denofgeek.com/movies/13543/the-den-of-geek-interview-mark-herman

"The Story of Hudson Hawk", Hudson Hawk special-edition DVD

WHERE DOES A MOVIE BUDGET GET SPENT?

20
Los Angeles Times, 15 April 2007, articles.latimes.com/2007/apr/15/business/fi-movie15

HOW ALIEN: RESURRECTION LED TO THE ICE AGE MOVIES

30
Chris Wedge interview, www.denofgeek.com/uk/movies/animation/42116/how-alien-resurrection-led-to-the-ice-age-movies

UNMADE STAR WARS & STAR TREK MOVIES

33
"The New Heroes of Hollywood", *Preview* magazine, 1980

35
Matthew Graham interview, www.denofgeek.com/uk/tv/star-wars/42348/matthew-graham-interview-the-star-wars-live-action-tv-show

37
"Tom Cruise Not Made of Iron", *Sci-Fi Wire*, article no longer online [www.canmag.com/news/4/3/590]

STRANGE OR ILL-ADVISED MOVIE SEQUELS THAT NEVER WERE

39
San Diego Comic-Con panel, July 2013, jimhillmedia.com/editor_in_chief1/b/jim_hill/archive/2013/07/28/p-p-p-please-say-it-isn-t-so-roger-rabbit-sequel-is-stalled-or-so-says-veteran-disney-producer-don-hahn.aspx

THE MOVIE SEQUELS YOU MIGHT NOT KNOW EXISTED

44
Chiller Theater magazine, October 2002, www.chillertheatre.com/prog/33.htm

45
Amazon review, *Addams Family Reunion*, www.amazon.co.uk/review/R2P08RJVEEFU72

HOW A HE-MAN SEQUEL & A SPIDER-MAN MOVIE BECAME A JEAN-CLAUDE VAN DAMME HIT

47
Gary Goddard interview, www.motumovie.com/2010/02/q-with-director-gary-goddard.html

"Incredibly Strange and Ridiculously Cheap: Albert Pyun's 30-Year Career in B-Movies", io9.gizmodo.com/5966375/incredibly-strange-and-ridiculously-cheap-albert-pyuns-30-year-b-movie-adventure

49
"Bodybuilder Wins $487,500 for Injury by Van Damme", *Orlando Sentinel*, 27 February 1993, articles.orlandosentinel.com/1993-02-27/news/9302260751_1_damme-jean-claude-van-cyborg

WHY THE 1980S WERE SO GOOD FOR FANTASY MOVIES

53
Kael, Pauline, "Why Are Movies So Bad? Or, *the* Numbers", *New Yorker*, 23 June 1980

THE 1990S SPEC-SCRIPT GOLD RUSH

60
"Million-dollar Babies", *New York* magazine, 18 June 1990

62
"When the Spec Script was King" *Vanity Fair*, 8 February 2013, www.vanityfair.com/culture/2013/03/will-spec-script-screenwriters-rise-again

"Script Fee Vomits Upward For Mayhem-Meister", *Variety*, 8 August 1994, variety.com/1994/voices/columns/script-fee-vomits-upward-for-mayhem-meister-1117859467/

THE MAN WHO SOLD $26M OF MOVIE SCRIPTS

65
Eszterhas, Joe, *Hollywood Animal*, Knopf, 2004

articles.latimes.com/1992-02-09/entertainment/ca-3230_1_eszterhas

variety.com/1993/film/news/gangland-deal-may-bring-scribe-up-to-3-4-million-105682/

MOVIE SCRIPTS THAT CHANGED CONSIDERABLY FROM THEIR ORIGINAL DRAFTS

66
Simon West interview, www.denofgeek.com/movies/stolen/26723/director-simon-west-stolen-con-air-rick-astley-and-more

Nicolas Cage interview, www.whyy.org/flicks/Cage_Interview.html

"Commando at 30", www.denofgeek.com/movies/commando/35060/revisiting-commando-at-30

67
Marconi Film, www.marconifilm.com/marconifilm-livefree.html

"Fox Eyes WW3", *Variety*, variety.com/1998/film/news/

fox-eyes-ww3-com-as-tentpole-for-1999-1117467113/

"The True Story of *Pretty Woman's* Original Dark Ending", *Vanity Fair*, 23 March 2015, www.vanityfair.com/hollywood/2015/03/pretty-woman-original-ending

68
Brendan Hood interview, www.joblo.com/arrow/interview74.htm

THE COMIC-BOOK MOVIE THAT WAS MADE NEVER TO BE SEEN

71
"Fantastic Faux", *Los Angeles* magazine, vol. 50, no. 3

THE CHANGING PRICE OF BLOCKBUSTER MOVIES

77
Sandra Bullock's deal for *Gravity*, *Hollywood Reporter*, www.hollywoodreporter.com/news/gravity-sandra-bullock-make-70-683561

HOW TINY DETAILS MADE A HUGE STAR WARS UNIVERSE

81
Fon Davis interview, www.denofgeek.com/movies/star-wars/36528/fon-davis-interview-greebles-miniatures-star-wars-and-more

Visible V8, www.partsofsw.com/v8parts.htm

82
"Ask Brian Johnson", www.space1999.org/features/ask_brianjohnson/2001-11a.html

FILMS RUMOURED TO BE GHOST-DIRECTED

85
"The Western Godfather", *True West* magazine, 1 October 2006, www.truewestmagazine.com/the-western-godfather/

"Q&A: Bob Hoskins", *Guardian*, 18 June 2011, www.theguardian.com/lifeandstyle/2011/jun/18/bob-hoskins-interview-neverland

86
Leguizamo, John, *Pimps, Hos, Playa Hatas, and All the Rest of My Hollywood Friends*, HarperCollins, 2006

Mark Jeffrey Miller interview, www.smbmovie.com/SMBArchive/specials/interviews/4_MarkM_MikeH_8-31-10.html

87
Brode, Douglas, *The Films of Steven Spielberg*, Kensington Publishing Corp., 2006

"Director Drama Heats up on Dredd", *Los Angeles Times*, October 2011, latimesblogs.latimes.com/movies/2011/10/director-drama-heats-up-on-dredd.html

FILMS THAT CHANGED DIRECTOR, ONCE FILMING HAD STARTED

89
Douglas, Kirk, *I Am Spartacus! Making a Film, Breaking the Blacklist*, Open Road Integrated Media, 2012

90
Jumpin' Jack Flash: "Marshall Comfortable Filling Director's Shoes", *Chicago Tribune*, 16 October 1986, articles.chicagotribune.com/1986-10-16/features/8603180096_1_laverne-de-fazio-shoes-jumpin-jack-flash

Goldman, William, *Which Lie Did I Tell? More Adventures in the Screen Trade*, Pantheon Books, 2000

THE BLOCKBUSTER MOVIE WITH 35 SCREENWRITERS

93
"Bringing the Flintstones to the Big Screen", *Entertainment Weekly*, 3 June 1994, ew.com/article/1994/06/03/bringing-flintstones-big-screen/

"Screenwriters Follow a Rocky Road for *The Flintstones*", www.highbeam.com/doc/1P2-4208482.html

FILMS THAT FELL APART MID-PRODUCTION

98
"*Chronicles of Riddick*: New Movie Shut Down", www.tmz.com/2011/10/29/vin-diesel-chronicles-of-riddick-movie-production-money-shut-down/#.Ts10elaZh8E

"Wake: No Second Take", deadline.com/2015/04/wake-no-second-take-bruce-willis-and-director-leave-project-1201403390/

99
Gore Verbinski interview, www.denofgeek.com/movies/the-lone-ranger/26750/gore-verbinski-on-rango-lone-ranger-bioshock

100
Catmull, Ed, *Creativity Inc., Overcoming the Unseen Forces That Stand in the Way of True Inspiration*, Bantam Press (April 2014)

THE PERILS OF PRODUCT PLACEMENT

104
Man of Steel: Ad Age, adage.com/article/news/superman-reboot-man-steel-snares-160m-promotions/241822/

Man of Steel: PQ Media, www.pqmedia.com/about-press-20150313.html

105
Natural Born Killers: Associated Press, www.apnewsarchive.com/1994/Coke-Officials-Concerned-About-Commercial-in-Natural-Born-Killers-/id_9c993c1823d52cf7139dc017eaed0a53

Mac and Me: Maltin, Leonard, *Leonard Maltin's Movie and Video Guide 2004*, Plume, 2003

INCREDIBLY ARDUOUS FILM PRODUCTIONS

106
Harris, Mark, *Scenes from a Revolution: The Birth of the New Hollywood*, Canongate Books, 2008.

Doctor Dolittle: "I Am Not a Madman", *Guardian*, 5 October 2007, www.theguardian.com/theguardian/2007/oct/05/features11.g21

107
Jaws: "Shark Tale that Changed Hollywood", news.bbc.co.uk/1/hi/entertainment/4600557.stm

Sorcerer: "Roy Scheider, *Sorcerer* Star, Talks of Thrillers", *New York Times*, 21 January 1977

Documentary about making of *Apocalypse Now: Hearts of Darkness: A Filmmaker's Apocalypse* (1991)

108
Ishtar revelations from director Elaine May, movieline.com/2011/05/18/ishtar-revelations-from-director-elaine-may/

Waterworld: Kevin Reynolds interview, www.denofgeek.com/movies/13508/kevin-reynolds-the-den-of-geek-interview

109
The Island of Dr. Moreau: John Frankenheimer interview, *Premiere* magazine, April 1997

BIG PROBLEMS ON THE SETS OF MODERN MOVIES

110

"*Police Academy* forced to play by Moscow rules", *Los Angeles Times*, 10 October 1993, articles.latimes.com/1993-10-10/entertainment/ca-44101_1_police-academy

111

Mad Max: Fury Road: "It's Mad Max out of Africa", *Sydney Daily Telegraph*, www.dailytelegraph.com.au/entertainment/its-mad-max-out-of-africa-and-broken-hill-isnt-happy-about-it/news-story/2746c27623e7973da3b2508cc1867bf7

Waterworld: Kevin Reynolds interview, www.denofgeek.com/movies/13508/kevin-reynolds-the-den-of-geek-interview

112

The Addams Family: Barry Sonnenfield interview, *Empire* magazine, January 1991

THE MAN WHO'S MADE THE WORLD'S MOST EXPENSIVE FILM: FOUR TIMES

120

Keegan, Rebecca, *The Futurist: The Life and Films of James Cameron*, Three Rivers Press, 2010

Potter, Maximillian, *Back To The Future: The Terminator Returns*, Premiere magazine, July 1996

IS MOVIE MARKETING SPOILING FILMS?

124

Terminator Genisys: "No, 'Terminator: Genisys' Director Alan Taylor Doesn't Like That Spoilerish Trailer, Either", uproxx.com/movies/terminator-genisys-alan-taylor/

How to Train Your Dragon 2: A113 Animation, www.a113animation.com/2013/12/new-how-to-train-your-dragon-2-trailer.html

INCREDIBLY LATE CHANGES TO MOVIES

126

Clash of the Titans review, www.denofgeek.com/movies/6939/clash-of-the-titans-review

127

Louis Leterrier interview, www.huffingtonpost.com/2013/05/28/louis-leterrier-now-you-see-me_n_3333311.html

FILMS THAT REMAINED UNRELEASED FOR YEARS & WHY

128

Effie Gray: "Emma Thompson's Effie cleared for release after winning second lawsuit", *Guardian*, 21 March 2013, www.theguardian.com/film/2013/mar/21/emma-thompson-effie-cleared-for-release

SECRETS FROM THE BBFC & MPAA EXAMINERS' ARCHIVES

130

Alien (1979), www.bbfc.co.uk/sites/default/files/attachments/Alien-Final.pdf

Braindead (1992), www.bbfc.co.uk/sites/default/files/attachments/Braindead%20reports.pdf

131

Carry On Up The Khyber (1968), www.bbfc.co.uk/sites/default/files/attachments/Carry%20On%20Camping.pdf

132

Dr Who And The Daleks (1965), www.bbfc.co.uk/sites/default/files/attachments/Dr%20Who.pdf

Gremlins (1984), www.bbfc.co.uk/sites/default/files/attachments/Gremlins.pdf

133

Terminator 2: Judgment Day (1991), www.bbfc.co.uk/sites/default/files/attachments/T2-final.pdf

All accessed May 10 2016

WHY TERRIFIC MOMENTS END UP ON THE CUTTING ROOM FLOOR

134

King, Stephen, *On Writing: A Memoir*, Hodder & Stoughton, 2000

THE CHANGING FACE OF MOVIE MARKETING

139

"Movie Stars, Social Media, and a Shifting Balance of Power", www.denofgeek.com/movies/social-media/39097/movie-stars-social-media-and-a-shifting-balance-of-power

WHEN A FILM STAR TURNS ON THEIR OWN MOVIE

141

Daniel Craig interview, www.timeout.com/london/film/daniel-craig-interview-my-advice-to-the-next-james-bond-dont-be-shit

142

Reynolds, Burt, *But Enough About Me: A Memoir*, G P Putnam's Sons, 2015

"Me and Marlon, Just Talking", *The Globe and Mail*, www.theglobeandmail.com/arts/me-and-marlon-just-talking/article1137888

143

"*Babylon A.D.* Director Mad as Hell", www.slashfilm.com/babylon-ad-director-mad-as-hell-calls-movie-stupid-fox-gut-less/

Batman & Robin: George Clooney on *The Graham Norton Show*, BBC Television, 22 May 2015

Terminator Salvation: The Hollywood Reporter, www.hollywoodreporter.com/news/sam-worthington-titans-i-i-61491

Daily Beast, my.xfinity.com/slideshow/entertainment-starswhoslammovies/3/

"Cool. Excellent. Thanks.", *Newsweek*, europe.newsweek.com/cool-excellent-thanks-174870?rm=eu

Stop! Or My Mom Will Shoot: "Stallone's Rocky V regret", *Toronto Sun*, www.torontosun.com/entertainment/movies/2010/07/08/14645536-wenn-story.html

HOW FILMS WERE AFFECTED BY THEIR TEST SCREENINGS

146

For Love of the Game: "In New Film, Costner's Part Is Cut", *New York Daily News*, www.nydailynews.com/archives/gossip/new-film-costner-part-cut-article-1.856935

Seven DVD commentary track

FILMS THAT CHANGED DRAMATICALLY IN POST-PRODUCTION

148

The Avengers: Jeremiah Chechik interview, www.denofgeek.com/movies/chuck/16963/jeremiah-chechik-interview-diabolique-chuck-and-what-went-wrong-with-the-avengers

149

Jonah Hex: "Hated It", www.indiewire.com/2016/02/hated-it-josh-brolin-talks-jonah-hex-says-they-reshot-66-pages-in-12-days-272606/

Rogue One: A Star Wars Story: "Making Star Wars Is a Team Sport", *Los Angeles Times*, www.latimes.com/entertainment/movies/la-ca-mn-rogue-one-gareth-edwards-20161201-story.html

Mathews, Jack, *The Battle of Brazil*, Hal Leonard Corp., 2000

THE LITTLE MOMENTS THAT CHANGED A FILM'S FORTUNES

150

Kuhn, Michael, *One Hundred Films and a Funeral*, Thorogood, 2002

152

The Business of Film with Mark Kermode, BBC Radio 4, 5 August 2015

153

Beresford, Bruce, *Josh Hartnett Definitely Wants to Do This…True Stories from a Life in the Screen Trade*, HarperCollins, 2007

Hart Bochner interview, www.denofgeek.com/movies/23335/hart-bochner-interview-ellis-in-die-hard-directing-and-more

DO BOX OFFICE FLOPS ACTUALLY FLOP?

170

"Disney Could Lose $140m on *Tomorrowland* Flop", *Hollywood Reporter*, www.hollywoodreporter.com/news/disney-could-lose-140-million-801244

171

"Top 10 Disappointing Blockbusters", *Entertainment Time*, 28 August 2009, entertainment.time.com/2009/08/28/top-10-disappointing-blockbusters/slide/waterworld/

"The 15 Biggest Box Office Bombs", CNBC, 20 March 2012, www.cnbc.com/2012/03/20/The-15-Biggest-Box-Office-Bombs.html

173

"Mark Wahlberg Explains Why his Planet of the Apes Reboot Failed", www.mtv.com/news/2440584/mark-wahlberg-planet-of-the-apes-tim-burton/

HOW DOCTOR STRANGE AND PINK FLOYD ARE CONNECTED

182

Scott Derrickson, Twitter, twitter.com/scottderrickson

183

"'Dr. Strange' & 'A Saucerful of Secrets': Storm Thorgerson's Clever Cover", nightflight.com/dr-strange-pink-floyds-a-saucerful-of-secrets-storm-thorgersons-clever-cover-design/

A FEW REMARKABLE THINGS ABOUT REMARKABLY BAD MOVIES

193

Radford, Benjamin, *Tracking the Chupacabra: The Vampire Beast in Fact, Fiction, and Folklore*, University of New Mexico Press, 2011

194

Reeve, Christopher, *Still Me*, G K Hall & Co., 1998

THE SUBTEXTS OF FAMILY MOVIES

200

Don Hahn interview, www.denofgeek.com/movies/16583/don-hahn-interview-beauty-and-the-beast-howard-ashman-the-lion-king-south-park-and-frankenweenie

THE DARK ARTS OF THE MOVIE POSTER QUOTE

209

"The reviewer who wasn't there", *Newsweek*, europe.newsweek.com/reviewer-who-wasnt-there-153387?rm=eu

BIG BOX OFFICE HITS THAT WERE UTTER SURPRISES

212

Goldman, William, *Which Lie Did I Tell? More Adventures in the Screen Trade*, Pantheon Books, 2000

213

"Adam Sandler Heads to Netflix", media.netflix.com/en/press-releases/odoyle-rules-adam-sandler-heads-to-netflix-migration-1

215

Jason Blum interview, www.denofgeek.com/movies/jason-blum/31398/jason-blum-interview-the-purge-anarchy-paranormal-activity-5-and-more

OLD REVIEWS OF CLASSIC FILMS

220

Psycho: www.nytimes.com/library/film/061760hitch-psycho-review.html

The Wizard of Oz: newrepublic.com/article/95059/tnr-film-classics-the-wizard-oz-and-the-adventures-sherlock-holmes-september-24-1

221

The Godfather Part II: www.nytimes.com/movie/

The Empire Strikes Back: www.nytimes.com/library/film/061580empire.html; www.nytimes.com/movie/review?res=9801E6DA103BF936A15755C0A964948260

The Thing: https://archive.org/stream/starlog_magazine-064/064#page/n65/mode/2up

INDEX

PICTURE CREDITS

All stills are the copyright of the respective film studios and distribution companies. Every attempt has been made to credit these and we apologize if any omissions have been made.

123RF Paisan Homhuan/Illumination Entertainment for Universal Pictures 212

Alamy Stock Photo AF archive: 18br, Columbia 75, 146, 208, Constantin Film 161, Dreamworks 103a, 187, Lionsgate 181b, Lucasfilm 80, MGM 46, 48, 192a, MTV Films 56, New Horizons 70, 71, New Line Cinema 213, Paramount Pictures13, 39, 62, 181br, 215, 238, Touchstone/Buena Vista 186, Tristar Pictures 16, 55, 20th Century Fox 17, 27, 29, 31, 45l, 74, United Artists 176, 190, Universal Pictures 43, 102, 157, 167, 172, Walt Disney Pictures/Buena Vista 219, Warner Brothers 30, 40, 90, 133a, 193a, Archives du 7e Art: Paramount Pictures/Hasbro 76; Archives du 7eme Art/Photo 12: Buena Vista Pictures 86, DreamWorks 117a, Paramount Pictures 112; Atlaspix: Universal Pictures 138, 139, Walt Disney Pictures 171; Broccoli Photography/Walt Disney Studios/Pixar 160; CBW/Scholastic 94b; Collection Christophel: 81a, Amblin Entertainment / China Film Co/Universal Pictures 42, De Laurentiis Entertainment Group 193a, Lux Films 58, MGM 82, 20th Century Fox 143, RnB/Sanford Productions/Warner Brothers 18a, TriStar Pictures 137, Universal Pictures 144, The Walt Disney Co France/Marvel 24; Dominic Harrison 83; Entertainment Pictures: Atlas Entertainment 140l, Buena Vista 203, Columbia 147, DreamWorks 72, Focus Features 237, IFC Films 214, Legendary Pictures 127, Lucasfilm 148, MGM 91, 128, New Line Cinema 45r, Optimum Releasing 99, Paramount Pictures 20, 20th Century Fox 140r, United Artists 88, Warner Brothers 54; Everett Collection: Alchemy/Millennium Entertainment 129, Bryanston Pictures 181a, Cannon Films 49, Lionsgate 125, Marvel Studios/Walt Disney Pictures 178, MGM 87, 221bl, New Line Cinema 28, Paramount Pictures 25, 155, 20th Century Fox 106, 179, 236, The Rank Organisation 132, United Artists 202, Universal Pictures 44, 107, 113, 183, Walt Disney Pictures/Buena Vista 163, 210, Warner Brothers 14, 59, 104, 111, 119, Zespoły Filmowe "Tor" 205; Jeff Morgan 01 © EMI Records 1968 182; MARKA: 20th Century Fox 108, Warner Brothers 23; Moviestore: Buena Vista 67, Entertainment Film Distribution 156a, Fox Searchlight Pictures 156, Lucasfilm 189a, Paramount Pictures 34, TriStar Pictures 64b, 20th Century Fox 103, Universal Pictures 36, 221br, Walt Disney Pictures 73, Warner Brothers 50, 115, 116, 173, 175; Nancy Kaszerman/Zuma Press 19b; Photo 12: CBS TV Distribution/NBC 33, Lucas Film 169, New Line Cinema 63, Paramount Pictures 220bl, 221a, 20th Century Fox 96, 217, 20th Century Fox/Universal Pictures 121, Walt Disney Pictures/Buena Vista 224, Warner Brothers 218; Pictorial Press: Marvel Studios/Walt Disney Pictures 184, Polygram 152, 20th Century Fox 15, 100, Warner Brothers 123b; Reuters: 64a, Matt Dunham 37; ScreenProd/Photononstop: MGM 125a, 20th Century Fox 189, Warner Brothers 61, 196; Uber Bilder / Marvel Comics 183; United Archives GmbH: Buena Vista 84, 162, Impress Movie TV/MGM Artisan Entertainment 59b, MGM 49, New Line Cinema 141, Paramount Pictures 41, 51,Trimark Pictures/PolyGram 131, TriStar Pictures 142, 20th Century Fox 118, 188, 222, Universal Pictures 92, 216, Walt Disney Productions/Buena Vista 53, Warner Brothers 135; WENN UK: Lionsgate Films 95r; World History Archive/MGM 220br

Avalon Photoshot/Warner Brothers/photo David James 195l

Getty Images Aaron Rapoport/Corbis 185; Ebet Roberts/Redferns 225; Francois Guillot/AFP 35; John Kobal Foundation 18bl; Lawrence K Ho/Los Angeles Times 26; Sunset Boulevard/Corbis 81, 89, 134

REX/Shutterstock Lorey Sebastian/Dreamworks 117, Lucasfilm/20th Century Fox 199; Luke Wynne/20th Century Fox 103; Snap Stills/Lionsgate/The Weinstein Company 97; Stephen Morley/Polygram/Channel 4/Working Title 151; 20th Century Fox/Paramount Pictures/Digital Domain 109; Universal Pictures 174

Via **Wikipedia**: Constantin Film AG/New Horizons 69; Fine Line Features/Lionsgate 101

Additional image credits:

123RF ayphoto 158; Boris Rabtsevich 78; Enrico Lapponi 95l, Fabrizio Troiani 193b; gavran 333 18 ar; Gina Sanders 206; Hctor Snchez 207b; Michael Gray 207bl; Photodeti 195b; Ruslan Kudrin 64ar, bl; Scott Betts 194l; Stocksnapper 181a; Tarzhanova 207a; Vectomart 210; Yuliia Davydenko 19ar

Alamy Stock Photo Andrew Twort 180r; Arco Images GmbH 192b; Artem Povarov 94a; blickwinkel/Teister 180a; D Hurst 180l; David Wall 194r; johnanthony 18cr; Jvphoto 220a;

Radharc Images 164a; Ruslan Kudrin 18cl, 65, 207a;

iStockphoto mariapazmorales 19c

Shutterstock Matjaz Preseren 10; Graeme Dawes 122

23 OF THE BEST POST-CREDITS SEQUENCES IN THE MOVIES

There can't have been too many people left in the cinema when the credits for 1980's Airplane! drew to a close. But those who did sit it out were rewarded with the wraparound to a joke that had begun at the start of the movie. Airplane II: The Sequel, meanwhile, would end with a tease for the never-made Airplane III. Post-credits sequences are now very common, but here's a selection of some of the finest, less well-known ones.

LETHAL WEAPON 3 (1992)

This one's really great. At the start of the otherwise hardly memorable *Lethal Weapon 3*, Danny Glover and Mel Gibson – particularly Gibson – are instrumental in destroying a building. Come the end of the credits for the movie, and we see them encountering another building under threat. This time, they prove they've learned their lesson!

STAR WARS: EPISODE I – THE PHANTOM MENACE (1999)

Sometimes, an effective post-credits sting needs to be heard and not seen. At the end of the exhaustive credits for *The Phantom Menace*, the sound of Darth Vader breathing sent people's nerd-bumps off the scale. Not that he'd appear back on screen in his more familiar guise until 2005's *Star Wars: Episode III –Revenge of the Sith*.

Ben Stiller in *Dodgeball*.

DODGEBALL: A TRUE UNDERDOG STORY (2004)

A nice comedy coda, this. We get to see what has happened to Ben Stiller's White Goodman in the time following the end of the film's story. Let's put it this way: he's a very hungry man.

The Boxtrolls' end credits lift the lid on stop motion animation.

FERRIS BUELLER'S DAY OFF (1986)

Starring Matthew Broderick, this 1986 classic contains one scene, featuring Mr Rooney (played by Jeffrey Jones), that plays in the midst of the final credits. But, even better, Ferris Bueller firmly breaks the fourth wall when, once the credits have finished, he orders you all to "go home".

THE BOXTROLLS (2014) AND *KUBO AND THE TWO STRINGS* (2016)

Animation studio Laika make some truly beautiful movies, and if you stay seated through the credits for *The Boxtrolls* or *Kubo and the Two Strings*, you'll be treated to a behind-the-scenes glimpse of just how intricate and demanding the craft of stop-motion animation is.

MARRIED TO THE MOB (1988)

An overlooked comedy from *The Silence of the Lambs* director Jonathan Demme, *Married to the Mob* has plenty to keep you entertained throughout the credits. But wait until the end and you get Michelle Pfeiffer and Matthew Modine in the midst of a full-on dance routine.

AUSTIN POWERS: THE SPY WHO SHAGGED ME (1999)

"Is the movie over?" screams Will Ferrell's Mustafa, from the bottom of a cliff. It's a little extra gag, and a hint at the chaos that Mike Myers's Austin has a habit of leaving behind.

THE UNFORTUNATE ADDITION

Every now and then, you get a mid- or post-credits sequence that sets things up for a sequel that never happened. Step forward one of the most recent examples: *Terminator Genisys* (2015), the poorly received fifth instalment of the *Terminator* movies.

It had been intended to set up a fresh trilogy, which is why during the credits we get a ten-second tease that Genisys hasn't actually been destroyed. Assuming decent box office and audience reception, the adventure was set to continue, but at the time of writing there was no sign of this happening.

A KNIGHT'S TALE (2001)

The Hollywood breakthrough movie for the late Heath Ledger is a fun movie that still stands up well. After the credits, mind, you'll find a desperately immature, and in no way funny, farting competition. Obviously, you need to tut as you watch it.

SAVING MR BANKS (2013)

This is truly spine-tingling. *Saving Mr Banks* tells the story of author P L Travers, and her resistance to Disney's adapting her novel *Mary Poppins* for the big screen. Playing over the end credits is a real recording of the late Travers, leaving the Disney animation team in no doubt as to her feelings on certain matters.

YOUNG SHERLOCK HOLMES (1985)

A sinister little extra sits at the end of *Young Sherlock Holmes*, setting things up for a sequel that never followed – after the credits have rolled, we get our first glimpse of Holmes's most notorious nemesis.

ADVENTURES IN BABYSITTING (1987)

For a light comedy, there's a tremendously dark post-credits sting for director Chris Columbus's *Adventures in Babysitting*. That's when we discover that one of the characters in the film has been left on top of a tall building, all by himself, with nobody knowing he's up there. Chipper stuff.

WINNIE THE POOH (2011)

Ah, this is lovely. Go past the end credits of the delightful *Winnie the Pooh* feature, and you get a valuable extra moment with the Backson. What's more, director Don Hall would go on to make *Big Hero 6* for Disney, and that would sneak a special Marvel guest into its post-credits scene.

IRON MAN (2008)

It's worth tipping the hat to the one that really started the current craze: 2008's *Iron Man*. Stick past the credits and you get the first appearance of Samuel L Jackson as Nick Fury, who's babbling on about something called "The Avengers Initiative". Nothing will ever come of that, of course…

PLANES, TRAINS AND AUTOMOBILES (1987)

Cinema has given us few finer Thanksgiving movies than John Hughes's *Planes, Trains and Automobiles*, and the union of Steve Martin and John Candy is sublime. Stick to the very end, though, and you get an added gag:

Planes, Trains & Automobiles finds space after its credits to top one gag off.

there's Candy's boss, still hunting through the photos we get to see earlier in the movie.

CRANK (2006)

The most fundamentally, gleefully bonkers movie featuring the mighty Jason Statham, the first *Crank* holds a special treat right at the very end. It's a wonderful 30-second sequence that basically reimagines the film you've just seen as a 1980s video game.

BEAN (1997)

Taking a leaf out of Ferris Bueller's book, Rowan Atkinson returns as Mr Bean at the very end of his maiden movie adventure, declaring, "Yes, I normally stay till the end as well. Bye. You can go now if you wish. Bye!" The sequel, *Mr. Bean's Holiday* (2007), would feature the word "Fin" being written into sand following the credits, only for the sea to wash it away.

HARRY POTTER AND THE CHAMBER OF SECRETS (2002)

The *Harry Potter* movies aren't known for their post-credits stings, but the second film in the series does add an extra scene for Kenneth Branagh's Gilderoy Lockhart. Suffering from amnesia, he has now written a new book, we learn: *Who Am I?* Indeed.

THE A-TEAM (2010)

For a movie based on a 1980s TV show, *The A-Team* was fairly shy about bringing back the original team in guest roles – unless you make your way to the end of the credits, where you get an added extra with half of the original gang.

X-FILES: I WANT TO BELIEVE (2008)

The second *X-Files* movie has a secret scene right at the very end, which makes good on something mentioned earlier in the film. We basically see our heroes, Mulder and Scully (David Duchovny and Gillian Anderson), rowing off toward a deserted island. This story thread wouldn't, though, be picked up when we next met the pair, in 2016's TV show revival.

MOANA (2016)

This is one to flush out the Disney nerds of the world. After the credits crawl for the studio's 2016 animated treat comes to an end, we find Jemaine Clement's Tamatoa still stuck on his back, spitting out a pun relating to the 1989 Disney film *The Little Mermaid*…which, like *Moana*, was directed by John Musker and Ron Clements.

MASTERS OF THE UNIVERSE (1987)

This always makes us chuckle. With a bit of a nod to *Carrie* crossed with a soupçon of *The Terminator*, Skeletor briefly returns at the end of *Masters of the Universe*, promising "I'll be back…"

THE GRUMPY SIGN-OFF

A modern variant on Ferris Bueller telling the audience to "go home" and Mr Bean politely saying "you can go now if you wish", in *Absolutely Fabulous: The Movie* (2016) that job goes to outspoken journalist Jeremy Paxman, who declares "People should be back to watching videos of kittens. Now bugger off!"

ACKNOWLEDGEMENTS

Crikey, where do you start?

Back in 2007, when Den of Geek began, it was thanks to Mat Toor that I even got, as a then-web novice, the basics I needed to get going with the site. And without James Tye's steadfast support, advice, guidance and never-ending stories of how he was once the UK Doom Champion, it would never have kept going either. It'd be remiss to start by not thanking both of them.

This book, then.

Its genesis lay in Trevor Davies of Octopus approaching us, and then talking us through his view of the project, and kindly leaving some free books behind. It was he, along with Nicola Bates, who pushed for this to happen, and Trevor has put up with plenty since, including the moment he gave me a big lollipop for hitting a final deadline. Nice man.

On the Dennis Publishing side, the mantle has since been taken up by Dharmesh Mistry, Kimberly Stone, Emma Turner and Jerina Hardy to varying degrees. On the US side, a huge thanks as always to Mike Cecchini (even if he does have questionable views on certain *Superman* movies), Bob Bartner and Jennifer Indeck Bartner, too.

I've kept telling the team at Octopus that working with book people is lovely, and they look at me like I've lost my mind. But to the following people who spend their lives actively bringing more books into the world, my heartfelt thanks...

There's the design team of Jaz Bahra and Siaron Hughes, not to forget Giulia Hetherington who hunted down pictures and then replaced them when I grumbled. Stephen Blake at MFE Editorial Services had to put the index together, and I don't envy him one bit.

This book features no shortage of superheroes in its pages, but surely a space in someone's cinematic universe needs to be saved for Alison Wormleighton and Karen Rigden. Lord knows just what bobbins you'd be reading if they hadn't picked up all the stuff that was clearly wrong on what I insist was only a first draft.

Then there's Pollyanna Poulter. The capacity of Polly's brain, and the calmness with which she processes information, means that she's a candidate for medical science investigation as far as I'm concerned.

To Trevor: thanks for sticking with us. Hope it was all worth it.

To Jason Statham: we love you.

To Mark Kermode, who has been banging our drum for years: thank you. I still think you're fundamentally wrong on *Superman III*, but to have such a loud cheerleader for the website – and book! – has meant a lot.

And then there are the people who wrote the words in this nerd tome. As well as myself, there's Ryan Lambie, Louisa Mellor, Mike Cecchini and Andrew Blair. They, plus the people who write for Den of Geek and pour their heart and soul into it, are the lifeblood of what we do. You can't beat good nerds.

To the families who support us: thank you. And apologies for buying you this book for Christmas.

And finally, to the people who came to what was once our little website and encouraged us to keep going, who backed us, championed us, supported us, criticized us, commented and fought for us: we owe you everything. Thank you so much.

Now I'm off to eat the lollipop that Trevor gave me...